8 — $\frac{2}{17}$

THE RELUCTANT PRESS LORD

THE RELUCTANT PRESS LORD

Esmond Rothermere and the *Daily Mail*

S. J. Taylor

Weidenfeld & Nicolson
LONDON

First published in Great Britain in 1998 by Weidenfeld & Nicolson

© 1998 S.J. Taylor

The moral right of S.J. Taylor to be identified as the author of this work has been
asserted in accordance with the Copyright, Designs and Patents Act of 1988

A CIP catalogue for this book is available from the British Library.

ISBN 0 297 91654 3

Typeset by Selwood Systems, Midsomer Norton
Set in Stone Serif
Printed in Great Britain by Butler & Tanner Ltd,
Frome and London

Weidenfeld & Nicolson

The Orion Publishing Group Ltd
Orion House
5 Upper Saint Martin's Lane
London, WC2H 9EA

*This book is for the late A.J. Fritz,
my mentor and my friend*

CONTENTS

ILLUSTRATIONS

Sections of photographs appear between pages 52 and 53 and 148 and 149

The Publishers wish to thank Associated Newspapers, the *Daily Mail* Library and individual members of the Harmsworth family who have kindly made available photographs from their personal archives. The Publishers also wish to thank Robert Morrow, QC and *UK Press Gazette*.

ACKNOWLEDGMENTS

I would like to thank Peter Beal and Colin Franey for reading early versions of this manuscript and, most especially, Vere Rothermere for his thoughtful reading of the final draft.

I am also grateful to Paul Rossiter for his unflagging assistance on this volume as well as the first. Paul recently completed forty-five years service with the company, making him the longest-serving employee at Associated Newspapers. As well as helping me with research, he was kind enough to read a draft of this manuscript.

Otherwise, I am indebted to Kathleen Wareham, who lent me the unpublished memoirs of her late husband Arthur, editor of the *Daily Mail* from 1954 to 1959. The late Peter Black spent a long afternoon with me talking about inconsequentials then, at the end, produced an unpublished manuscript, *The Saving of the Mail*, written in 1976 about the events of 1971. It included a copy of the McKinsey Report, long since lost, and a number of memoranda that were also destroyed in Associated Newspapers' move from Fleet Street to Kensington – all very helpful. Bert Irvine, too, lent me his diaries, again giving me special insights into the workings of the *Daily Mail*. I also appreciate the detailed accounts of life on the Street given me by Tom Pocock and Jeffrey Blyth. Ian Jackson gave access to the Minute Books of Associated Newspapers and Peter Lewis gave me his book *The Fifties* – a very readable record of the era. And Mike Randall lent me a copy of his rationale for the *Daily Mail* under his editorship, the publication *Why, Why, Why*.

Of the many I interviewed, I am especially grateful to Rhona Churchill, Louis Kirby, Neil Swindells, Monty Court, Brian MacArthur, Donald Todhunter, Reg Foster, Howard French, Alwyn 'Robbie' Robinson, John Winnington-Ingram, Jonathan Harmsworth, Charles Wilson, Barry Norman, Anthea Disney, Sir Edward Pickering, Marmaduke Hussey, Robert Morrow QC, Sir David English and again, Vere Rothermere. All these sources, many of them involved with other pressing commitments, were willing to spend a great deal of time giving me important information.

My editor, Ion Trewin, a realistic man, has been supportive over a very long haul.

I would also like to thank my great friends Anna Webster, Linda Melvern, Kathy Campbell, Genevieve Cooper, Peter McKay, Claudia Harmsworth, Susan Kyle, Ann Leslie and Sherrie Good for their continuing interest and support.

PROLOGUE

Armageddon ... Again

By September of 1994, it was necessary for Ralph Izzard – former chain-smoker, former alcoholic, former womanizer and celebrity stuntman for the *Daily Mail* – to fold his long and bony hulk into a wicker wheelchair. Coffee he tried to drink ran out the corners of his mouth and down his chin, soiling his fresh shirt. There was some question as to whether he was continent. He was, by the age of eighty-three, barely audible and easily fatigued. Yet scholars still plagued him with visits, hoping to hear about the time he scaled Mount Everest, reaching the first station ahead of Sir Edmund Hillary, or his trek over the Himalayas, or his search for the Yeti.

Izzard had originally been hired by the *Mail* through nepotism. He was the first son from the first marriage of Percy Izzard, agricultural and horticultural correspondent for the newspaper since 1909. Of Percy it was said that soldiers fighting the Great War had written letters to the editor affirming that his column, 'A Countryman's Diary', helped them to understand 'what they were fighting for'. It appeared to be something to do with gardening.

Percy Izzard's son Ralph had read forestry at Queen's College, Cambridge, and at the end of the first year of his studies, he travelled to the Black Forest to observe the exemplary system of forestation that had been developed there by the Germans. As soon as he arrived, however, Izzard abandoned his studies for a job as an assistant in the *Mail's* Berlin Bureau. He was chosen for the coveted position because of his father's friendship with the foreign editor Douglas Crawford.

This was 1931. The Nazis were on the rise, the Communists in direct conflict. But Izzard, aged twenty-one, could find no reason for alarm. He had joined a boxing club in the Communist district and a soccer team in the section of the city where the Nazis lived. He boxed with the Communists, played football with the Nazis. The sport was good on both sides. In the next few years, though, when he was transferred, first to Vienna and then to Prague, he became increasingly aware of anti-German sentiments among the people whose lands were threatened by Nazi ambitions. There were demonstrations, clashes in the streets, riots.

It was Izzard's job to cover them and as he did so he began to grasp the notion that some sort of great upheaval was at hand. By 1939, Rothay Reynolds, chief of the Berlin Bureau, had been dismissed by the *Daily Mail* – most probably because he was homosexual – and Izzard was hired to replace him. He was twenty-nine years old at the time.

Now, in 1994, remembering all this, he stirs in his wheelchair and with appalling effort steadies his shaking chin and leans slightly forward. He begins to whisper hoarsely. There is something he wants to say before he dies.

The *Daily Mail* office was staffed by a secretary and a man named Maximillian Bott, known as 'Smacksamillian' Bott. There were White Russians in and out of the place. A lot of journalists went to Berlin to change their money there. Whenever they could, they passed their straight currency on to individual Jews to help them get out of the country. This went on the whole time. These currency exchanges were local gathering points.

Selkirk Panton, an Australian on the *Express*, he was interned. I left thirty-six hours before the war broke out. I went to Denmark, there were five of us. Me, Panton, Ewan Butler of *The Times*, Anthony Mann from the *Telegraph*, Ian Colvin with the *News Chronicle*. We could have gone to Holland but there was a long train journey. The nearest place was Stettin, a port in north Germany on the coast. There we got a ship straight to Denmark. Then we got a train to take us to Copenhagen. We were all friends, we were all about the same age. We stayed in the Hotel Angleterre. It was built around a courtyard. I was staying in a corner room and I could hear all the telephoning going on throughout the hotel and I heard an American making a call to another American and he said, 'Well, the war's on,' and that's how I found out the war had started.

I went from Copenhagen to Holland. I speak Danish but not well enough to understand the newspapers, but I can speak quite a lot of Dutch and I could read the newspapers so I moved over there. I was in Amsterdam. The Amsterdam paper still had people in Berlin so I was able to update my dispatches home. I was several months in Holland.

I was staying at the Carlton Hotel. Panton and Anthony Mann were arrested by the Germans who had taken over Denmark. They were interned on an island in the Baltic called Bornholm. They were there for the rest of the war. I avoided that as I had gone to Holland.

I was still there when the first paratroopers were coming down. It was very odd because they were very low. Henry and Clare Luce motored up from Paris to Amsterdam to see it. Bill Murray was there too, the newsreel man from Pantheon News.... They all left the same day. The planes kept going overhead to bomb the airport. I kept badgering the British consul as to how we were going to get out. Were there any arrangements for the British?

Well, there weren't. They finally rang us up and said, 'There's one last hope, we had a motorlaunch down the canal, to a little port in the North Sea called Ijmuiden. We had the last ship to leave Holland. The British consul had a ship in Rotterdam, a rendezvous for the escapers. We got in this launch, desperate, Nazi paratroopers all around the canal on both sides. We had to go right through it, it was at night. I was very uncomfortable when I saw the paratroopers, I could see them all around dropping. Well, we made it. Then in Ijmuiden we had to get out. There was a tiny little ship to get on to, they were all British, Morley Richards, myself and about three more. We got on the ship and we started to go down into the hold, we had to climb down a ladder into the hold, a lot of straw was down there. You'll never guess. Down there on the straw was the Sadler's Wells Ballet Company that had been sent over as a Hearts and Minds cultural exchange with the Dutch. They sent the ballet corps to the Dutch. All their tights were all laddered and torn.

That was all he could articulate on this sunny afternoon three months before his death, but to Ralph Izzard it seemed important to get it on record. This was the way the Second World War started for the Berlin Bureau Chief of the *Daily Mail*.

At about the same time Ralph Izzard and his fellow correspondents were evacuating Berlin, the *Mail*'s correspondent in Poland, Cedric Salter, was making his way out of Warsaw across the only bridge still standing. Pre-dawn air bombardments had knocked out all telephone and cable communications into and out of the city and, with no way to report back to London on the massive German invasion of Poland, Salter had volunteered as a driver to help evacuate British refugees over the frontier.

Salter joined up with two other correspondents and five British women, commandeered a Mercedes and two Hillmans, and, each car heavily laden with luggage, the refugees travelled out of the city in pitch darkness.

The next day they made it to Naleczow, a meeting place for all the correspondents who had just evacuated Warsaw. There, Salter's little caravan joined up with a convoy of fifty vehicles, all waiting for a petrol delivery in order to proceed. Around 3 a.m. on the morning of 7 September Salter received his forty-litre ration and, along with the legendary *Daily Express* correspondent, Sefton Delmer, who had taken the front seat beside him, Salter continued on to Lwow.

By now, with no proper sleep for over three days, Salter had passed the early stages of exhaustion and found he was no longer tired, so he continued driving. For his part, Delmer began a long, eloquent and detailed discourse 'upon the tapeworms from which we should inevitably suffer as a result of the sausage, purchased in a small village in lieu of lunch and tea, [and he then] proceeded to render Nazi songs in a powerful but unexpectedly tuneful baritone'.

Predictably, once they reached the border they were faced with bureaucratic obstruction and it was necessary for them to use all their journalistic wiles to get the Poles travelling with them safely into the country. This accomplished, Delmer left for England, where he had been recalled by the *Express*, and Salter, having filed his stories, travelled some five days later back into Poland.

The city of Lwow, which Salter and his compatriots had so recently travelled through without mishap, was now in flames, and Salter found that Poland had been transformed into 'a terrified and broken country, falling rapidly into complete chaos. I met whole detachments of deserting troops.... They wished to fight on, but their officers had deserted them and, leaderless, they did not know what to do.'

In defiance of the first German blitzkrieg, women had fought beside their men, roads were overflowing 'with hungry and destitute refugees fleeing to the east' and Poland was growing weaker and weaker. Only ten days before, Salter had left 'a people hard pressed but supremely confident'. Now he found that confidence shaken, replaced by the grimmest determination merely to survive.

Poland was falling. The only hope was England, and not because the Poles had any expectation that they could or would be rescued by British troops. It was because England was now the best last hope for civilization in Western Europe.

As for Salter, a hard-bitten veteran reporter who had covered the Spanish Civil War, he was surprised by the emotionalism of the Polish people, who openly showed affection for an Englishman in their midst. In the street, he found himself standing next to an old man who grasped his hand and with tears in his eyes repeated over and over, 'God save England, God save England.'

Thus did the *Daily Mail* record the devastating blitzkrieg of Poland by Hitler's troops.

Poland's collapse in 1939 was followed during the spring of 1940 by that of Denmark, Norway, Holland and Belgium, bringing some 320 radio stations under Nazi control, and back home in London the *Daily Mail* established a 'monitoring' service. Its brief was, in the words of its organizer Alec Rutherford, to 'listen at the keyholes of the world'. A staff of multi-linguists was recruited and a vast system of eavesdropping on foreign wavelengths began.

The listening post was installed in an air-raid shelter that had been purpose built on the first floor of New Carmelite House. It was connected by teleprinter to the sub-editors' room, so that translations of anything newsworthy could be transmitted to the night staff within minutes of being received.

'Radio Polskie Warszawa' died within the hearing of the listening post, as the mayor called on the population to stand fast against the Nazi onslaught. There followed a few bars of the Polish National Anthem and the last lingering call signals of the station.

Later, Radio Brussels and Radio Amsterdam described the unstoppable German blitzkrieg across northern Europe. A warning came over the earphones, 'Bombers over Lieg'. Then, as refugees were warned 'to take to the fields and leave the roads clear for troops', the *Mail* staff heard sirens sounding in Brussels and Antwerp. The announcement that Brussels had been declared an open city came over the wires, as well as the massacre by bombing of 30,000 people in Rotterdam.

By June, the listening post was reporting the fall of France: 'The German troops are now at the gates of Paris. . . . Tomorrow they will enter the city.'

As the Luftwaffe speedily turned their full attention towards England, their approach was heralded by a remarkable broadcast heard on the first floor of New Carmelite House. '*Bitte kommen!*' said a voice. He identified himself as 'Cerberus', the name of the many-headed dog that, according to Greek mythology, guarded the gates of hell. He called his squadrons 'Falcons', 'Pigeons', 'Eagles' and 'Seagulls'. 'Where are you, No. 6?' Cerberus asked. 'Why do you not answer my signal? Cloud cover at ——, searchlights just switched on at ——. Come in at 2000 metres and bomb. Action in one minute.'

The reception of the air fight taking place somewhere overhead the site of the *Daily Mail* signalled the beginning of the air battles that would determine whether England would stand or fall.

Young, pregnant and still considered something of a novice reporter at the *Daily Mail*, Rhona Churchill was given an office car and a driver to travel 'to the scene of the most spectacular overnight bombing – to the City, the docks, St Paul's, etc.' In this way she saw much of the carnage caused by the blitz. It was, in her words, 'harrowing and devastating, yet also inspiring'.

> For, uppermost in my mind and in that of everyone I talked to was still the memory of the enormous relief we had all felt at Dunkirk time when we heard Mr Winston Churchill on the radio telling us we were all going to fight on, and that was the spirit still dominant throughout those dark days. I spent several

nights sleeping in the Tube and caves where Londoners were sheltering and was amazed by the pervading 'good neighbour' atmosphere.

In peacetime city dwellers tend to keep themselves to themselves. In bomb-ridden London the barriers were down and total strangers were treating each other as long-lost friends.

It became a point of pride to her to make it into the office, 'regardless of what happened overnight'. And as she walked to work through the confused clean-up efforts of the next morning, Rhona often saw 'firemen still out with their hoses strung across Fleet Street'.

The paper's male and female staff shrank rapidly, as did the paper (owing to newsprint rationing). Men who joined the Territorial units found themselves guarding the vital bridges over the Thames against potential saboteurs instead of reporting....

Our Social Editress, Barbara Armstrong, became redundant, as did our Women's Page Editor. There very quickly wasn't any newsprint for their kind of copy. Barbara joined the newly formed Women's Army Corps. Many of the remaining editorial day staff did night duty as air-raid wardens, fire-brigade auxiliaries and first-aid workers. A Fleet Street women's rifle unit was formed and an army sergeant gave us rifle training. I think the *Daily Mail*'s Phyllis Davies was the reporter who got this going.

I was by then too pregnant to attend the classes for more than a few weeks, but rolled on my extended stomach at target practice for as long as I could stand it.

Inside the offices of the *Daily Mail*, one of the great dangers every staff member shared was of becoming a 'bomb bore'. One night Rhona Churchill was assigned to spend time sheltering with Londoners in various places, one of them 'a restaurant in London where they danced all night and anyone who wanted to could sleep in the cellar on mattresses'. On a whim, her husband decided to join her, so neither of them was aware that a bomb had fallen through the roof of their house and landed in the bathtub. Trained to fill up their baths with water in order to cope with any fires in the home, they suffered no damage. But though this was an innocuous tale with a happy ending, Churchill by then knew better than to tell it round the office. People had become indifferent to near hits and misses, there were so many similar stories. Then, too, she had no wish to be identified as a 'bomb bore'.

She was nevertheless, as everyone must have been, still greatly affected by what she was seeing day after day:

I remember ... at this time, watching the firemen pouring water into John Lewis's in Oxford Street, which had been set alight overnight. I was emotionally involved because it was the store where my mother had bought our school uniforms and other clothing and I thought, 'There goes my childhood.'

The bombing of Oxford Street became commonplace. Before long, the *Mail* was reporting 'Bomb Sales' wherein goods that had been damaged in air raids were 'offered to the public in a new sort of autumn bargain sale'. Cleaning up wreckage and salvaging what they could, shop assistants quickly learned to treat the bombings as 'business as usual'. They worked with look-outs perched on the roof to keep watch and warn them of any approaching danger.

Another staff member, veteran reporter Paul Bewsher, who flew with the RFC in the First World War, was astonished at the way in which the night-life of the West End continued as if nothing were happening. He had been out one night, meeting friends at a 'cocktail club' when an air raid began:

There was an incessant roar of gunfire and the great white flashes leapt up again and again at the end of the small, dark street. Sipping iced cocktails at the bar were three smartly dressed women and their conversation, to my astonishment [contained] no reference to the turmoil and uproar of the gunfire outside.

Sometimes I think the whole thing is not real. I mean the way in which the night-life of the West End is still going on ... as if nothing unusual were happening.

In the meantime, the evacuation of children was being speeded up. Before the raids on London began in earnest only a hundred children were leaving each week. Now, with the constant bombardment, registration reached 2500 per day as parents hurried to the LCC schools organizing their children's speedy exit.

Those youngsters lucky and wealthy enough to secure a place in America or Canada faced other perils. German U-boats made no distinction between ordinary ocean seafaring vessels and the so-called 'mercy liners'. In one case, eighty-three of ninety children drowned when the ship carrying them in a heavy gale was torpedoed.

Those whose parents decided to keep them behind would be deprived of any of the treats usually associated with a normal childhood. The *Mail* sponsored a salute to these children, a special poem in their honour. It was only a bit of doggerel, but for those growing up during the war years it set the spirit of the times:

There's no ice-cream for you to eat
No sugar biscuits, crisp and sweet,
No quivering jelly, all a-shake,
Not a single creamy cake,

No holidays upon the sands,
No donkey-rides, no jolly bands,
No gay balloons to toss about,
So many things you've gone without;
No Easter eggs, exciting, gay,
No crackers for your Christmas Day,
Oranges? Well, just a few,
But no bananas all year through.
No thrilling toys, no birthday treats,
Not much chocolate, too few sweets!
We grown-ups think we've lots to bear,
But, boys and girls, you've done your share!

Everyone was doing his share, like it or not, as the imposition of full rationing came into force. The *Daily Mail* published 'Seven Ideas (for ration-saving meals)' from recipes developed by 'London's greatest chefs'.

From the Dorchester came the 'Kent Hot Pot', calling for one cabbage, one swede and a few carrots. These were to be chopped together, blanched and cooked until tender in a casserole with bacon rind and a splash of vinegar. 'One hour before serving add one small sliced apple and one dozen small potatoes. Serve in casserole. (Enough for four persons.)'

The Café Royal added its recipe for 'Potato Dumplings'. It called for one pound of potatoes, three ounces of flour, and one egg '(if possible, but not absolutely necessary)', salt, pepper, a little margarine and a 'small quantity grated cheese for flavouring (this also not essential)'. All of this was to be cooked, mashed and rolled into little balls for poaching.

At Grosvenor House, Chef G. Vallet offered vegetable cutlets – cooked, chopped vegetables of any kind, mixed with dry mashed potatoes, covered in breadcrumbs, then fried in oil. Or in a more fanciful vein, Frascati's suggested 'Timbales of Vegetables Royal', a cooked vegetable dish served in a potato-lined dish with white sauce '(made with the yolk of an egg, if possible)'.

Other serious shortages were being felt. The content of the *Daily Mail*, as well as other newspapers, was severely limited by a dearth of newsprint. In these early years the nation's supply decreased to twenty-five per cent of what it had been before the war. It would, by 1942, shrink to only fifteen per cent of pre-war availability. And as a result of agreements negotiated by the Newspaper Proprietors Association the *Mail* was reduced first to an eight-page, then to a six-page newspaper and finally, in 1941, to only four pages. At the same time the number of columns was increased from seven to eight, crowding in as much news as possible.

The effect on the *Mail*'s style was not totally disastrous. One young sub-editor on staff, Arthur Wareham, wrote, 'We became masters in the art of compressing a mine of information into the tidy wartime newspapers. This lesson in the economy of words was invaluable and as a result there is no doubt that post-war daily journalism has been superior to the brand we inflicted on our readers before 1939.'

As well as crowding and shortening, fewer copies of the *Mail* were being printed. The newspaper urged its readers to 'share your *Daily Mail*.... Do not leave it in the train or lying about when you have finished with it. Pass it on to one of your friends who has been unable to get one.'

The shortage also brought about another major improvement, the publishing of news on page one. Before the war the *Mail* lagged behind its major competitor, the *Daily Express*, by continuing to publish advertisements on page one, as the paper had done since it was founded in 1896. Now, space was too precious.

Other changes were mandated by the blitz. The first floor of Northcliffe House, the production site for the *Daily Mail*, was transformed into a hotel of sorts, with bedrooms for editors, directors, mechanical managers and anyone else directly responsible for production. When a raid was on they could work late into the night, then stay on at work in relative safety.

Such precautions were necessary because when the blitz was at its height, between November 1940 and May 1941, 43,000 civilians would lose their lives and 51,000 would be seriously injured. And the bombs would fall perilously close to Northcliffe House.

Bill Benbow, an electrician in charge of a fire party, received a call on 29 December 1940 saying that incendiary bombs were falling on the *News Chronicle–Star* building.

> I took the party out on the roof. When we got there we heard a high explosion bomb coming down, they really whistle, and so I said to the crew, 'Scatter away from the flames and lie down on the roof.' We lay down as we had been trained and I'll tell you what I did, I really prayed that night, that the pilot would be a good shot. I knew there was nobody in the building he was bombing, but if he was a little bit out he would hit us. And he was a good shot.
>
> The bomb landed in the building, and we stood and watched. I've never seen a scene like it in my life. As the flooring gave way under the intense heat, machinery on the fourth floor fell through the various floors, creating a great inferno in the basement of the *News Chronicle* building. It was an awe-inspiring sight.

Indeed, all across London the bombing had been devastating. From their vantage point atop the roof of Northcliffe House the fire crew could see the smoke rising all round. One of the crew said, 'I wish I had a camera,' and went down to find a photographer. A few minutes later Herbert Mason appeared with his camera. 'I took the photo', Mason said later, 'when I caught a glimpse of St Paul's Cathedral in a momentary gap in the smoke and I recorded the scene for all time.'

The *Daily Mail* would describe the event in more florid terms: 'Incendiaries fell around him. Starlings wheeled in the air. Buildings crashed. Firemen struggled with hoses. Flames reddened the night sky and at that moment Herbert Mason looked across Ludgate Hill and saw the great dome of St Paul's standing firm amid the smoke and destruction.'

This was the single most famous photograph of the Second World War, and it was destined to personify England's survival and triumph during the blitz.

1

The War Lovers

Whatever people had been, they tended to be more so once the war began. The urgency and uncertainty of England's effort to survive lent dramatic impetus to every event, and there was an almost euphoric heightening of feelings.

The Chairman of Daily Mail & General Trust, Esmond Rothermere, was not exempt from the chaotic emotional terrain produced by the war. He had been in love, deeply and seriously, since the summer of 1936, when he met Ann O'Neill in Austria.

According to Ann's account of their meeting they had become acquainted beside an Austrian lake, where Ann was sunbathing. Esmond offered to put sun oil on her back and that simple act resulted in a physical attraction so overwhelming that the young matron, four years married but as yet innocent of desire, was willing to abandon both convention and morality, to lose herself entirely in love.

The Esmond she lionized was a highly romantic figure and a man of the world. He was rich and handsome, a friend of the Prince of Wales, popular, droll, sensual. He had himself married young, had three children and was going through a highly controversial but infinitely interesting divorce, his former wife citing over two dozen co-respondents. By the same token, he was heir to the Harmsworth publishing dynasty, a man who would soon become the proprietor of the *Daily Mail*, one of the most powerful voices in the kingdom.

In November 1940, when the blitz was raining down death and destruction on London, Esmond's father Harold died in Bermuda and Esmond succeeded to the title of Viscount Rothermere of Hemsted. With such power and prestige, Esmond was surely the most eligible semi-detached man in the land.

Only two things now stood between Ann and Esmond.

The first was her marriage to Lord O'Neill. But Ann's husband, and the father of her two children, had joined the North Irish Horse Guards and left to serve in northern Africa, where he quickly rose to command his own regiment. His absence afforded Ann almost unlimited licence to pursue her love affair with Esmond Rothermere, an opportunity she seized.

The second impediment to her relationship with Esmond was perhaps more unusual. Two years after her love affair began, in 1938, Ann had fallen in love with yet another man, this time Ian Fleming, troubled black sheep of the Fleming banking family. Unbeknown to Esmond – or indeed to her husband Shane – she and Fleming embarked upon a highly complicated and dangerous psycho-sexual liaison.

By the start of the war Ann had unleashed her emotions, giving full vent to her passion for Esmond and her dark attraction to Fleming, pairing the two of them against her husband Shane. In this, she was not unlike others who compressed their lives in the face of the exigencies of war. Where she differed was in the easy nonchalance she exhibited in conducting the complicated series of betrayals she seemed to require.

Indeed, to a woman such as Ann, romance and love presented her with the only opportunity to exercise power. It lent her dull life the illusion of drama and significance and, well, a great sense of fun.

On her father's side, Ann Charteris, later O'Neill, descended from an upper-class côterie known as the 'Souls'. They were a clique of aesthetes who were aristocratic but Bohemian, insular but intellectual. At the centre of the group was her grandmother, Mary Wyndham, who had been personified as one of the Graces in the well-known painting by Sargent. She had married a Charteris and as her husband was an unrepentant philanderer, often absent because of frequent visits to his mistress, the lightly assembled group assumed a consuming interest for his neglected wife. Mary easily replaced her husband with her long-time companion, the politician Arthur Balfour who, in his attendance upon her, showed a constancy and affection most husbands do not.

As self-styled intellectuals, the Souls were known for 'lightly skimming the cream from the surface of life'. They delighted in unrestrained eccentricity, as demonstrated by George Wyndham turning somersaults across the drawing-room floor while quoting Virgil, then singing 'The lark now leaves his wat'ry nest' to an unembarrassed Balfour. The Souls met by preference at Stanway, Ann's grandparents' home, a house of particular architectural interest located in the Cotswolds. (Inigo Jones was said to have designed the gatehouse.)

Ann's mother was Frances Tennant, who came from the Glasgow chemical manufacturing family. Ann's great-aunt Margot married H. H. Asquith, Liberal leader and later Prime Minister; her aunt Cynthia later married the Asquiths' son, thus making Ann's lineage so impeccable that her behaviour came to be accepted as above reproach for the duration of her life. It was an advantage much welcomed by Ann and her younger sister Laura, both of whom certainly made the most of their important social placement.

In her autobiography, *Laughter from a Cloud*, Laura admitted being born 'into what is known as the privileged class', although she preferred the old-fashioned word 'aristocracy', most probably because of its rich connotations of social superiority.

Licence was what Ann and Laura each in her own way sought, and each in her own way achieved. It was a quality admired for its own sake, without unnecessary recourse to responsibility, guilt or remorse. High on Laura's list of favoured predecessors, for example, was

the notorious Colonel Francis Charteris who succeeded in being drummed out of three regiments in his lifetime for cheating at cards, theft and embezzlement. Later he took to gambling and money-lending, on which he founded his vast fortune. His character did not improve in his later years, and at the age of fifty-five he was put in prison for raping his maidservant – a recurrent vice of his. When he died in 1732 his body was savagely mutilated by the mob on the way to his funeral.

This was Laura talking, but both Ann and Laura affected this lively, brittle tone, somewhat childlike, somewhat cynical, always understated. There was a sense of birds hopping from one branch to another, trilling.

Perhaps the brittleness resulted from an unconscious desire to distance themselves from their emotions. The girls both remembered the death of their mother from cancer when Ann was only twelve and Laura ten. Ann later wrote to a relative, 'I was too old not to remember it well and remember minding very much when she went to the nursing home – curiously much.' It seemed a thing of wonder to Ann that she could feel so deeply, but something in her remembrance shows an unwillingness to be a dupe to grief or to unhappiness. Everything *could* be kept in its proper place, if only one adopted the proper attitude.

Ann, in her diaries, letters and conversations, sounded like a character in a Noël Coward play – or perhaps Noël Coward, one of the great friends of her later life, had simply lifted the cadence of her speech, using it to present the new modern woman. At any rate, whether on stage or in real life, it played. And it played well.

In the early days of the war, urged on by her friends to marry, divorce and secure an enormous settlement from Rothermere (surely a joke), Ann acted seriously to force Esmond's hand:

In the spring of 1941 Esmond was persuaded by me that we must marry or part, so we went through the rigmarole of giving evidence at Bournemouth (Esmond went back on this two months later). The evidence coincided with one of Ian's forty-eight-hour leaves [from the Naval Intelligence Division] and he persuaded me to continue from Bournemouth to Cornwall for a day's golf. Ian met us at Bournemouth and we motored (press lords had plenty of petrol). I was being sick every twenty minutes from nerves and guilt. Ian told Esmond I was not to be indulged. We were to stop at no more inns and I could damn well be sick in the hedge. This had a curative effect!

When we arrived I went to bed. Ian came to my room, told me I was behaving very badly and must return to Shane. I burst into tears.

The raw brutality and ruthlessness with which she was treated by Fleming had rather an unsettling effect upon Ann, though she was candid in her estimation of Esmond's love-making skills. There could be no doubt, she was fond of saying, Esmond was quite the most accomplished lover she had ever had. But Ian's cruelty created its own sensation. It would develop into something rather more interesting to Ann than simple love-making.

But the Esmond whom Ann misunderstood as simple, because of his unwavering affection and dependability, was a good deal more complicated than a young woman in her early twenties might have imagined. She saw him as a towering figure of strength and power. In fact, the events in Esmond's life had mostly conspired to undermine his confidence in his own judgement and competence.

His two elder brothers who had died in World War I, Vyvyan and Vere, had seemed to him to be his superiors in every way. He confided to a friend that his father had once said, 'If only those two were still around he would have nothing to do with the newspapers and the newspapers would be better off.'

Esmond's father had been almost a crushing force in his life and despite having no intentions of overpowering his last surviving son, Harold had done so – often unwittingly. After the death of his second son Harold suffered a nervous collapse and transferred all his ambitions for the three boys on to the one surviving, creating a suffocating sense of pressure. It was now Esmond's duty, as his father saw it, to 'inherit all the sacrifices of those great personages your two elder brothers. They would have wished for you a great career and sometimes through my tears I see in your future an ample vindication for what they – and I – have suffered.'

If Esmond had been close to his mother he might have found the responsibilities he faced more bearable. And she might have been able to build up his confidence. But Lilian's way of dealing with the deaths of her sons was to cauterize her feelings. When her eldest boy, Vyvyan, lay dying in hospital she didn't bother to visit him. Instead, she gave herself over entirely to pleasure, following her inclinations towards the literary, forgetting the past and leaving the responsibility of dealing with her remaining son to Harold.

By the time Esmond had grown to manhood his many gifts were apparent to all. He was tall, graceful and uncommonly handsome, and he had a sense of humour sophisticated beyond his years. To an outsider, evenly evaluating the man he had grown to be, it appeared he embodied every grace that fortune can bestow. Regardless of this, his sense of self had been seriously impaired. Anything he achieved, he had come to believe, derived from the great energy and drive of his father and his Uncle Northcliffe, who had come up the hard way, advancing from abject poverty to enormous power and wealth in only a few decades.

He had constantly to live up to their expectations. By his conduct and his gentlemanly behaviour he had to compensate them for real and imagined snubs from the British upper classes. He had to fit in where they had been excluded. Esmond learned to be a gentleman, to ride, to excel in sports, to dress well, to speak well and, above all, to represent the family with panache. But always, behind the veneer lay the nagging fear that his brothers could have managed better, that his uncle and father had made the real climb: he was only the figurehead.

In reality, his father was taking almost every decision about his life and Esmond's own wishes, as they so often did, fell by the wayside – in a way, without Esmond actually realizing it. He campaigned for office under the aegis of his father's anti-waste policy 'Squandermania', becoming, at twenty-one, the youngest MP in the House. He loved being a Member of Parliament and he turned himself into a persuasive speaker. He told his friends he would have been quite happy to carry on for the rest of his life in politics.

But his father's prejudices prevented him from advancing. After Bonar Law became Prime Minister in 1922, it was widely rumoured that Harold had threatened him with withdrawing the support of his newspapers if Bonar Law did not give Esmond a Cabinet position, and that the Prime Minister had pretty well told him to go to hell. But this was not actually what had happened.

Bonar Law had no objection whatever to Esmond and, in fact, wanted to take him on in a junior capacity. But Harold had decided Bonar Law was a weak and ineffectual leader and Esmond would do well to wait for a better opportunity. Again, when Bonar Law's successor, Stanley Baldwin, showed an interest in putting Esmond to work, Harold vetoed his accepting a position.

Baldwin, Harold wrote to Esmond, had 'neither the imagination, decision nor courage' to see the nation through any of the difficult times that lay ahead. 'Stand out,' he advised his son in 1924. 'Your time will come. You can only hurt yourself by making an alliance with a fiasco.'

Esmond's time never came. Baldwin was destined to become the dominant force in Conservative politics for the next fifteen years. By shutting his son out early with Bonar Law and making an enemy of Baldwin, Harold had effectively destroyed any chances Esmond might have had for high-level political office.

Esmond began to speak wistfully of what it would take to make him really happy, and this presupposed he was not happy with the way things were. He fretted and his fretting caused worry among the family. In an unforeseen way, his complaints only brought him more problems. His father became concerned about what he perceived as a new danger and spoke of what he regarded as Esmond's weakness: 'YOU SEEM EXCITABLE AND WORRIED,' his father wired him in January of 1924. 'CAN ALWAYS SELL PAPERS AND ... SHALL PROBABLY DO SO YOU DEAREST BEN* COULD NOT STAND MY DAILY STRAIN.'

Esmond retired from Parliament in 1929, no doubt to please his father, and began what was to become his life's work, managing Associated Newspapers. It was thought this hand-over, while Harold was still living and in charge of the Daily Mail Trust, would prepare him for his eventual role as the head of the entire company. Instead, it brought Esmond a sense of impotence and even embarrassment, as he watched the company decline and endured the publication of his father's unpopular views in the *Daily Mail*. Although he knew Beaverbrook's *Daily Express* was overtaking the *Mail*, he was powerless to convince his father.

On his mother's side things were even less satisfactory. Lilian was flighty. During the early years of her marriage she had conducted an affair with Harold's younger brother St John and a rumour continued to circulate through the family that St John was Esmond's real father, though whether this was true was never established.

She and Harold separated soon thereafter and she began to pursue a literary career in France, making early translations of Gide and eventually becoming the patron of T. S. Eliot's quarterly review *The Criterion*. Throughout this period she seemed to grow more and more self-absorbed, distancing herself further from Esmond and blaming him for remaining close to his father.

Alternately frivolous and condemnatory towards her last remaining son, she became more capricious. When in a gay mood, she signed herself 'Bluebell' and chatted in her letters about her many projects. But

---

* Harold often addressed his son as 'Ben' in his letters.

in the last decade of her life, after disappointments began to accumulate, she became embittered, blaming Esmond for his failure to live according to her dictates. The letters she sent then were written in a shadowy hand and signed only 'Your Mother':

> There is only one life to be lived and you are only half living and it makes my heart ache as your mother – regretfully it seems – in name only! I am grieved beyond words – I have tried to be your friend but that also seems to have failed. That is to say: you do not want me – My own life fortunately is so full and complete so perfectly happy that I can live without your love and 'attention' but it overflows to you and to all who are not so fortunate as I am and in spite of everything I am very grieved that you and I are not more united. I could have been of so much use to you in so many ways....
>
> I have never interfered or proffered advice – well, there it is and so it is – friends real friends who are able to advise and tell one another the truth without fear are rare – and in your position they do not exist.
>
> Your Mother

By late February of 1937 Lilian had been diagnosed as having cancer and had undergone painful surgery as a result. Her letter to her son then reflected a lifetime of suppressed anger.

> Dearest Esmond
>
> Thank you for your chatty letter.
>
> I am very sorry I cannot write in the same strain and that is why I have abstained from contacting you but I am still bruised and shaken by the cruelty of your father – who seized the occasion of my very serious illness to persecute me – last time at Marseilles – your father said to me complacently: 'I don't think Esmond has made the most of his life, do you?' Feeling very indiscreet I said: 'My dear, he has been terribly handicapped' (meaning to continue and tell him what I thought about his part in it!).... I hope I shall never set eyes on him again.
>
> He has been the evil genius of your life as well as mine and has imagined it well compensated for by money – Oh, how mistaken he is! – but you my dear boy also ever at his side – money is your 'God' also and neither you nor your father ever had or ever will have any real joy in life....
>
> I am fed up with both of you – you have no 'guts' and no imagination so there it is – I pity you both.
>
> Your Mother
>
> PS   I do not mention my health – as obviously it is a matter of very secondary consideration with you both and you have no doubt reports from all your 'spies'—PS   You no doubt think I shall 'forget' all this don't delude yourself on that matter – the surgeon said too when I was screaming in agony: 'She will

forget all this when she is better, it is nerves and she is hysterical'! Alas! I remember all that horror, every moment of agony and so it will be with this—

Lilian's cruel letter was tantamount to a curse. Esmond was 'handicapped', he had no 'guts'. He had never nor would he ever have 'any real joy in his life'. It was a strange legacy for a mother to leave to her only son.

But there was a second, unintended legacy, one that no doubt had far-reaching consequences in Esmond's dealings with the opposite sex for the rest of his life. He should seek no mercy from the feminine psyche. Whimsy and caprice was the province of woman.

And her dying word was rage.

When she first clapped eyes on Ian Fleming in the same summer she began her affair with Esmond Harmsworth, Ann O'Neill described him in her diary as 'a handsome, moody creature' and indeed, far more so than Esmond, Ian was wont to wrap himself in his complexity, as if it were an outer garment that enhanced his appearance. He was exceedingly handsome and very troubled, and apt to be ruthless with women – a very attractive quality for those of them who, in whatever circumstances, had been bored in an earlier relationship.

His inability to cope with the traditional jobs thrown his way by his mother, a constant interferer, made him more interesting still. He was a misfit who didn't make the grade at Reuters or in the City. The first position his mother conspired to sabotage, the second he managed to fail at without her assistance. The fact that he was so well born meant he was less likely to be thought of as being feckless, though he was, and much more likely to be considered merely indifferent – a quality that would not adversely affect his social standing.

Somewhat unexpectedly, Fleming *did* find his *métier* in July of 1939, when he was enlisted by Admiral John Godfrey, the director of the Naval Intelligence Division (DNI), into his newly formed Special Branch which dealt with intelligence and meteorology. Fleming had a distinctive turn of mind for this rather specialized work, bringing to it a mature and keen intelligence, along with the originality of a fecund adolescent sensibility.

In some ways he seemed not to have entered into the adult world, for he continued to be dominated by his mother, so much so that he didn't even leave her London house to take up his own bachelor quarters until he was twenty-eight. Once esconced there, he set about fulfilling his teenage ambition of having a lot of different women and treating them badly.

He was very fond of showing these would-be lovers his extensive pornography collection, described by one girlfriend as 'variations on a theme about flagellation.... [There were a lot of] books about women dressed up as a schoolmistresses in lace collars, standing over manacled men with a whip.'

'I say,' he asked one girlfriend hopefully as she leafed through the collection. 'Are you getting a kick out of that?'

A recurrent event in his adult life was the seduction of an attractive woman and, in the immediate aftermath, the dumping of her unceremoniously. Perhaps his intention, conscious or unconscious, was to communicate to the woman that she had been important to him only insofar as his pressing physical need was concerned. Once that was assuaged, satisfaction was derived by savagely humiliating her and by letting her know the low esteem in which he held her.

The women in Fleming's life who escaped this vicious humiliation were generally his older lovers, of whom there were several. All of them were rich and powerful and likely to be of help in one way or another in his career or otherwise.

A certain set of circumstances in Fleming's life seemed to have contributed to his ambivalence towards the opposite sex – a competent, talented father who died heroically in World War I and who was held up to him constantly for emulation; an overbearing mother under whose complete control Ian lived during his formative years; and a sense of continuing inferiority to his gifted older brother of whom he was inordinately jealous.

Ian Fleming was born into the important Scottish banking family of Robert Fleming & Company. His grandfather, after whom the bank was named, had been the main financier to bankroll the major American railways, among them the Pennsylvania, Union Pacific and Atchison, Topeka and Santa Fe lines. This side of his family displayed the stolid, dour Scottish characteristics of thrift and responsibility. But his mother's side, though distinguished and highly intelligent, also showed a flamboyance for living that bordered on the eccentric.

With her big dark eyes, high cheek-bones and trim figure, Evelyn Beatrice Ste Croix Rose was the very antithesis of Fleming thrift and heartiness. She played the violin and was a good water-colourist for a start: none of the Flemings had any pretensions to music or art. She was frivolous, snobbish and vain. Money, as far as she was concerned, was for spending rather than saving. One of her extravagances was her wardrobe; she dressed with a theatrical originality which later often caused Ian and his brothers acute embarrassment. Gold, purple and green were her colours; billowing crinolines and outsize hats her style.

Almost from the moment Ian's father was killed in action in World War I, his mother Eve began to visit upon her sons her own peculiar type of humiliation ritual. She played the boys off against one another, Peter, Ian's elder brother, being deemed the more talented and gifted. To Ian she mercilessly praised Peter's exemplary conduct, reminding him of his own inadequacy. His youth was riddled with embarrassing incidents blown out of all proportion. For example, when his 'find' of ambergris along a beach turned out to be a large lump of New Zealand butter from a recent shipwreck, he suffered public ridicule for his stupidity. He was only nine and her reaction was a model of cruelty.

Later, Eve became enamoured of Augustus John and, ever obliging, John made her pregnant. She went away for the confinement, but returned with an 'adopted' daughter, Amaryllis. This was in 1925.

By 1927, the lack of balance in Ian's relations with women was becoming obvious. He had fallen in love, but his mother had decided Monique was unsuitable and she broke up his engagement. When he was at Sandhurst, a girlfriend refused to cancel a previous date with another suitor and he threatened to go to London and 'find myself a tart'. He made good his threat, finding his way to Club 43 in Soho and for his trouble got a serious case of gonorrhoea.

> Ian was no stranger to his mother's wrath. This time she tore into him mercilessly. He had let down the family, the regiment, her friends, all that she held dear. She had obtained royal patronage for him, her reputation at court would be in ruins. Apart from that, gonorrhoea was a dangerous and antisocial disease. Taking every opportunity to humiliate her son, she booked him into a nursing home in Beaumont Street for a residential course of treatment.

Yes, his mother was a monster. Yes, he had been badly let down. One need look no further than to his mother in order to chart the progression of Ian Fleming's need viciously to humiliate members of the opposite sex. A strong case can be made that he was transferring an unconscious anger towards her upon the women he met, making them pay for her outrageous conduct.

This must have been the reason why he found himself inexplicably attracted to Ann O'Neill. She was able instinctively to fulfil his need to be simultaneously savaged and admired. She operated in her own interests, as his mother had, and she was capable of the same acts of caprice and whimsy. And she was an intelligent woman with it – clever and witty – so that her ability as a destroyer was keen.

These qualities of Ann's may have gone a long way towards explaining Esmond Rothermere's devotion to her as well. He had never got much from his mother; he would get less from Ann. He knew what to expect, he felt comfortable.

It wasn't that Ian and Ann wished Esmond ill. It was that, along with all his money and his unaccountable need to please, he was just so madly helpful.

Even as the war intensified the already overwrought emotions of those at home, it created unexpected dependencies among those whose job it was to cover the actual fighting.

Despite the fact that they were completely different in terms of outlook and personality, Alan Moorehead of the *Daily Express* and Alexander Clifford of the *Daily Mail* had become inseparable – 'Mutt and Jeff', the other members of the press corps called them. Thus began the famous friendship of two rivals, the basis of which, Moorehead speculated, was the war. 'It isolated us from our past lives. We were like two strangers who clung together in a shipwreck.'

While at home Fleming, Rothermere and Ann O'Neill were trying to find their way towards some sort of emotional balance, Moorehead and Clifford strove to make sense of the progress of the war in Europe. They sat far away in northern Africa, dangling their legs in the swimming pool of the Gezira Sporting Club in Cairo. They were drinking Pimm's No. 1 and listening to the Club's wireless as it charted the fall of France.

Sedan had been overrun and the two correspondents, both in their early thirties, understood it was 'the end of the world as we had known it', the beginning of 'something different, a more dangerous, infinitely harsher existence'. The scene behind them was of gardens, waiters in cummerbunds and fezes, golf, cricket, green grass and date palms. Without either of them saying a word, both knew this world was 'unreal in the sense that it was already out of date and doomed'.

Their first meeting, in 1937, had not been auspicious. Moorehead had just arrived in Spain to cover the Spanish Civil War for the *Express*. Not knowing where to stay for the night, he went to the Bar Basque at St-Jean-de-Luz, a well-known watering spot for journalists. There, the barman pointed out Clifford, who was reporting for Reuters at the time, and Karl Robson of the *News Chronicle*. Clifford, it seemed to Moorehead, had a 'rather forbidding' manner, 'a round head, a broad cerebral brow and a tight-looking mouth. He peered in an uncompromising way through his glasses.' He had obviously attended public school in England, for he had the cool, unruffled manner that Moorehead, an Australian, particularly disliked. While Clifford appraised Moorehead distantly, leaving it to Robson to answer Moorehead's question about where he might stay for the night, Moorehead vowed to leave a wide berth between himself and a man he considered to be insuperably rude.

A chance meeting in Athens a few years later would change all that. They had both been to visit a sick friend and agreed reluctantly to go out to a taverna together afterwards.

> We argued then for three hours or more, sitting at the rickety wooden table, drinking ouzo, turning away the boot-blacks, the sellers of pistachio nuts and lottery tickets, and watching the evening transformation of Athens when the dust and the heat subside at last and for half an hour the air achieves the clear and buoyant colour of a rock pool in the tropics. The bright lamp of the moon came up over Hymettus as we went on talking.

Clifford had indeed attended public school and gone on from Charterhouse to Oriel College, Oxford. He was fluent in French, German, Italian, Spanish, Greek and Swedish, and able to communicate in twelve other languages. Along with his intellectual precocity Clifford was terribly shy, whereas Moorehead, even by his own reckoning, was brash, dominant and outspoken. Clifford was tall and ethereally handsome but, strangely, not very attractive to the opposite sex, while Moorehead's optimism and lively sense of humour gave him great appeal with the ladies.

Clifford had just joined the *Daily Mail*, the *Express*'s main rival. But despite the fact that they were expected to compete with one another on a cut-throat basis, neither was inclined to do so. Instead, they threw in together to outsmart their editors back in London. Aware that Cairo was the gateway to coverage of the British Expeditionary Force in the desert, both were eager to get there. So they worked out a ruse whereby each cabled his editor that the other was being sent to the Egyptian capital. It was the first time they contrived to manipulate their editors in order to work together. It would not be the last.

At the time, the forces in the desert had been quickly assembled from General Sir Archibald Wavell's Middle East Command and several small garrisons of British troops from various surrounding African countries. Off shore was Admiral Sir Andrew Cunningham's Mediterranean Fleet. Prime Minister Churchill added Britain's only remaining armoured division and with this force Wavell was expected to ward off Mussolini's designs on the Suez Canal, which he planned to seize by a pincer movement. In this way Wavell was to protect the short sea route from England to India and Australia, England's so-called 'lifeline'.

On 22 June Mussolini sent the first of literally hundreds of raids against Malta, the primary source of Wavell's petrol supplies. By the end of July Clifford had gone there, to determine what morale was like on the beleaguered island. 'Malta Awaits 90th Raid; Housewives go

Underground, Carry On; 3000 Live in Giant Shelter' read the headline. Clifford was billed as 'the first British correspondent to visit Malta since Italy entered the war'. Clifford wrote:

> When I toured this most bombed place in the Empire today, I wished that Mussolini were with me.
>
> He would have seen how his bombers, swooping over day and night from Sicily, have left the Maltese with their morale utterly unshaken and with a deep hatred of Italy ... Malta is giving the dictators a great example of how the British Empire stands up to 'lightning war'.

It was one of the last successful attempts on the part of the *Mail* to get a scoop out of Clifford, whose special friendship with the rival *Express* reporter Moorehead meant that both now made no apologies for the fact that they visited the British Embassy and Allied Armies General Headquarters together, pooling their information. It was enraging to their editors back home. Later on, the *Express* editor would express his displeasure by sending cables with identical congratulations to both war correspondents, who chose not to acknowledge them.

Rivalry in the desert was to a large degree a lost cause anyway, since the war there was so difficult to follow. Movement across large expanses of sand took on a ghostly dimension and all the correspondents had to place a great deal of reliance on official reports. The copy then passed through four censors. Under these conditions, coverage could be varied, but scoops were rarely possible.

In Cairo, Clifford and Moorehead depended upon one another to preserve their sanity, and their dependency developed to the point that they were rarely apart. They soon took lodgings together and were able to invest their lives with a familiar rhythm. Whenever they returned from the front, they went that evening to the Turf Club, where they had one drink and played a game of billiards, which Alex invariably won. In the daytime they played tennis at the Gezira Sporting Club. At night they listened to the Palestinian German-Jewish orchestra playing Beethoven and Wagner with the same enthusiasm as they watched the belly dancers in Cairo's hottest night-clubs.

At the front Clifford could be 'irritable and sometimes mean'. He nursed a kind of continuing pessimism and made no bones about the fact that he believed the war was 'a lost cause'. 'Stupidity,' Moorehead wrote of Clifford later, 'was apt to send him into a sudden quiet rage ... often he seemed arrogant and overbearing, and I found myself constantly trying to smooth down the feelings of some ruffled lieutenant ... or official to whom he had been rude...'

By the same token, he gave money to beggars and always 'made an effort to speak with native Egyptians and other Africans in their own language'. He would stop to talk with Italian and German POWs, probably, Moorehead mused, because he 'considered himself to be something of an underdog, or at any rate some sort of a misfit'.

In July of 1940 Clifford was in an RAF Sunderland flying-boat that had been attacked by Italian fighters near the island of Sicily.

> When a gunner had been hit, Clifford had taken his place and was thought to have shot down one of their attackers before the Sunderland managed to land at Malta, riddled with shot-holes and sinking...
>
> As the fighters attacked, Clifford had just begun writing a letter to his mother: 'Dear Mama, I am writing this high above the Mediterranean, where I am out on patrol with the RAF.' When the battle was over, he continued: 'I had just got as far as that when alarming things began to happen ... I cannot tell you more about them now but will reserve the full story until we meet...'
>
> This exploit would have to be kept quiet or Clifford could be executed if captured for having broken the non-combatant rules of the Geneva Convention that applied to war correspondents.

This was only the first time Clifford would carry out such an exploit. To Moorehead's astonishment, he often went along with aerial raids, leaving him to speculate that his friend Alex was the sort of man who sought out fear as a kind of antidote to fear.

Now a change in the terms of their relationship occurred when Moorehead's wife, who was seven months pregnant, came to Cairo. Moorehead believed at this point

> that our friendship could not admit a third person without falling away or breaking up altogether. Neither of us spoke of this, but as the day of Lucy's arrival approached Alex began to retire into a defensive reserve. He arranged to be away for a few days.... Nothing was decided.... We had not even settled the question of whether or not we should continue to live together.

Moorehead left, going on special assignment at the front. When he returned to Cairo he was astonished to hear his wife say 'that she and Alex had already been looking for flats together'.

As it turned out, Lucy and Clifford were both very domestic, Alex buying the furniture for the flat and getting up in the night to give the baby a bottle while Alan slept on. It was a domestic *ménage à trois*, with Alex the strangest volunteer nanny imaginable. The three became inseparable, undismayed by the gossip their strange relationship engendered among the press corps.

That was in Cairo, where Clifford and Moorehead made the best part of their lives. The worst part was spent in the desert, with General

Wavell's Desert Force. In September, the Italians had entered Egypt with five divisions. They immediately set up a series of fortified encampments that spread over a fifty-mile area. Wavell and his men settled seventy-five miles to the east, with the intention of attacking without further delay. But this plan was put aside when Wavell was ordered to make a foray into Greece, where the Italians were also invading. It was not until December that Wavell's Western Desert Force, consisting of 31,000 men, 120 guns and 275 tanks, were able to carry out the attack planned earlier. The Force found a gap in the Italian defences and, though completely outnumbered, succeeded by mid-December in kicking the Italians out of Egypt completely.

The jubilant headlines in the *Daily Mail* back home cheered a populace wearied by the blitz. 'Britain Strikes in Egypt: 1000 Prisoners', one headline read. 'Italian Camp Taken: General Killed', ran another. In the attacks against Bardia and Sidi Barrani the paper told of '30,000 Italians Captured and More are Coming in'. The Highlanders had taken the town at bayonet point, charging forward into the Italian lines 'and after fierce hand-to-hand fighting, cleared the trenches'.

Clifford and Moorehead always approached the front with a sense of dread and, although the action was wholly successful, in this case their sense of foreboding was justified, the pair of them facing untold hardships. Camped in seaside sand-dunes, they at first felt the full triumph of the action when Libyan and Italian soldiers surrendered to them. Further south, near Buq Buq, they were awakened when three armed Libyans approached their campsite, 'utterly dejected and miserable', and surrendered. While the correspondents finished their breakfast the Libyans waited, then got into the back of their truck, and Clifford and Moorehead drove them to the prisoners' depot.

But the exhilaration of easy defeat quickly evaporated when they ran out of food and petrol. It became necessary to search for abandoned dumps for supplies. In the midst of this, Clifford became ill. They would find out later he had been struck with sand-fly fever and jaundice, but for now Moorehead and his fellow correspondents were forced to leave Clifford in the lee of a sand-dune, wrapped up in a blanket, not knowing how serious his condition was. When they went back to search for him, they couldn't find him for an hour. That night, the scorching heat turned to freezing cold, with 'a wind so sharp and piercing that one could not imagine it had ever been hot in the desert. Goose flesh pockmarked our bare sunburnt arms and stunned our eyelids until we ... reached for towels or waterproof sheets to bind round our heads.'

They then prepared what Moorehead would later refer to as the best meal of the campaign: a stew of tomatoes, bully beef and parmesan, served with mineral water. Clifford, however, was too ill to eat.

Despite this, they pressed on. The goal was to reach the front near Bardia, but the trucks broke down and the cold, windy night-time weather made travel difficult. Drawing matches to see who would carry on, Clifford and Moorehead were elected. They 'crept on into Sollum', amid the falling shells, as they watched their colleagues hitch-hike back to their camp. They found a clump of palm trees and camped under them for the night. All they had carried with them was 'a tin of plum pudding and half a bottle of whisky', and as they sat there eating and drinking, a flight of Italian Savoia began an aerial assault overhead. 'In the night they came again, their flaming exhausts making weird flashes above our heads as we crouched in that frozen wadi. Clifford had not eaten for three days and clearly we could not go on. In the first grey light we turned back.'

In terms of the massive bombardments and important battles that would follow in the war, this was only the first campaign the two men would follow together. It would turn out to be little more than a minor skirmish in the lives of these famous correspondents whose fates were now intertwined by the war.

2

Bruisings

The destruction of Coventry, followed swiftly by a raid on Southampton, made it clear that no part of the country was immune to German bombers. In London on December 1940, the largest raid yet destroyed three hospitals, several churches, a convent, a block of flats and other surrounding buildings.

The *Daily Mail* reported:

> the attack grew in ferocity after the earliest London night alert ever sounded. It ended a quiet spell which had lasted for two days and a night. The heaviest barrage for more than a fortnight rocked London as the attackers came in at high speed. Some very heavy guns were in action and the whole skyline was constantly lit by gun flashes.

In the light of the increasing danger from German raids, Esmond determined that his estate, Mereworth, was no longer safe, since it was in the direct line of the aeroplanes as they flew over England. And he had given over his London home, Warwick House, to the Red Cross for the duration of the war. Two of his children, Esme and Vere, had been evacuated to the other side of the Atlantic, although both would soon work their way back home.

He and his eldest daughter, Lorna, had therefore encamped at his father's house at 79 Avenue Road, along with the managing director of Associated Newspapers, Stanley Bell. One evening Lorna had been dining at the house next door and had only just returned home, when a bomb dropped across the street. Stopping to pick up only her fur coat and jewellery, she fled to the cellar where she slept in the chauffeur's room, all the servants having gathered in the air-raid shelter that Harold had had built near the house.

But this only proved to Esmond that no place inside London itself was safe. He decided that if the family had to stay there, they could put up at the Dorchester, which was thought, wrongly as it turned out, to have been built with special protection against bombs. Meanwhile, Esmond rented a small cottage in Ascot.

Despite these good intentions, it was here that Ann O'Neill, who was his regular visitor, experienced her first bomb. 'Went to bed early,' she recorded in her diary, 'was woken by ear-splitting crash and opened my eyes to a sea of flame and broken glass. I lay speechless with terror but thank God only one bomb fell near, the rest several hundred yards away in the wood. I tiptoed over debris to the landing and met the hysterical pantry boy, flashing his torch.' The boy was in a state near hysteria because Esmond had been buried in the rubble. 'Put that torch out,' Ann told him sharply, 'we must find him in the dark.' Just then, according to her account, Esmond arose from under a piece of plaster ceiling, unhurt but annoyed, Ann wrote, by her cowardly speech.

These near escapes and others, which became commonplace throughout the country, made it imperative to protect those whose business it was to produce the *Daily Mail*. Although New Carmelite House was not used as a publication site during the war, it did provide space for a bomb shelter for staff and, during daylight hours, the accounts department was still housed there.

The building had a light well in its centre and maintenance staff thought it safest to cover the shaft with armoured sheeting, to prevent the building from splitting if it was hit by a bomb. Between the light well and the sheeting, however, there was a four-foot gap and it was through this that incendiary bombs fell during one raid over the city, penetrating the bomb shelter below. The mattresses caught fire, thus setting off the sprinkler system, and the basement was flooded. Electrical staff had to go into the shelter, sweep up the shards of broken glass and mop up the water. If this had happened at Northcliffe House production of the *Daily Mail* would have been halted.

Now, the Manchester office assumed more importance because of the relentless bombing in London. Under normal conditions the Manchester publishing facility provided a regular service to Ireland, Scotland, Wales and the north of England. But during the worst of the blitz it also supplied copies of the newspaper to South Wales and the Midlands and even parts of southern England. It appeared to the management of Associated Newspapers that the facility was well beyond the enemy's range.

But in December 1940 that myth was dispelled, when fire raids rained down hundreds of incendiaries on the city. That night had been a bad one, but for the Manchester-based Northcliffe House, Whit Monday 1941 was the moment of crisis.

At 3 a.m. a high-explosive bomb hit a building right opposite the *Daily Mail* premises in Deansgate. It set fire to a gas-main, which was soon roaring like a furnace and eventually destroyed several suites of *Daily Mail*'s offices. The explosion of the bomb killed one of the *Daily Mail*'s ARP staff, and several others were blown through the front door of the building by the blast. A moment later, a large printing-works standing next to Northcliffe House suddenly flared up. It had been set on fire by incendiaries, so that the *Daily Mail* building was now sandwiched between two conflagrations, with the flames licking its roof. This was soon smouldering in several places. . . .

Apparently, the water hydrants had been damaged by the explosion, for there was no water pressure. So staff formed a bucket chain until the City Fire Brigade could establish what course of action to follow.

The blast of the bombs had blown off the sprinkler heads inside the building and the streaming water soon converted staircases into cascades which poured down towards the basement. If this had become flooded, the machines would have stopped, and all the electrical apparatus would have been short-circuited, with considerable danger to the men working in contact with it.

The men forming the bucket chain were now called to sweep away the water with whatever implements they could find at hand. They pulled up the carpets to make dams and, along with rolled-up coconut matting, managed to direct the flow of water out of the building. Thus the staff contrived to get out the *Daily Mail*.

At the end of the day the business offices were demolished, the outer façade of Northcliffe House was destroyed and every window blown out. Although water was being successfully diverted away from the production facility in the basement, it had done enormous damage to the interior of the building. But, more serious than all this, the black-out shutters had been destroyed.

Now the same men who had been fighting fire and water since the early hours of the morning began working to put the black-out back together. With only a few minutes to spare, the staff managed to cover the last window in time to get the paper out.

For those living and working in wartime England, superhuman effort became commonplace and people prided themselves on their ability to cope. For Rhona Churchill, who was pregnant with her first child, it was time to leave her job on the *Daily Mail*. Her husband Alfred had joined the RAF in Fighter Command and was directing flights at Biggin Hill fighter station as he awaited overseas posting. The couple knew he would be sent abroad before the baby was born. Rhona went to stay with her mother at Bromley, Kent, near Biggin Hill, so they were able to be together when Alfred had leave.

But this area was known as 'Bomb Alley' and for good reason. So Rhona reluctantly moved again to her mother-in-law's house located in the 'relative safety of the Midlands'. These were troubled times and the young couple decided they would work out a way to find one another if Britain lost the war.

> We devised a code so that when Alfred wrote to me he could always tell me exactly where he was – a simple one used by his stepfather in the First World War. Based on the word Chelmsford, it had ten different letters and made use to the one to ten numbers in latitude and longitude. Thus, if he was in, say, Cairo (30 latitude, 31 longitude), he would write 'My love to Elsie, David, Eileen and Charles' – 'E' standing for three (the third letter in Chelmsford, D for zero or ten, C for one). This way I could pinpoint him in Durban, Cairo, Jerusalem, Cyprus, or Sicily.
>
> He came on embarkation leave three times.... Each 'final' parting was a tremendous strain for his stepfather for he had experienced the trench-warfare of the 1914–8 war and been shell-shocked. I still vividly remember that third and really last parting – Alfred in RAF uniform standing waving from the step of the bus, his stepfather bursting into tears, me now eight months great with child and his mother close to tears. But she was a strong woman. When we got home she merely said, 'Now, George, no more tears,' told me to put my feet up, made us a cup of tea and started to clean the house rather strenuously.

Rhona delivered without her husband there, as so many wives did during the war. She went to the Ministry of Health Centre for Wartime Babies at Northampton and, during her stay, discovered that the nursing staff ran a betting book, gambling each day on how many little newcomers would be black, 'there being a lot of American soldiers in the area. One unfortunate unmarried mother produced three black triplets.'

Not too long after Rhona's delivery, her mother-in-law suggested she should keep the baby with her, so that Rhona could go back to work as temporary staff on the *Daily Mail*. Her mother-in-law 'became a wonderful granny and mother to John for the next fifteen months', as Rhona rejoined the *Mail* and became quietly indispensable, as was her way.

The office had been streamlined for fast-breaking war news and one of the subs who had managed to survive several different editorial regimes, Arthur Wareham, had been promoted to splash sub-editor. He had impressed his immediate superior, Stanley Horniblow, with his ability to condense 'a mass of material' into a coherent account filling about two and a half columns.

> I co-ordinated the news of the Battle of Britain, the Battle of the River Plate, the fighting in Norway and many other campaigns.... The sinking of the German pocket battleship *Graf Spee* by the cruisers *Exeter* and *Canberra* was a moment of exhilaration. The sinking of the *Prince of Wales* and *Repulse* by the Japanese off

Malaya was a moment of despair. Pearl Harbor was the night that changed the course of the war. Up to then I had been sending off a brief cable each day to a Japanese newspaper, the *Hochi Hochi Shimbun*, containing the highlights of the day's war news. The message I sent on the night of Pearl Harbor was too rude, I am afraid, to be repeated here but it ended the contract in no uncertain way.

Wareham was to become the *Daily Mail*'s chief armchair strategist. In the Russian counter-offensive, all the *Mail* received was a communiqué that gave a list of the cities – 'populated places' – that had been liberated. That sent Wareham to the map to try to figure out where the Russians were and how the advance was proceeding. Despite the imprecision of the method used, the *Mail* did seem to get it right an astonishing number of times.

Even as their colleagues back home struggled with bombs and deadlines, Alexander Clifford and Alan Moorehead were following the actions of the 7th Armoured Division, soon to become famous as the 'Desert Rats'.

On 1 January 1941 General Richard N. O'Connor began to push across northern Africa, continuing with the British campaign to defeat the Italians by traversing the desert bulge of Cyrenaica. After smashing Bardia the Desert Rats, assisted by intensive air and naval bombardment, succeeded in taking Tobruk, the main supply link for the Axis powers, most notably of oil and petrol.

Clifford and Moorehead followed the British troops into the desert, eating the 'gusty, gritty fog' caused by the troops and their vehicles churning up the sand into their faces as the 'lorries ploughed slowly through a rutted morass of dust'. At night, they cooked 'desert style': 'You cut a four-gallon petrol tin in half with a jack-knife, fill one half with sand, pour petrol on it and set it on fire. Then you cook in the other half ... you must finish by sundown, for the fires can be seen for miles.'

They then settled in for the night. Clifford developed a ritual in which he laid his sleeping bag on top of a mat on the sand, then put his blankets across it. Wrapping 'my leather jerkin round my feet', he put his greatcoat 'on top of everything'. He always wore heavy long under-wear below his pyjamas and 'sometimes a sweater above, and always bedsocks'.

My day clothes were kept dry in a large cylindrical RAF flare-case beside me, carefully stacked so that I could dress in three or four swift, painless motions in the morning. My boots went under the bed to prevent them getting filled with dew. It was always agony getting undressed. But it was delicious to wriggle down into the sleeping-bag and gradually to warm up. I used to lie looking straight up

above me, watching the falling stars sliding down the sides of the sky.... Sometimes it was so still you could swear you heard the music of the spheres. On cold
nights like this the stars shone with an extraordinarily clear, frosty glint, and
looking at them steadily had a queer mesmeric effect which sent me quickly to
sleep.

He was awakened smartly at 4.30 a.m. by the sound of gunfire and, half
asleep, he would jerk on his clothes. He and his fellow correspondents
would then get ready for another day in the desert.

The tank silhouettes showed everywhere ... the cold stuck to the bone ... the
chill metal numbed men's fingers as they packed up hastily. They would probably
be in action within an hour. But they had already been in action so long that it
had come to seem the natural condition of their lives.

They stretched themselves, hunted for lost socks and mufflers, opened packets
of dry biscuits, did a thousand trivial things. They shouted from tank to tank ...
joking, cursing, borrowing things, asking questions. There was nothing whatever
to suggest they were setting out to face death....

We raced along behind the brigadier, bumping across a battlefield which
seemed familiar.... The tanks threaded their way among slit-trenches ... petrol
cans, fragments of clothing, charred trucks, piles of shell-cases and green ammu-
nition boxes, and all the mess and litter of war.

The troops crossed the northern deserts of Africa, advancing 500 miles
and destroying in the process nine Italian divisions. By early February,
Benghazi had fallen in what the *Daily Mail* hailed in front-page headlines
as the 'Greatest Blow to Hitler'. Alexander Clifford's story, datelined
'Beyond Cyrene', described the push into Libya as a 'Pleasure Tour'.
Clifford's lead began thus:

Grim, sun-tanned British troops are streaming 10 miles beyond the ancient city
of Cyrene on their way to Barce and Benghazi as I write this tonight.... There
had been reason to expect powerful resistance in the fortified line four miles
beyond Giovanni Berta. But the British Army stormed through this little white-
washed hamlet without a sign of opposition.

Moorehead would later describe the fall of Benghazi with a new enthusiasm, the army overrunning 'one enemy camp after another'. Thus were
he and Clifford given the chance to discover 'the immense joys of
looting. We looted parmesan cheeses as big as cartwheels, and tins of
strawberries, barrels of wine and cases of chocolate, binoculars and
typewriters, ceremonial swords and Italian money galore.' This took
place on 8 February. By the eleventh Moorehead and Clifford would
have been ambushed, as the 'Italian troops made a last desperate attempt

to save Barce'. Their parmesan cheeses, Moorehead reported sadly, 'would be pitted like gruyere' and the biscuits they had plundered shaken to a fine sand. In the end, they would have nothing to eat.

It had started on 29 January when, as the papers reported, 'Italian troops evacuated Derna', the first desert town in O'Connor's push across the bulge of Cyrenaica. Fresh from the desert Clifford and Moorehead craved some kind of luxury and finally managed to locate a villa that had not been looted. It was 'close to the sea, richly hung with bougainvillaea ... we had good wines on the table and a fire going'. The villa, Moorehead discovered, had been occupied by Marshal Rodolfo Graziani, the head of the Italian forces, and the correspondents basked in drinking his wines and eating from his dinner service. Moorehead took his first bath in a week, later hailing some soldiers marching by and asking them in to take baths as well. They sent two officers who had left cards 'a couple of bottles of the Marshal's better brandy'.

Every day Clifford and Moorehead, accompanied by their conducting officer, Captain Geoffrey Keating, would drive out to the front in order to write their pieces for their papers back home. Given the speed of the British advance, it was not always possible to determine 'whether the forts and villages off the main line of advance had been taken or not'. But as they travelled along the road, it seemed as if they were getting warmer and warmer.

> And then at last we were on the enemy. A group of Italians in green uniforms were laying mines in a bend in the road. They dropped the mines and fled into the bushes at the sound of the leading armoured car and our truck following next in line. There were two more armoured cars following immediately behind us....
>
> British officers and men jumped out of the vehicles and began tearing up the mines to make the road safe for the Australian troops now advancing up the road some miles farther back. As they worked, the Italians, about half-a-dozen in all, emerged on to the road a little higher up and stood watching us. It was strange they did not surrender. 'Give them a burst,' someone began to say, and then from the hill ahead a long whining scream of bullets came at us down the roadway. We were ambushed.

As Clifford and Moorehead rushed towards a wooded bank to the left of their vehicle, hoping for cover, 'the enemy ... firing almost at point-blank range', unlashed a burst of fire at one of the armoured cars beside the correspondents. It burst into flames, killing those inside. Moorehead saw another man hit in the legs by machine-gun fire, heard his terrible screams, before one of his comrades dragged him out of harm's way. The enemy were strafing the road with bullets.

Then I saw Keating, full in the face of the fire, running down the line of empty armoured cars trying to get a first-aid kit. Our driver had been cruelly hit on the arm by an explosive bullet as he had leaped from the truck. I ran over to him, tearing off a bandage from a sore on my knee, but he was huddled crookedly in the shallow drainage gutter, quickly drenching in his blood. Clifford joined me, and together we tore off his greatcoat and cut away his sweater and shirt. But then the Italians creeping closer saw us – the last of the British left around the cars. They blew our truck to bits while we lay four yards away trying to stem the wounded man's flow of blood.

Then Keating, who had somehow got up the roadway, joined us with a first-aid pad which we fixed in the wounded man's arm. The fire was very close and very heavy and our cover not more than eighteen inches, so we had to stop and lie still from time to time. Then a piece of shrapnel struck Keating in the forearm, while a bullet tore a ragged hole in his leg. He fell forward softly upon the driver in the shallow trench. Clifford was nicked neatly in the behind. Another bullet passed through the folds of the sleeve of my greatcoat and, certain I was hit, I remember waiting frigidly for the pain to come.

The two correspondents watched as a soldier moved past them, 'dragging the torso of one of his companions, and presently he too was killed'. Then Moorehead took a phial of iodine from the first-aid kit, and held it over the enormous wound of the driver, but his hands were shaking so badly that the phial fell broken into the wound. As he picked up another phial, 'Alex took it away from me and broke it in the proper way.'

But the Italians wouldn't let up, and so half dragging the boy, with Keating following as best he could, the four of them moved pathetically, crouching and darting from one bush to another. Suddenly, Moorehead heard English voices and 'with a rush of gratitude', he and the others were hoisted on to a Bren-gun carrier. They were carried to a small cottage where the two wounded men were operated on, and Clifford and Moorehead were given a swig of water and some tuna fish.

The next day they returned to the spot where they had abandoned their truck, but it was little more than a charred skeleton. 'We were sitting forlornly there among our wreckage when the other war correspondents arrived, and we clambered aboard their vehicles. There was no time to lose. The advance was going very quickly now.'

A year later the correspondents would still be in northern Africa, numbed by the continuous warfare they had witnessed. Faced with the endless suffering, they tried to occupy their minds with domestic arrangements. Christmas would find Clifford and Moorehead 'in a bombed and desolate Benghazi', where they had managed to commandeer two turkeys. Clifford, the cook, considered 'boiling them . . . in a hip-bath, cooking them on spits over a bonfire or coating them in mud and building a fire around them'. At last, they managed to find a stove working in an abandoned hotel.

By now, Hitler had decided to redress the balance of power in the Mediterranean by sending in the Luftwaffe's Air Corps X and General Erwin Rommel, along with his Panzer Afrika Korps. The long-range German bombers prevented Wavell's Desert Force from using the port of Benghazi as a supply base. But Wavell held Tobruk, denying Rommel's entry and thus a land-based supply link.

It was a gritty and determined decision, one that kept Tobruk under alert for some nine months. In December Clifford and Moorehead made their way to the city, not bothering to record what they saw around them, for the gruesome sights they were witnessing as a matter of course could never pass the censors. Later, Clifford wrote of what they had seen:

> Our route lay through the vast, stretched-out rubbish-heap that had been the battlefield.... Alan and I argued about Jane Austen as we bumped past little groups where violent action had been suddenly frozen by death into grim, silent tableaux. We found several British tanks – one contained two roasted bodies and an Edgar Wallace – and not a few Germans. I acquired a German rubber ground-sheet fitting into a neat sachette – most useful. I got it from a truck where a young fair-haired hero was sitting at the wheel with his brains piled on the seat beside him. On the floor of the cab was a postcard from his mother saying that she would bake him another cake when she could but there was nothing to make it with in the house at the moment.

Life had become a grim and determined effort to get through the day without thinking too much. Clifford and Moorehead were by now war-weary veterans who avoided the front whenever they could and who occupied their minds with whatever banter they could manage. Jaded and disillusioned, the pair had nothing except each other.

Back home in London, the proprietor of the *Daily Mail* was involved in a love affair that, more than the reportage of Alexander Clifford or Esmond's many other war correspondents, would affect how the newspaper prospered over the next three decades.

Ann O'Neill, the young matron who had captured Esmond's heart, was weighing up her alternatives. Her most secret lover, Ian Fleming, was mysterious, tentative, irrational, flamboyant, secretive and cruel. Her conventional lover, Esmond Rothermere, was handsome, rich, intelligent, witty and kind. Over and over she asked herself which of them she preferred. Which of them could *help* her more? But the real question was, 'Why choose?'

The complexity of what had developed, full-blown, into a *Jules et Jim* relationship, was attractive to Ann and she enjoyed mulling her situation over in her diary: 'Shane was abroad. Ian by then spent all his leaves wherever I was. I never showed Ian I was in love with him. I knew instinctively it would be fatal. But I did know he was becoming more and more dependent on me. He said I had the heart of a drum-majorette which offset his melancholy.'

In October 1944 Ann's husband, Shane O'Neill, was killed and, in an unlikely scenario, Ann played out her new role as grieving widow with a good deal less heart than any self-respecting drum-majorette:

I was with Esmond and Ian at Esmond's house at Ascot when the telegram arrived to say that Shane had been killed in action in Italy. I was extremely distressed and went immediately to Ian, asked him to tell Esmond, asked him to arrange for my two children to be sent to me, one from home, one from school.... I was thirty-one when Shane was killed and all my family expected me to marry Esmond. Esmond was very anxious to marry me, I was fond of him – very – but no longer in love. I knew he had not wanted the divorce because he thought Shane might be killed – he had always wanted to wait until the end of the war before we took any legal steps. The night before I married Esmond I dined with Ian, and we walked and walked in the park. He said several times 'I want to leave some kind of mark on you'; if he had suggested marriage I would have accepted.

Ann was one of nature's predators. Unable to imagine what anyone else felt, or even that they could feel at all, she was herself unable to experience the normal human emotions of guilt and remorse. When Shane died, she was heard to say, over and over, 'Death is the best revenge.' By this, she intended to convey the idea that by dying, Shane had extracted the cruellest final revenge upon *her*.

For Ann's part, her husband's death had mainly underlined the most pressing issue in her life: the question whether or not she 'could get' Fleming. And if she couldn't, she reasoned pragmatically, she would marry Esmond. How had a woman capable of such logic cast a spell on Ian Fleming and Esmond Rothermere, two intelligent men of the world?

According to some descriptions rather a hatchet-faced woman, Ann did not enjoy a reputation as a great beauty, though she was trim and presentable, with a taste for smart clothes. As for intellect, she was untrained and ill-educated, though she was widely read and reputed to be unusually clever – for a woman. Certainly, she had the considerable advantages of her birth. But the source of her appeal lay elsewhere. Her absolute indifference to the feelings of her contemporaries gave her the crucial advantage in her manipulations of them.

In Ian's experience the person most like Ann had been his domineering mother. In Esmond's, it was largely the same – although he had retained a good deal more balance, probably because his father, though dominating and worrisome, did actually wish him well. No one in his youth had thought to wish Ian well. Ann fitted both men's emotional expectations and, sadly, their emotional needs. Additionally, her illustrious background made both men feel she was 'the immortal garland to be run for'.

So Ann, the centre of her own world, had at last contrived to use Rothermere's resources in order to become the centre of the world at large – the beau monde. Thus did her married life begin. As one of her friends put it: 'It makes perfect sense. She's marrying Rothermere and Ian's round the corner in a flat.'

Determined to become the premier social hostess of London, she reopened Warwick House in the autumn of 1946. One of her closest friends, Peter Quennell, said, 'It must have been almost the last big London house to be kept up in the affluent pre-war style; and the parties she held there were even more diverse than her crowded wartime routs.'

Quennell thought it would have been appropriate to inscribe the maxim, 'Do as you will' above the door. Coincidentally, this had been the one chosen by Aleister Crowley, a.k.a. Beast 666, 'the wickedest man in the world'. Ann's idea of a party, while not quite as decadent as the ritualistic psycho-sexual 'Paris Workings' staged by Crowley in 1913, did have a tendency to get out of hand.

On the first Christmas after the war, Ann and Esmond rented Lord Moyne's house, Bailitts Court, near Bognor Regis, and invited her sister Laura and her husband Lord Dudley to join them. The photographer Cecil Beaton was also asked, as were Loelia Duchess of Westminster and a number of others. On Christmas night there was a fancy-dress ball and Laura later wrote, 'Cecil of course appeared in some splendid get-up, while my sister and I resorted to stockings and suspenders and not much more than a skimpy scarf.' Before dinner, a game of bridge quickly degenerated into one of forfeits, wherein the penalty was 'to find Cecil Beaton and kiss him'. Laura's stuffy husband, Eric Dudley, lost and, in a fit of rage, paid the forfeit, but later wanted to leave the house party. Rothermere took this all in blandly, deserting the crowd to read a good detective novel.

There was another pre-Warwick House party, in July 1945, arranged to celebrate, so it was thought, Churchill's triumphant return to office. Held at the Dorchester, the *Daily Mail*, according to Peter Quennell, had provided enough champagne to celebrate the Second Coming ... [but when] results flashed on to the lighted screen, and one after another Tory strongholds fell, faces lengthened, jubilant voices sank, and the mood of a primitive wake submerged the atmosphere of carnival. Through the crowd stalked Lord Dudley, Ann's hot-tempered brother-in-law, furiously prophesying revolution; our host observed that now we were 'all finished'.

Once into Warwick House, Ann endeavoured to give her parties an intellectual tone and at first organized lecture platforms, where a panel of guests would discuss important political issues. Such debates were usually sandwiched between an elegant dinner and a dance that lasted until the early hours of the morning. She called these gatherings 'brain trusts', but her great friend Evelyn Waugh described them as utter failures. One at which he spoke was boring beyond description, he recorded in his diary, and another that featured a really first-rate panel of political wits also fell flat. If anything, it was a greater failure even than the one he had been a party to.

Those entertainments that centred around films were sometimes more successful, but just barely. In June 1948 Noël Coward wrote in his diary that he attended 'an enormous party' at Warwick House, and afterwards everyone adjourned to Alex Korda's projection room where *Le Diable au Corps* was shown. Directed by Claude Autant-Lara and starring Gérard Philipe and Micheline Presle, the film was a tragic World War I love story, during a large part of which a couple, unclothed, sit before a gas fire, while outside rain pours down relentlessly. The nudity caused considerable embarrassed laughter among the younger male members of Ann's audience. But Noël Coward thought this crowd of sceptics boorish, adding in his entry, 'It is rather frightening to see something fine and imaginative and true torn lightly to pieces by these sophisticates.' A memorable moment occurred when Lord David Cecil, who had been seated in the front of the auditorium, was asked, 'What did you think of the film?' And he answered 'in his high precise voice, "I thought the weather was perfectly beastly."'

Otherwise, a light sense of decadence pervaded most of Ann's parties and this was probably intentional. The same woman who as a girl had watched a relative turn somersaults while quoting Virgil wouldn't blanch when her great friend Lucian Freud ate priceless orchids from a bouquet. And if something genuinely untoward occurred Ann could be counted upon to call attention to it. At one party she was summoned at nearly 5 a.m. by Esmond who 'said he must immediately talk to me alone', Ann wrote to her brother Hugo,

which filled us all with curiosity, but he was insistent and pompous so I meekly went into the hall where I found Martin [Charteris] and with exaggerated solemnity they told me a man and woman were asleep in Martin's bed and what should be done; of course I told everyone and we rushed upstairs, but Esmond so seriously insisted on discretion that I finally went alone to identify the bodies, and found passionately entwined not a man and a woman but two men; they looked so happy that I left them and put Martin in Nanny's bed for what remained of the night.

In the background at almost all these parties was Ann's lover, Ian Fleming, whom she was meeting on a regular basis whenever she could. At first the couple maintained a pretence of discretion, but as they remained undetected they became careless. On one occasion when they could be together for some length of time, Ann wrote instructing Ian to 'kindly write "A" in his book in red letters'.

On this occasion, Ian was immediately to abandon all his other lovers, and if he did not, she joked merrily, 'I shall start our longest honeymoon by hurting you where it hurts most so that you will only be able to write letters to me like Abelard did to Héloïse; and I shan't really mind because I shall have been your last woman, which will give me enormous satisfaction because I have such an unpleasant character.'

This was the first of Ann's light-hearted 'castration jokes', which appear from time to time in her letters to Fleming. In another she will rip the antennae off the troublesome lobsters she is preparing for him. These references may be taken lightly, as whimsical japes, or they can be seen as a kind of bizarre complement to the couple's descent into actual sado-masochistic practices, most especially the 'bruisings' they both enjoyed inflicting upon one another. The couple preferred 'the lash', sometimes referred to as 'the raw cowhide' by Ann.

For his part Fleming complained of her keeping him awake all night: 'You have made bruises on my arms and shoulders,' he wrote. He added the titillating love-threat, 'All this damage will have to be paid for some time.' On offer from Ian at any time was an allotment of twenty lashes, 'ten on each buttock'. For her part Ann professed to like it. On one trip to New York she wrote to Ian, complaining, 'It's very lonely not to be beaten and shouted at every five minutes. I have no bruises and I am basking in flatterers. [I] must be perverse and masochistic to want you to whip me and contradict me, particularly as you are always wrong about everything and I shall go on saying so for ever and ever.'

Fleming, who had never shown the slightest hesitation in demeaning women, romanticized himself as an all-powerful sadist. He was anxious, perhaps too anxious, to show his superiority over the inferior sex (his mother?). Women were, in his book, devalued human beings. He told his male friends, 'Women were like pets, like dogs, men were the only real human beings, the only ones he could be friends with.' But there was every indication that in spite of himself, he was the one who had been enslaved by Ann. She had bound him by means of his vice, one nurtured secretly for years before he found his willing 'victim', and he was oddly compliant in following her dictates. As usual, Ann was the one firmly in control. Wrote the macho Fleming: 'You are like a piece of barley-sugar in my pocket which I can lick at without it getting any smaller and I simply want to hug you until you squeak every time.'

The simpering Ann replied: 'This dear familiar face is not accustomed to neglect, / and still has the capacity to make other men erect. / So if by chance you meet a pretty Biarritz slut, / just pause for thought and hesitate before you stuff her up, etc.'

Thus the affectionate couple.

Through all of this, Esmond suspected nothing. And realistically, who *would* have suspected what was actually taking place? For the behaviour of Ann and Ian beggared all imagination.

From Boodles, Ian would saunter down St James's to Warwick House, where Rothermere, always the gracious host, was happy to welcome him as the spare man at a dinner table or a partner who knew the rules in a bridge rubber. Ian became an honorary member of an extended family that included Loelia Westminster, Ann's brother Hugo, who lived at Warwick House briefly after he married Virginia Forbes Adam in 1948, and Ann's sister Laura, who was in situ during the latter stages of her troubled marriage to Eric Dudley. But it was a curious schizophrenic existence. Whenever Esmond was away or simply at the office, Ian found his way up the stairs to milady's bedroom, and that caused all manner of tensions and confusions. Virginia Charteris recalled inadvertently surprising the two lovers during the 'cinq à sept' period. 'There was an atmosphere you could cut with a knife. Ian said apologetically, "I'm just going." They'd just had the mother and father of all rows. Clearly they thrived on it. They liked hurting each other.'

The full extent of the couple's folly became apparent when Ann became pregnant with Ian's child. She wrote to her sister-in-law, who was also pregnant, in March 1948, 'I hope your situation is as interesting as mine.' The sad irony of Ann's words was realized beyond even her own intentions when, in the eighth month of her pregnancy, she began having labour pains at the Gleneagles Hotel in Scotland where Esmond had taken her and the usual entourage of friends on a short holiday aimed at relaxing her before the birth. But instead she was rushed to hospital in Edinburgh, where she gave birth to a baby daughter by Caesarian who lived fewer than eight hours.

Although Esmond mourned the child as his own, it was Ian Ann longed for. He was working through a game of golf as she wrote a pathetically disconnected note to him from her hospital bed:

My Darling

There was morphia and pain and then you were here and now you've gone and there's nothing except the grim realisation of what happened in the last ten days.... I feel full of remorse towards Esmond and yet my grief and loss is entirely bound up with you; and both are too feminine for you to understand; the loss of a baby of 8 hours' age cannot be a grief to a father, so I mustn't get ideas about Esmond's feelings, or get hysterical about it all.... I hope you are playing wonderfully and feeling well, it's the greatest comfort to know you are near me, and thank you for your sweetness all this year and for your letters....

Goodnight my sweet

Ann

In the aftermath of the tragedy, Esmond decided that Ann needed to get away, and he took her first to Paris and then to Portofino, where Alexander Clifford, the former Mediterranean war correspondent, had bought a villa overlooking the sea. In this small fishing village 'the hills rose up from the sea in sparkling terraces of vines and bright rocks with the contadinos' cottages in between, the Castello was deserted, and the village life revolved around the cycle of the seasons'. The gorgeous bay attracted a circle of impressive visitors and expatriates – Joe Alsop, Osbert Lancaster, Truman Capote, and many others. Esmond thought the lively company would help Ann forget about the ordeal she had just been through.

Since the war, Clifford had become an important figure. His coverage of the desert war in North Africa had been followed by the Allied invasion of Salerno and later the D-Day invasion. Along with Moorehead and Christopher Buckley of the *Daily Telegraph*, Clifford now became known as part of a 'trio' who were famous for their reportage. But of the three, Clifford was surely the most famous. His shy, self-effacing manner had won the hearts of the reading public, but though he still worked for the *Daily Mail* he preferred to live in anonymity in Italy. In addition to his special assignments on the newspaper he was working on a political book that would bring him even greater fame, *Enter Citizens*.

Clifford had married author Robert Graves's daughter Jennifer Nicholson. Jennifer's surname was Nicholson because her mother refused to give her father's name to her daughters, a sign of the girls' colourful background. In describing Jennifer to his mother, Alex had written that she was twenty-six and had had 'a bizarre and curiously unsuitable career'. She had worked as a cabaret performer, a ballet dancer, a chorus girl, an actress and a radio writer for the BBC. Moorehead had said of the improbable match that it was 'the least predictable of attachments and the most inevitable.... [She had a] touch of recklessness and eagerness for life.... Alex rose from the depths like a leaping trout.'

Alan Moorehead and his wife Lucy did not like Alex's new wife, describing her as 'temperamental and too assertive'. But they came to Portofino anyway to see Alex, and in fact had visited the couple and departed only a short time before Ann and Esmond arrived.

On one cloudy and rather depressing day Ann received a letter from Ian that included articles from American magazines. When she showed one of them, written by Alan Moorehead, to Jennifer, she 'put her head in her hands and burst into tears, occasionally uttering imprecations and curses against Alan Moorehead, while Alex sat scarlet and shamefaced'. According to Jennifer's version of why she was upset, she and Alex had lent their villa to the Mooreheads, sacrificing a great deal of money from Italians who wanted to rent the house, and in a moment of foolishness Jennifer had confided to Alan that she was writing a book on Portofino. She had read him sections of her manuscript and the article published in the *New Yorker* that Ann now held in her hands was based on Jennifer's research.

> It cast a great shadow over the day for whenever we passed a post office Jenny sent abusive telegrams to Alan while Alex was dumb and miserable but unable to save the Clifford–Moorehead axis from becoming an Italian vendetta.... Esmond added the *coup de grâce* by becoming absorbed in the article and pronouncing it interesting and excellently written.

Ann wrote of these matters to Ian with much amusement. Such a fracas was to her liking and, since the split between the Mooreheads and Cliffords was soon mended, little lasting damage was done to the deep friendship between the two war correspondents.

Just as Esmond had foreseen, the change of scene had done Ann good. More or less fully recovered, she was soon meeting Ian again, in one or another of their hideaways. Their passion was now strongly grounded in mutual grief, or so Ann believed, for she said it was the kindness which Ian showed her during the death of their daughter that convinced her he loved her. So far as Ian was concerned, their passion was as irresistible as ever.

Only one thing bothered him about the clandestine relationship – the unsightliness of the scar Ann now carried as a result of the Caesarian. He could not help feeling repugnance whenever he happened to catch sight of it. For Ann was no longer perfect and this was the sort of thing Ian found very difficult to cope with – although it would be a long time before Ann found that out.

3

'The Monster'

Esmond had a propensity to please that had landed him in trouble a number of times, both with women and with work. And if that weren't enough, he had an exaggerated sense of fair play that often put him at a disadvantage.

He had very early in life become acquainted with the discrepancy between the artificial public lives led by great men and their private failings. When he was barely twenty-one years old, Esmond had attended the peace conference at Versailles as ADC to Lloyd George. In later years he would entertain his dinner guests with humorous stories of the Prime Minister's many peccadilloes and his own duties of keeping track of the frequent comings and goings of Lloyd George's mistresses. Lloyd George had viewed his relations with women as a kind of relaxation after the pressures of office. Esmond's father, too, had his share of involvements with the fairer sex.

It was only natural that Esmond's own conduct would be affected by the behaviour he had witnessed among the men who were his models. And while he had no capacity for the darker aspects of the relations between the sexes, he did have a complicated nature.

He was certainly precocious where women were concerned. His early marriage to Margaret Hunam had been a passionate alliance, intensified by the fact that Esmond and Peggy, as she was known, were both so young. But despite adoring her, he still could not resist flirtations with other women, some of them serious. Infuriated that her young and good-looking husband was the centre of attention with other women, Peggy, herself a beauty, found no difficulty in carrying on flirtations of her own. The result was domestic disaster, with Peggy eventually bundling up the couple's three children and making her way to Claridge's. Though she continued to nurse hopes that they would put the marriage back together, the young couple's relationship degenerated still further and they found themselves embroiled in one of the longest divorce proceedings in history, lasting some eight years.

This was the denouement of the marriage. But in their early years together Esmond had coddled Peggy, planning their cottage on the Isle of Wight down to the last detail, playing games with the children, dancing attendance on her every wish, and lavishing gifts and flowers upon her. This gave the impression that he was an easier man than was actually the case.

Again, after he resigned from Parliament in 1929, assuming more duties at Associated Newspapers, he brought an eager enthusiasm to the job. But his own rigid code of ethics prevented him dealing as ruthlessly as his major rival Beaverbrook. Time and time again, he would be outfoxed by the *Express* proprietor, and it was often his own doing.

By the time he had been in the job for two years, it had become obvious to Esmond that something had to be done about the *Daily Mail*. He wrote urgently to his father on 'the decline in the sale of the "DM"'. The *Express*, he told him in a private and confidential memorandum, was inching up on the *Mail* and the reason, Esmond wrote conclusively, was that 'the "DM" is not the best morning paper of its kind in London'. At the moment the *Express* was within 20,000 copies of the *Mail* and, when the circulation of the *Express* did top the *Mail*, 'Northcliffe House prestige will have suffered a blow from which it may never recover'.

In Fleet Street and beyond, Esmond warned, 'All kinds of people are waiting for this moment to jeer.' But despite the impending crisis he disagreed with his father's intention of throwing half a million pounds into give-aways and competitions. He believed the money would be better spent on upgrading the news department, which was slipping badly. He also thought the newspaper was being poorly edited and that a new man must be found. As Esmond wrote to his father, the key was first the *Sunday Dispatch*.

> A young man of thirty-five [who] should be given the editorship of the "Dispatch" with complete independence to make or mar his career, and let him introduce new blood. There is no such man on the Staff at present – Fleet Street will have to be scoured for him. . . .
>
> Men should not be got rid of because they have independent views, or are difficult to get on with. Most men worth anything are difficult to get on with. There have been many people sacked in N. House for insufficient reasons. This has not helped the atmosphere. There should be only one criterion – 'Is the man a success at his job?!'

Throughout the company, Esmond told his father, 'there is a great feeling of alarm' and he advised his father not to react to his memo immediately, but to take time to reflect upon what was the best course of action.

The memo did have an immediate effect, however. When Bernard Falk, the editor of the *Sunday Express*, retired, a young assistant editor at the paper was summoned to Carmelite House by the then managing director of Associated Newspapers, Sir George Sutton. The young man, just twenty-six years old, had recently distinguished himself with his coverage of the crash of the R101. Years later, Arthur Christiansen would remember what happened next.

Sir George asked him whether he had handled the coverage of the air crash himself.

Yes, Christiansen answered, the editor had gone home early because it was a slack news day.

Sir George had one other question and that was how much Christiansen earned. 'Thirty-seven pounds per week,' Christiansen answered. With that Sir George excused himself from the room and when he came back in he was with Esmond Harmsworth.

Christiansen thought Esmond 'a monosyllabic giant ... as shy of me as I was of him'. He was very shocked when Esmond, after only the most cursory of greetings, asked him 'how [he] would like to be the editor of the *Sunday Dispatch*.' 'I said I did not know. "Esmond" said that if I accepted the job I would be paid £3000 a year. I reeled inwardly at this, but tried to look calm and said I would like to think it over.'

Here, then, was Esmond's 'young man' – the twenty-six-year-old he believed could boost circulation, first of the *Dispatch* and eventually of the *Daily Mail*, thus leading the paper's revival against the competition of the *Express*. But Christiansen already worked for Beaverbrook and it was Esmond's sense of ethics, his feeling for fair play, that now prevented him pressing his advantage, instead extracting a promise from Christiansen. He was to go away and think about the offer, but he was not to use the offer to get his salary on the *Express* jacked up. To this a confused Christiansen readily agreed, thinking he was greatly overpriced by Esmond and Sir George Sutton.

But when he returned to his own office and told his editor what had happened the latter rang Beaverbrook and the pair were immediately summoned to Stornaway House, Beaverbrook's home near Green Park. There they talked, the details of Christiansen's meeting with Esmond and Sir George being repeated and Beaverbrook listening gravely. At last the press baron asked him baldly whether he would stay or 'are you going to cross to the shadows?'

Christiansen blurted that he would stay, and the men sat drinking and talking of other things. Then, when he rose to go, Beaverbrook said as an aside that his salary would be put up to £3000 per year. Christiansen objected, saying he had agreed he wouldn't use the offer to get his money upped. But Beaverbrook said, somewhat impatiently:

'Let us go through our conversation from the beginning. I told you that I would like you to stay with the *Express*. You said that you would. We then abandoned discussion of your situation and talked about next Sunday's paper. Then I said to Gordon "Put Christiansen's salary up to three thousand a year..."'

Did I, or did I not, agree with his version of the sequence of events? Finally I had to agree that I did.

'Very well. Gordon, put Mr Christiansen's salary up as from the first of January – back-date it to January for good measure. Goodbye to you.'

It was in this way that Beaverbrook put a halt to Esmond's poaching his promising young editor, an exercise that must have seemed like child's play to the wily Canadian. In two more years Christiansen would become the editor of the *Daily Express*. Under his leadership the *Express* would become a force in Fleet Street, just as Esmond feared.

Some seven years later, in 1938, Esmond would again come face to face with Beaverbrook, and although he now understood the ruthlessness and egotism of his rival he would again he outsmarted. This time, it was because of Esmond's honest desire to be of service – to the Prince of Wales.

After he separated from Peggy, Esmond had become a close friend of the Prince. It was a relationship that had started on the Riviera but quickly changed scene to England. As Esmond became more and more a familiar figure in the Prince's intimate circle, Edward and his constant companion, Wallis Simpson, motored to Mereworth for a pleasure outing. In return, Esmond was a guest of the newly crowned king in the autumn of 1936, when he joined a shooting party.

'Balmoral was delightful,' he wrote to his daughter Lorna on 7 October. 'I went stalking most days but the deer were very difficult to get. We had good weather and the scenery is very beautiful. The King is always a perfect host so we were all very comfortable.'

All was not as idyllic as Esmond's letter to his daughter seemed to indicate, however, for within three weeks, Mrs Simpson would be granted a decree nisi on the grounds of her husband's adultery, thus freeing her for marriage. King Edward VIII intended to marry the twice-divorced American.

The American press was well informed on the possibility, anticipating the marriage of one of its own to the British king with eager anticipation, and speculations began spewing out of the American media. But the British press was far more reluctant to report what, in the first instance, appeared to be little more than one of the King's more serious flirtations. The turning point had been the granting of the decree nisi, signalling a change in the terms of the affair, and the King prevailed upon Esmond to advise him what was the best way to proceed with the British press.

Esmond believed that he could convince his fellow proprietors that discretion on their part might prevent a full-scale constitutional crisis. As the chairman of the Newspaper Proprietors Association, a post to which he had been elected in 1934, he was in the perfect position to do so. But Esmond knew Beaverbrook would never agree to co-operate with him in such a venture. For a man like Beaverbrook nothing would do except that he be at the centre of the storm. Esmond's counsel to the King then was that he ask Beaverbrook's advice on how to proceed, allowing him to co-ordinate any press response.

Thus was Beaverbrook drafted one more time into a role he much enjoyed – that of go-between. The King responded to the charismatic personality of the press baron positively and when the crisis grew out of all control requested Beaverbrook come to his aid. In the winter of 1936 Beaverbrook, who suffered from asthma, was mid-Atlantic on a trip for a rest-cure in Arizona, but returned to England as the King had asked.

So it happened that Beaverbrook and the Harmsworths stood staunchly supporting the monarch against a mutual enemy of long standing – Stanley Baldwin. In an effort to defuse the situation, Esmond's father Harold suggested a morganatic marriage; that is, a marriage in which Mrs Simpson and the King were permitted to wed, but she would not be entitled to become his queen. Esmond duly forwarded the suggestion to the King, then to the Prime Minister, where it was rejected on the basis that there was no legislative precedent for such an arrangement.

Winston Churchill, very sympathetic to the King's cause, suggested he wait for things to cool down, to accustom the British public to the idea of Mrs Simpson, but the King remained intractably committed to proceed with his marriage without delay. Given this, all that was left to Esmond was to provide what support he could.

On 4 December *Mail* columnist Margaret Lane published a chirpy interview with Wallis Simpson, beneath a flattering drawing, that was intended to create the image of a woman who would be acceptable to the British populace. On the same day a *Daily Mail* leader wrote of 'the determination of the country ... that no development of the present extraordinary situation shall be allowed to part it from its beloved King'.

'Abdication', the editorial continued, 'is out of the question, because its possibilities of mischief are endless. The effect on the Empire would be calamitous.' Esmond was effectively showing his support for the King by every means at his disposal.

By 10 December the *Mail* published a leader entitled, 'The Nation's Hope'. It pictured a country united in its wish that the King would delay wedding Mrs Simpson. 'Unhappily,' the leader read, 'the indications late last night were not such as to encourage optimism, though until the last minute of the last hour the nation will continue to pray that the King's final decision will be against abdication.' At last, on 11 December, the *Mail* published the outcome: 'The King Has Chosen'. In far-flung prose, the *Mail* wrote:

> We have passed through the most anxious and astounding day in the history of our Empire. At its close no longer did King Edward the Eighth hold the most glorious heritage that ever fell to the lot of a ruler. His 'final and irrevocable' abdication fills every heart with an overwhelming sense of tragedy. Indeed, the event far transcends man's capacity to realise it and all that it implies.

Esmond remained staunchly loyal to the end, but finally he was not the man to see how best to position himself in terms of events so that any benefit from the sensational affair fell to him and his newspapers.

Beaverbrook was. If he could not save the King he could at least help himself. He eventually persuaded Edward to sell him the serial rights to *The King's Story*, putting forward in 1956 in his own version an account of the events that led him to abdicate. For this, Edward received a record £200,000 and the *Sunday Express* experienced a circulation boost that left Esmond's rival *Sunday Dispatch* in the dust.

Esmond had again failed when pitted against the wily Beaverbrook. Did this mean Esmond was a willing dupe to any ruthless foe who happened to be at odds with him now and then? There was certainly that side to his character.

Esmond could be as ruthless as the predatory types who surrounded him when his back was to the wall – but only then. He could act quickly and efficiently, but only in a case where his own survival, or the survival of his company, was at risk. And this 'last-chance-saloon' ruthlessness of Esmond's could come as a nasty surprise to those who had been taking it as a matter of course that they could manipulate him in any way they pleased.

To his subordinates Esmond was indeed the centre of power, but he was also a symbol of leadership and importance. His men sometimes went to amusing lengths to show obeisance to the name Rothermere. The secretary of Associated Newspapers, for example, always stood up out of respect whenever Esmond rang him on an extension line.

The reaction of a shareholder who gushed forth in a General Meeting of the Daily Mail & General Trust was not untypical: 'I always believed in the name of Harmsworth,' said one Mr Nicholson, 'and it is one of the finest firms to work for. The industry as a whole owes a great debt to the name of Harmsworth. We admire the strides you have made and the work you are doing. The newspaper world owes much to the name of Harmsworth. . . . They were the pioneers, and I think you are a worthy successor to a worthy father.'

Esmond, not one to lose his poise even in the face of this remarkable public praise, could only answer, 'Thank you very much indeed. Thank you for coming here and making such a charming speech. We very much appreciate it.'

But the same position of power that caused one man to subjugate himself would cause another to plot and scheme in order to occupy the position himself. In 1944, just before Esmond married Ann O'Neill, a crisis occurred within the ranks of the *Daily Mail*. On the floor the full details were not known. But the gossip mill ground out a story that seemed plausible. The night editor, Arthur Wareham, kept a personal account of the rumours that pitted the managing director of Associated Newspapers against the chairman of Daily Mail & General Trust.

'Stanley Bell, a brilliant management man,' Wareham wrote, 'had risen rapidly from very lowly beginnings to become Managing Editor and was a tremendous power in the organization. It is possible that he overestimated his power.' The story circulated that the editor of the *Evening News* wanted to get rid of a long-serving executive and Bell rubber-stamped his agreement without consulting the chairman. The upshot was that the man was dismissed from the company. Lord Rothermere objected and, wrote Wareham,

> Bell, from all accounts, seems to have taken up a rather aggressive attitude by suggesting that if Lord Rothermere doubted his judgment then he (Stanley Bell) would be prepared to resign, never thinking that Lord Rothermere would accept his resignation. Lord Rothermere, for reasons of his own, did accept, and Bob Prew, who had always been very close to Stanley, resigned with him.

This was the story that was put about, but it was a far cry from what had actually happened. A few days after the crisis, on 2 August 1944, Esmond wrote to a close business associate, Frank Humphrey, in New York that 'Stanley Bell has retired from his position as Managing Editor'. He went on to say that he had no plans to fill the vacancy for the moment, but eventually he would put William McWhirter in Bell's place. 'You will not expect me to enter into the reasons for the change in a letter. These matters are better left to discussions and so you will have to wait until we meet. . . . Stanley Bell's resignation took effect as from the 26 July.'

The dismissal had been a hot one, according to a source very close to the chairman. And the man, Percy Hobson, who was Esmond's secretary and who overheard part of the argument between Bell and Rothermere, reported it thus:

Well, Stanley Bell had a stand-to with him in Esmond's office and Esmond said 'No, I'm sorry I'm not having it. I have your contract in my drawer here and here it is and you're gone.' That's all Percy could hear. Stanley Bell gave the impression that he was chairman and Esmond said, 'You're not chairman, I am.' That was the hearsay from Howell.

The story behind what Hobson overheard, never committed to paper but passed down by word of mouth through the decades, held that Stanley Bell and Bob Prew, along with a handful of others, found out that Esmond did not own fifty-one per cent in the company and began buying up shares in order to control it. One person in the cabal apparently reported this to Esmond and was amply rewarded. It may even have been McWhirter, the man who replaced Bell. The others involved were all sacked and Rothermere reviewed his ownership to be sure this couldn't happen again.

A second rumour circulated on the other side of the Atlantic – that Frank Humphrey, the business associate in New York to whom Esmond had written the day after the resignations of Stanley Bell and Bob Prew had been announced, had been one of those fomenting the overthrow of leadership. Humphrey was a complicated man, given to moralizing about the necessity of young people to walk the straight and narrow, while at the same time keeping three mistresses in New York City. Such a one was quite capable of organizing a secret coup. If Humphrey was involved, then Esmond's letter was an effectively sinister way of announcing the failure of the cabal to achieve its desired goal.

It wasn't the last time Esmond would face an attempt to take over the company right under his nose, but it was the most dramatic. Now it was important to put an unexceptional spin on what had happened and, to this end, nothing could have been more prosaic or less informative than the announcement of Bell's departure that appeared in *The Times*. 'The board of Associated Newspapers', *The Times* wrote, 'announces that Mr Stanley Bell, having expressed his desire to retire from the position of managing director, his resignation has been accepted with regret.'

A few days later *The Times* announced that Bell would continue as the chairman both of the rationing committee of Associated Newspapers and the Wastepaper Recovery Association.

Now Esmond went about tying up every loose end and he wrote to Beaverbrook explaining that it had been necessary 'to make certain changes at the *Mail*'. Stanley Bell, he explained 'had become extremely swollen headed and loyalty was never his strong point. He has now left the business.' As for a suggestion made by members that Bell might possibly be given the position of managing director of the Newspapers

Proprietors Association of which Esmond was the head, 'this would create an impossible situation and I am sure that should such a situation arise I could count on your friendship and support.'

None of this was known on the editorial floor, but the swift demise of two such important figures as Stanley Bell and Bob Prew had a great effect on the staff. 'If both the Managing Editor of Associated Newspapers and the Editor of the *Daily Mail* could depart in this way overnight, anything could happen in our organisation. One must never for a moment assume that one is indispensable,' Arthur Wareham entered in his diary.

When Northcliffe had been proprietor of the *Daily Mail* the same editor, Tom Marlowe, ran the newspaper for twenty-seven years. As soon as Northcliffe's brother Rothermere took over the helm the editors began to change more rapidly: there were five, not counting 'acting' editors, in some eighteen years. It now appeared that Esmond might follow in his father's footsteps instead of Northcliffe's, changing his editors almost on whim. Surely Esmond, who had argued so forcefully with his father against a lack of continuity on the *Daily Mail* staff, would not himself perpetuate a similar reign of terror, and all that that entailed in terms of morale and loyalty among the staff.

On the other hand, men who were insecure about their own survival were the least likely to plot the overthrow of their superiors. Perhaps the rapid turnover of editorial leadership did have a certain logic all its own.

At about the same time that Esmond was fighting off the first attempt at a palace coup under his leadership, his new editor, Stanley Horniblow, and Charles Sutton, Horniblow's foreign editor, were plotting to get the best war coverage for the *Daily Mail*.

It so happened that each newspaper was allowed only one war correspondent at a base camp. Agencies, however, were allowed two. Sutton, who had good contacts at the International News Service (INS) and took the agency's wire, made a deal whereby he could send one of the *Mail's* correspondents, in place of an INS reporter, who would then wire the stories back to the INS in Fleet Street. The INS would in turn bounce them over to the *Mail* offices.

Sutton's plan was to send in a correspondent to follow the Americans across the Rhine and into Germany, and send back not the propaganda pieces that had nurtured the British populace during the dark days when it looked as if England might suffer defeat, but the truth. For this, he needed a correspondent who could speak German.

Rhona Churchill had spent a year as a student in Germany during pre-Hitler days and was fluent in German. So, after the birth of her son John,

The young Esmond. Handsome, rich, intelligent and powerful, he seemed to have it all. But the heroic deaths of his two elder brothers in World War I overshadowed his own sense of self.

DAILY
MAIL

SUNDA
DISPATC

Opposite
Above First precautions against the Blitz.

Below Whit Monday 1941, the bombing of the *Daily Mail*'s Manchester office.

This page
Right The *Daily Express*'s gregarious Alan Moorehead, with his introspective rival from the *Mail*, Alexander Clifford. The war, wrote Moorehead later, 'isolated us from our past lives. We were like two strangers who clung together in a shipwreck.'

Below Rhona Churchill, war correspondent for the *Daily Mail*, with Prime Minister Churchill and Field Marshall Montgomery, on the 25th of March 1945.

Right Esmond Harmsworth (second left) with Edward VIII, Wallis Simpson and friends, at Mereworth. Later, Esmond would advise against Edward's Abdication, to no avail.

Left Ann with her new husband, Ian Fleming, after leaving Esmond. Their ill-starred relationship would remain deeply troubled, both husband and wife eventually seeking the company of others, their only son Caspar ending his own life.

Below The flamboyant and talented *Daily Mail* editor, Frank Owen. At first friendly with Ann, he would learn to dread her interference.

Opposite The Rothermeres welcome actress Margaret Lockwood to the National Film Award ceremony in 1947. Soon after Emond's marriage to Ann, she became a glittering social hostess. But it wouldn't be enough for Ann.

Above *Mail* editor Guy Schofield in 1950 with senior editorial executives, in a posed photograph typical of the age. Billed 'a real gentleman', within two weeks of assuming control of the newspaper, Schofield had sacked ten top *Mail* men.

Left *Mail* editor Arthur Wareham. Self-styled as 'the quiet man of Fleet Street,' Wareham was stable, hardworking, conservative and capable. He lasted six years, a record in the troubled 1950s.

Opposite The Coronation issue of the *Daily Mail*.

Daily Mail

NO. 17,791   THREE HALFPENCE   FOR QUEEN AND COMMONWEALTH   WEDNESDAY, JUNE 3, 1953

The Queen's message: 'I thank you all from a full heart'

LET US CHERISH OUR OWN WAY OF LIFE

The Queen, who spoke **ng and confident** **broadcast this** **to Britain and** **mmonwealth at** **k last night after** **ronation :**

HEN I spoke to you last, at Christmas, I asked you all, whatever your n, to pray for me day of my Coro——to pray that God give me wisdom rength to carry out romises that I then be making.

out this memorable have been uplifted tained by the know- hat your thoughts ayers were with me. been aware all the that my people, d far and wide out every continents ean in the world. ted to support me task to which I have een dedicated with lemnity.

usands of you came on from all parts Com monwealth and to join in the cere- but I have been con- too, of the millions s who have shared means of wireless ion in their homes. ou, near or far, have ited in one purpose.

usband . . .

rd for me to find n which to tell you strength which this ge has given me.

emonies you have day are ancient, and f their origins are n the mists of time. ut their spirit and n e a n i n g shine the ages, never, more brightly w.

n sincerity pledged o your service, as so f you are pledged to Throughout all my with all my heart strive to be worthy trust.

resolve I have my to support me. He all my ideals and all tion for you. Then, h my experience is rt and my task to have in my parents andparents an ex- which I can follow rtainty and with ce.

ppes . . .

also this. I have be- e not only the splen- aditions and the of more than a d years but the trength and majesty Commonwealth and of societies old w; of lands and ifferent in history rigins but all by ill, united in spirit im.

I am sure that this. oronation, is not the f a power and a ur that are gone declaration of our for the future and years I may, by race and mercy, be o reign and serve your Queen.

en speaking of the gions and varied to whom I owe my ut there has also from our island theme of social and thought which ses our message to rld and through the g generations has acceptance b o t h and far beyond my

loyalty . . .

ntary institutions, eir free speech and for the rights of es, and the inspira- a broad tolerance in t and its expression ls we conceive to be ous part of our way and outlook.

cent centuries this has been maintained nvigorated by the contribution, in ge, literature, and of the nations of commonwealth over-

expression, as I pray ays will, to living y of it will be not the solemnity and Monarchy as to ny Parliaments and I ask you now to them—and practise oo ; then we can go s together in peace, Justice and freedom men.

ay draws to its close, that my abiding ys will, to living des as sacred to the Monarchy as to ny Parliaments and I ask you now to heir inspiration of your and affection.

you all from a full God bless you all.

Composed and sedate she drove to the Abbey.   With solemnity and great dignity she played her part in the long and moving Coronation ceremonies.   Radiant and happy she returned to Buckingham Palace.   Hundreds of pictures proclaimed that supreme happiness.   This one most of all.   It was taken on the balcony after nine tiring hours of ceremonial.

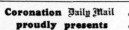

Coronation Daily Mail proudly presents

Two *Daily Mail* greats. Noel Barber (top), on the 16th of December 1957, in a story headlined, 'I AM AT THE POLE.' When Sir Edmund Hillary reached the South Pole, Barber was actually waiting for him. Four years earlier, the swash-buckling Ralph Izzard (right) had overshot Hillary's British Expedition of Everest at 18,000 feet.

when Charles Sutton cajoled Rhona back on to the *Mail* as temporary staff, he actually had in mind sending her overseas as a war correspondent.

My value, such as it was, really started in 1944 when the American First Army crossed into Germany and took Aachen.... I was put into American Army uniform and assigned as a War Correspondent to the US Ninth Army, who were then established in the German city. My instructions were to ignore the battle stories and roam at will concentrating on getting in among the German civilians and writing factual reports.... I think the *Daily Mail* was the first Fleet Street newspaper to adopt this policy and it must have taken courage and foresight. I was lucky enough to have this very fertile field almost to myself until the war ended.

Rhona Churchill had a good track record that made what looked like a gamble actually a great deal less risky than it appeared. As a young reporter, she had very much admired Margaret Lane, the star feature reporter on the *Daily Mail* in the 1930s. Rhona knew well that Margaret Lane had got her start when she travelled on her own to America and did some heavy reporting, including getting an exclusive with Al Capone after he had been imprisoned for evading taxes.

Rhona herself had therefore trekked to the United States to be like Margaret Lane. Offered a desk at the King Features Syndicate, she had a better offer when somebody got her a ticket that allowed visiting journalists to travel free by air anywhere in the country. Rhona thought this too good to turn down and left New York, touring America and sending back copy to the *Sunday Dispatch*. She returned when it became plain to her that there would soon be a war, 'and I didn't want to get stuck on the other side of the Atlantic when it broke out.'

Once installed in the INS in Germany, Rhona wore an American uniform because women sent out to cover the war under British accreditation were not given the same freedom as a man to do the job. They had to have an army driver, they weren't allowed beyond army Headquarters without special permission and they had to be accompanied by a conducting officer. 'In other words,' Churchill wrote later, 'they couldn't do their jobs.'

Since I was far more capable than most men at looking after myself because I spoke German, it all seemed quite ridiculous.

This of course also was resented. [And the arrangement] wasn't really quite fair. Noel Monks was the news man. Anything that was hard news, he covered and I covered whatever I felt was not hard news and in my field. We didn't clash very much. Occasionally we did because I would go off and do something I couldn't discuss with him and then find perhaps that he'd done something about it as well but this didn't happen very often because I didn't cover battles.

I did at one stage fly over a battle. I got myself into one of those little spotter planes that were flying over the battle and I wasn't allowed to cover the actual ground battle so I thought it might be fun to go up and watch it from the air and I wrote the copy and I got into trouble for that because I really shouldn't have done it, it wasn't my job. It so happened that Noel was flying through London and picked up a *Daily Mail* and saw that I was sitting up in a plane over a battle.

Rivalries aside, Rhona was typing an overnight report when the most memorable story she reported during World War II came her way. 'Your namesake's next door,' someone whispered to her and she abandoned her story, rushing out to see Winston Churchill and entourage leaving in army vehicles. At the end of the line was a jeep, empty except for a GI driver, and Rhona called out, 'Can I come with you?' He said, 'Sure. But I'm the spare vehicle and if they want me I'll have to dump you.'

Churchill was friendly to Rhona, but declined to give her an interview because he had turned down a number of her colleagues the day before. 'But stay close to me,' he said, 'and you'll hear all I say and get a good story, and I do congratulate you on being here.' Thus did Rhona cross the Rhine with Churchill and Eisenhower. The material he gave her was good, but the censor ended up cutting all the best bits.

What finally ran in the *Daily Mail* was a story-caption written by the sub-editor headlined 'Churchill is the name'. 'In the footsteps of the Premier planted firmly on the east bank of the Rhine goes the first British woman to cross the river – war correspondent Rhona Churchill whose dispatches appear in the *Daily Mail*.' Below the short piece is a picture of Winston Churchill in uniform, walking briskly with a cigar in his mouth, and Rhona, in her American uniform and heavy army boots, following close behind. But the story was hastily retracted about a week later in the pages of the *Daily Mail*, after the newspaper received an angry cable from Iris Carpenter who wrote, 'I was across Rhine at Remagen with attacking infantry less than 20 hours after the bridge was secured. What is happening to *Daily Mail* reporting accuracy? Or was there another Rhine for Rhona Churchill to cross?'

'Caption to picture page 3, March 27', the newspaper said, 'stated Rhona Churchill was the first woman across Rhine. *Daily Mail* and caption writer apologise to the *Daily Herald*'s able war reporter Iris Carpenter, first woman across the river.'

Even if Rhona Churchill was not the first woman to cross the Rhine, she was a trooper. She looked a strange sight in the cold spring of 1945, wearing army long-johns under her trousers, a US helmet and wrapped up in an army quilt. She sat atop a German jeep she had commandeered herself and painted khaki, with a big sign saying 'US Press'. It had been necessary 'to requisition the jeep' because the *Daily Express* had sent a reporter to join her in her official travels and Rhona had no intention of sharing her stories with the opposition.

Later on she learned from a friendly *Express* reporter that the *Express* foreign editor, Charles Foley, had warned him, 'Watch Rhona Churchill who has been a thorn in our flesh since D-Day!' To Rhona's mind the explanation for this flattering rivalry was simple. Although most of the war correspondents were men with vast experience, many having reported the Spanish Civil War and earlier battles of World War II, Rhona's brief was 'to rove among the civilians and leave covering the battles to the men'.

Very soon I was getting so much human-interest copy in to the *Daily Mail* that both friends and rivals were referring to it as the 'Churchill and Aachen Gazette'. Most of my stories at this time were collected from Aachen, the first German city occupied by the Allies....

It was mid-winter and I went out to Aachen each day in an open jeep in search of a story, and each day returned with a winner. Somewhat naturally, I became a bit unpopular. Our newspapers were reduced to four pages by newsprint rationing, and it was thought I was hogging more than my fair share of the newsprint available for war stories. But it wasn't my fault. My job as roving reporter was to supply the *Daily Mail* with all the copy I thought they might want, and the system worked too well.

Every day I found just what the *Daily Mail* wanted – a good human-interest story. One day I found a German, in his late forties, lying on a couch in a bundle of blankets in a home that had obviously been prosperous. 'The Americans have stolen my sheets to use as camouflage, and I've got flu,' he said. 'My government asked me to stay here until they re-take the town. I have written orders confirming this,' and he showed them to me.

The American Counter Intelligence Corps (CIC) had no knowledge of these orders and contacted Rhona after her story was put through the censor. From this point on, they did everything they could to open doors for her. 'I think they secretly hoped I might uncover something else,' she mused many years later.

It was the CIC who allowed Churchill to enter the cells where teenagers soon to be executed were being imprisoned. When she was let into their rooms, she found several 'on their hands and knees in their solitary confinement, praying to God to keep them alive'.

I could not save them, I could only try to comfort them. I still vividly remember one lad, down on his knees in his cell. He had come through our lines with his youth leader, who was also in a cell. He was a lad at the beginning of life who had been indoctrinated by the Nazi system and was prepared to cross the lines and spy for his country. He had only hours left before they shot him and I found myself feeling sorry for him.

But the CIC took a tough line on these infiltrators. If they didn't execute these spies, they reasoned, there would be many more, with the net result of more 'dead Americans'. The prevailing attitude at the time, Rhona noted, was that 'the only good German was a dead German'. It was an attitude that seemed 'a bit uncivilized' to Rhona. She did find, however, that the myth of 'the good Hitler' was prevalent among many of the Germans she interviewed. It was a hard belief to dispel. In speaking to one proponent of the theory, a schoolmistress, Rhona said, 'I showed her some photos I had taken of burnt corpses in a barn, and of skeletons in a concentration camp, but her mind was set on not believing.'

But even this did not mean 'one did not care. One cared a lot.' Rhona found that some of the stories involved her so much emotionally that she was unable to write about them at the time. On the day the Americans took Erkelenz, Rhona was standing on the steps of the town hall, watching 'spotter planes ... circling overhead'. Suddenly a pregnant woman approached her, saying, 'Fräulein, please help me. I'm about to have my baby. The pains have started.' With the memory of her own childbirth so recent in her mind, Rhona took the woman to the make-shift hospital where doctors were awaiting the fresh casualties. There she found a young, handsome American doctor and asked him to deliver the child. But it turned out he had been a German Jew whose parents had taken him to the United States where he had been educated. ' "You're asking me to bring into the world another Kraut who will probably want to kill my son on a battlefield," he protested. But he took her in, and a few hours later, while he was also dressing the wounds of GIs, he helped her give birth to a baby boy.'

Working on her dispatch that evening, Rhona found she was unable to write the story of the woman and her baby, and the young doctor who put aside his own prejudices to help her. She simply wrote up the day's happenings, leaving out the dramatic tale. But the incident did weigh on her mind. Years later, she decided to try to find this woman.

Even in the turmoil after the war, the Germans had kept such detailed records of every single thing that happened. It was the same when you went into places where they had slaughtered people. The records were still there, they hadn't burnt the records. When they'd done the actual killing, there was the list of the different people they had killed, who had been killed and on which day and how.

So it wasn't difficult at all to find this woman. I sought for and found that mother, only to learn that her baby died in infancy of malnutrition, as many babies did at that time.

Despite everything, Rhona could sympathize with the enemy and, at times, even identify with them. One day she was taking her US driver for a drink and when the pair of them entered the German inn, a family party stood up indignantly and, 'led by their women-folk, walked out. Good for them,' Rhona thought. 'I'd have done just the same if the conquering Germans had walked into the King's Head in my home village.'

Rhona's wartime editor, Stanley Horniblow, who stepped in when Bob Prew left so unexpectedly after the attempted palace coup, was not only a shrewd editor for these exciting last days of the war, he was also highly popular with the rank and file. It was thought he was capable of defending them against what they called 'that bullying regime above', meaning the managerial types whom Esmond had installed and who were becoming more important in the organization.

Horniblow, sometimes called 'Shanghai Horniblower' because he had spent a good deal of time in the Far East, was an athletic Australian known for dressing well and looking good. According to a member of his staff 'he was as handsome as a matinée idol with golden fair hair and he had the complexion of a girl'. Another of his employees said later that Horniblow, like many Australians,

talked with the most extraordinary upper-class accent. It was almost as though he was doing a role in a film in Hollywood, playing the part of an English aristocrat. He had one of these terribly plummy voices. He was a very relaxed and very amusing man to be with but this extraordinary voice emerged that didn't seem to have any association with the rest of the man.

An exceptionally able editor, Horniblow was to discover that he had one difficulty to cope with that the earlier editors of the *Daily Mail* had not – Lady Rothermere. Esmond's new wife Ann had decided to 'take a hand on the newspaper' and that appeared to mean that Horniblow would be eliminated.

The appearance of the well-known journalist Frank Owen as a columnist on the *Daily Mail* made many on the staff believe that Horniblow's days were numbered. Owen was a colourful Welshman who had been for a time the youngest MP in Parliament, then editor of Beaverbrook's

Evening Standard. During the war he had produced a Forces newspaper in Southeast Asia where he was a close friend of the Mountbatten family. Within a short time Horniblow was sent to the United States and Owen was put in charge of the *Daily Mail* while he was away. When he returned, Horniblow was given to understand that his authority had been undermined, and he resigned, returning to Australia.

Described by her friends as her 'latest adventure', Ann's interference on the *Daily Mail* had begun, although surreptitiously, even before her marriage to Esmond. In her mind a competition existed between her own family and that of Esmond and, to some extent, the contest appeared to be class driven. It had always irked her that Esmond tended to enjoy, as she put it, 'tennis tournaments and dances in Eastbourne, and I think he genuinely prefers that CLASS of society to our CLASS of society'. But her complaints about Esmond's social inadequacies were wisely kept within her own family circle and on these occasions she was writing to her brother Hugo. She would later complain to him rhetorically: 'all the shares belong to the Harmsworths so why should the Charterises get stomach ulcers on the outer perimeter of power?'

Hugo, a well-liked man with some talent but little push, had become her confidant on matters to do with the *Mail* because he was employed by them. Ann had got him the job. He had first been on the *Continental Daily Mail*, and there was something both endearing and ingenuous about the way he pressed the advantage of his position for the benefit of his friends.

'Hugo wasn't a schemer,' said one close friend, David Attlee. A group would simply be chatting, speculating about who the next foreign editor might be and someone would suggest a name. 'And Hugo would say, "I'll go and see Esmond about it." Hugo was completely open about it – a very endearing character.'

Tom Pocock, another friend of Hugo, concurred. 'He shamelessly used his influence,' said Pocock. ' "Oh, I'll talk to my sister about that," after I had mentioned I wanted a job. A telephone call and I was summoned to Rothermere's office, and I got a job, having been hired by Rothermere. I was handed over to poor Frank Owen who knew nothing about it.'

On his first day, Pocock was sent to see the forbidding Frank Owen – he was six feet four inches tall, with broad shoulders, 'very macho and tough with dark hair sprouting straight out of his forehead'. Pocock had heard he was 'a bit wild'. Since Tom had been hired on Features, Owen asked him for his ideas. Tom didn't exactly have any ideas, not expecting to come face to face with the editor on his first day. But he managed to come up with the rather lame, 'What about people who have terrible jobs but enjoy them?' Owen pressed him for an example, and at last

Tom suggested dustmen who were 'always smiling and singing'. 'He said, "So you think you would enjoy their jobs? Why?"

'I said "Well, perhaps when they're opening dustbins, they're always hoping they'll find a diamond necklace."

' "That's right, Tom," he answered. "Life is a dustbin. You go out and find me the jewels." '

That lunch-time, as Tom left the building, he happened to meet Owen on the stairs and the editor said: 'Come and have lunch with me.'

> We went off to El Vino's and various other bars and went to a very grand restaurant called Les Ambassadeurs, with some friends he had picked up and we didn't get back to the office at all. We ended up with some glamorous women in low-cut dresses in the Milroy nightclub. There were two wonderful dance bands. We were sitting there in the dark, bottles all over the tables. His link with the office was a white telephone among the bottles and every now and then a dispatch rider would come clumping into the night-club with page proofs for the *Daily Mail*, and the wine waiter would come over and shine his torch on it. Frank would read the proofs, ring up his night editor and tell him what to do. This went on until four in the morning. I thought, 'Gosh, I never knew Fleet Street was like this.'

Frank Owen proved to be one of the most popular editors the *Daily Mail* had ever had. Eccentric to the extent of driving his secretaries into a frenzy, it wasn't unusual for him to disappear for hours, only to reappear flushed in the face, with his shirt unbuttoned to the waist. 'Where have you been?' his secretary might ask him.

'Sunning myself on the roof,' was the unlikely answer. He was married to a former Cochran showgirl, a blonde nearly six feet tall, who often took friends and VIPs for tours around the building. Arthur Wareham recorded in his diary that 'her tour round the office always created a sensation.'

Meanwhile, Ann was getting in deeper and deeper, and amongst the editorial staff, she had been nicknamed 'the monster'. She had befriended Stuart MacLean the managing director of the *Daily Mail*, and even Frank Owen, whom she had helped put into the editor's chair, was feeling the constant pressure of her interference. Although she now pictured herself as an integral part of the organization, she blamed Esmond for 'the muddle' the *Mail* had become. She wrote to her brother,

> The *Daily Mail* can never be anything but a muddle, for even in the unlikely event of Esmond finding perfect lieutenants, the perfect lieutenants will be in the impossible position of quicksand power and no final responsibility; how can you completely trust or indeed help any person who will within cautious limits

invariably listen to the advice of the last acquaintance he meets? Frank [Owen] and MacLean must hate each other and me. Esmond has a wonderful memory but, I have come to believe, no capacity for thought and very bad judgement of human beings.

Ann then related to Hugo how she was tardily approached for a new name for the gossip column by MacLean and how, despite this, she saved the day by coming up with the title 'Who Why Where'. In her version of events it was virtually necessary for her to commandeer the column, and 'most of the news comes from me'. The heroic mould she saw herself in was not shared by others. Ted Pickering, then managing editor under Frank Owen, took many complaints from staffers about Ann's calls. He wouldn't allow them to run unless they could be made to stand up by the staff member. On one occasion he went into Rothermere's office and said, 'Look, really, this won't do. I can't have staff serving several masters, you know.' Although Rothermere was sympathetic, Ann's directives continued to bombard staff members.

The newspaper was enjoying a rise in circulation and Ann believed it could be traced to the gossip column she had started. She also believed Esmond was too polite and accommodating to run the paper; without her, it would sink.

Frank Owen was sacked. Internally it was thought there were many contributing factors, not least his propensity for drink, which was at last beginning to affect his ability to run the paper. Another line of gossip chalked his demise down to the visits of his mistress, a forceful left-wing lady, who was too often in the building during working hours. But all the staffers believed the root cause was a falling out with Ann Rothermere. The matter came to public attention on 5 June 1950, when *Time* magazine ran an article that sent shock waves through Associated Newspapers:

THE ELEVENTH MAN

Esmond Cecil Harmsworth, 52, second Viscount Rothermere, owns London's stoutly Tory *Daily Mail* (circ. 2,280,000) and for three years fiery, loquacious Frank Owen, 44, has been the editor. But it has long been common knowledge in Fleet Street that the real boss wears a petticoat. For several years, pretty, vivacious Lady Ann Rothermere, 36, has tried to run the *Mail* from Warwick House. Without consulting Editor Owen, she often summoned staffers to her home to assign stories or suggest new features. Six months ago, Stuart MacLean, advertising manager of the *Mail* and a friend of 'Annie's' was appointed managing director of the paper. Overbearing, tight-pursed Director MacLean moved in on editorial authority, in some cases firing, shuffling and promoting editorial staffers, without consulting Editor Owen.... Owen fought back, but fought a losing battle. In recent months, eight top editorial executives and writers and two directors have been fired or quit. Last week, as fed up with Warwick House as Warwick House was with him, Frank Owen quit.

With the demise of Owen, Ann's interest in running the *Daily Mail* seemed to wane. Her affair with Fleming was peaking; she had twice been to Jamaica on relatively extended holidays chaperoned by her close friends. Her social life now extended to New York and Miami, where, on various visits, she had made a huge hit. And, of course, parties at Warwick House still occupied a great deal of her attention.

She was so busy, in fact, that when Hugo and Virginia Charteris's two-and-a-half-year-old son drowned in a terrible accident she was late in getting a letter of condolence to her sister-in-law:

6 December [1951]

My Darling Virginia

I should have written sooner but there was a rush of plans for the holidays, a promotion party for Noël Coward, a television party to get funds for children's hospital and all the other dementia of Warwick Hut.

Darling, I have never suffered such grief as you; I held my baby's hand for one minute and was amazed how long the torture lasted, my deep love for Ian is based on his understanding of [my] mental condition at that time, so when I think of you it is by a large multiplication sum and I know how drab and remote all else must seem and I continue to mind for you quite dreadfully....

As her unfeeling letter shows, Ann had somehow travelled beyond the pale of decency in her own self-absorption. He relationship with Fleming had earlier in the year become open knowledge and Esmond, made aware of the fact that the daughter who had died in Scotland was Ian's and not his own, had given an ultimatum that Ann and Ian could not see one another for six months.

In one version the couple couldn't keep to it; thus Esmond made the decision to divorce Ann. In another Ann, realizing the marriage was all but officially dead, became pregnant by Fleming a second time to ensure that once Esmond filed, Ian would indeed marry her – something she was never sure she could count on. Whichever scenario is true, Esmond did divorce Ann. While Ann joked with her friends about the divorce, calling it 'the death of the golden goose', Esmond found it difficult to cope.

He joined his daughter Esme and her husband, Rowley Cromer, at Frenchstreet Farm, 'deeply wounded by his collapsing marriage'. Some of the family believed that Ann had been 'the love of Esmond's life'. That was one way of putting it.

A close friend, Aidan Crawley, was less sentimental. He believed that Ann had been a catastrophic element in Esmond's life. He had never been a man who bristled with confidence in the first place, Crawley believed, and Ann had robbed Esmond of the chance to achieve any lasting satisfaction from living.

Ann's son Caspar was born by Caesarian in 1952 and as she lay recuperating in hospital a large bunch of roses arrived from Esmond. 'Dearest Ann,' his note said, 'Best wishes to you and your son.'

Ann wrote to her brother, 'The hospital was awash with tears of what might have been. Oh what a strange character, in sixteen years that one line showed more feeling than when he took my body and vitality utterly for granted.' She then went on to compare Esmond's roses with the flowers sent by Beaverbrook – 'it's exciting to see £20 of flowers edged sideways through a sickroom door.' So much for the nostalgia of past love irretrievably lost.

But then, that was Ann.

4

'Ah, They're on the Woods'

Rhona Churchill's assignment to cover the movements of the US Ninth Army led her to witness at first hand the terrible misery Germany had inflicted upon the so-called 'enemies' of the Third Reich. On the same day Belsen was liberated, the little-known concentration camp at Nordhausen, located in the Hartz mountains, was also set free. Here, tens of thousands of male Jews had been worked and starved to death in a labour camp known as the 'Central Works', a factory housed in a series of caves and tunnels that had been carved into the peak called Kohlstein. Those who survived had lived under unspeakable conditions.

The first of the work-force had been requisitioned from Buchenwald in August 1943. Four-tiered bunks were set up in dank, unlit underground caves and here the slaves 'worked and slept in two shifts; when one went to work the other lay down on the same filthy litters and covered themselves with the same damp blankets. There were no latrines at all; empty carbide barrels, cut in half, were used; it was necessary to walk about a kilometre to the water-taps.'

Their day was divided into twelve hours of hard labour, with another six and a half hours spent travelling to and from their work place, lining up for meals, answering roll-call and attending to the other minutiae connected with the Nazi bureaucracy. Only five and a half hours were given over to rest. Under these conditions the prisoners died at a very high rate.

Because the men were so weakened that they could not perform their work well Albert Speer had encouraged the SS commandant in charge of the work-force to improve conditions. This was done and many of the workers were allowed to live in wooden barracks outside the caves, greatly reducing the death rate. Nevertheless, it was bad enough.

When Rhona arrived in the spring of 1945 she found the workers 'lying helpless six abreast on wooden bunks, or shuffling about like walking skeletons'. If one of them wanted to turn over, all had to do the same, but Rhona reckoned that 'a lot [were] not capable of turning over'. The American doctor assigned to caring for them said under no circumstances were they to eat normal food, as this would kill them.

Instead, a special diet was prescribed to restore slowly their ability to digest food. Rhona spoke at length to those who were able to talk and, despite their pitiful condition, they were the friendliest of any of the prisoners she was to meet.

> I remember one of them who was absolutely skin and bones looking at me sort of hollow eyed and saying, 'Why did they do this to me?' Also they wanted to touch me because they hadn't seen a friend for so long and they were lousy but one had to let them more or less hug one, and not cringe from it because they were so pathetic. I remember some creature, a bedbug or something, going down my neck and I had to fish that out rather rapidly.

Strangely, it seemed to Rhona, she was not allowed to visit the tunnels and the Americans, usually so helpful, would give her no background information. Instead, she was told she was 'off-limits' and the liberation of the camp was demarcated 'Top Secret'. Her stories were stopped by the censor, with no explanation.

Rhona was to discover much later that

> the whole of this area had been promised to the Russians at Yalta, but Nordhausen had replaced Peenemunde as the chief centre for the V1 and V2 (Buzz-bomb and Rocket) and at all costs the Americans wanted to keep their discoveries away from the Russians, so wanted no publicity for Nordhausen until they had time to confiscate its contents and clear its site.

Hitler had believed his rockets would save him and in September of 1943 Joseph Paul Goebbels had entered in his diary: 'England must be repaid in her own coin and with interest for what she has done to us.' The giant rockets, each of them weighing fourteen tons, would make 'an awe-inspiring murder weapon'. Goebbels himself believed that once these missiles began to fall by the thousands upon London the British would quickly capitulate. What prevented the plan from going forward were the many changes made in the design over the years from 1943 to 1945–65,000 modifications in all!

Altogether, the Americans carted away 300 railway cars filled with rockets and parts, sufficient to make seventy-five V2s. None of the specialists who directed the slave labour in the camps was made to stand trial at Nuremberg. As they themselves had anticipated, their knowledge made them inviolable. Eventually they found their way to cushy jobs of high prestige in the United States.

But at the time, Rhona knew little of this. And surrounding her were still many examples of the horror of the German regime, for even as the camp was liberated she and the others heard shooting from nearby.

They travelled to a valley less than a mile away and 'I came across one of these awful places in a barn, and it was chock-a-block full of bodies that had been burnt'. In their rush to get away the Germans had found it expedient to dispose of their prisoners – 'they just shoved them into barns and burnt them'.

Such things were difficult to forget and buried deep within her, even more difficult to remember years after she had returned to a normal life. However, there was one afternoon, she recollected,

> when some half-starved children surrounded my car and begged for food, and fighting back tears when a group of desperate refugee women begged me for English pound notes. I gave them what I had in return for currency they could not use, and they begged me for reassurance that it was real and not counterfeit, and I showed them the metal strip that Britain had recently started putting through her real notes after the Germans had flooded the Continent with counterfeit ones, and I remember saying, 'Don't let anyone take these from you, saying they are counterfeit money.'

The first British journalist allowed into Czechoslovakia and Poland, Rhona found it was also her fate to document the cruel treatment these victors meted out to the Germans, many of whom were incarcerated in concentration camps such as the ones where they themselves had imprisoned Jews and other 'enemies of the State'. In a piece entitled, 'I toured Germany in her misery', Rhona documented the atrocities being committed against the Germans inside Sudetenland, Silesia and Poland.

When the war ended Rhona's husband was demobbed and they began a normal married life together, with their baby John. Rhona was immediately invited by the *Daily Mail* to write a twice-weekly column on any subject not to do with fashion, cooking or any other traditional woman's topic. This she declined on the basis that she had already worked under sufficient pressure and wanted no more of it.

She was, by this time, suffering the nightmares that have plagued her dreams ever since. Oddly, they had nothing to do with the atrocities she had witnessed, but with a fear of her own inadequacy to do the job properly.

> I am covering a Royal Tour of India and the Far East. I am lost. I am directed to the wrong station in Delhi for the night journey to Prince Philip's next destination. I find myself alone surrounded by a seething mass of Indians, with no means of communicating with them. I've lost my luggage and my handbag, and with it my cash, cable card and passport. I'm going to lose the next day's story. I'm going to lose my job. I wake up.

Rhona did not lose her job. She asked to be assigned to the paper as a features writer and, although her request was frowned upon, since staff were expected to take a good offer when they got one, it was nevertheless granted. 'From then on I alternated between being on staff, full or part-time, or free-lancing from home, and between choosing my own assignments and being selected for them. This loose arrangement generally worked satisfactorily.'

Another war correspondent, the celebrated Alexander Clifford, would not fare so well. After the great success of Clifford's political tract *Enter Citizens*, he and his old comrade Alan Moorehead decided to try their hand at writing a play, provisionally named *Exit Citizen*. The plot involved a man suddenly told he has only a short time to live and the events that follow before his death. 'What does he do? We imagined that at first he went off on a debauch, indulging all his desires while there was still time. Next he turns to religion. In the end he wishes only to go back to his job and his normal life, and death when it comes finds him doing precisely the same things he always used to do.'

Ironically, this is what happened to Alex. Early in 1950 he was diagnosed as having Hodgkin's Disease and given two years to live. During the time he was undergoing radiation treatment, he and his wife Jenny moved back to England and Esmond Rothermere gave him 'a comfortable office with a carpet on the floor and an open fire'. Tom Pocock, the young reporter given his start by Hugo Charteris, was still working on the *Daily Mail* and his own office was only a short way from Clifford's. Stopping by one day, Pocock stuck his head in and remarked on what a nice room it was. 'Yes,' Alex answered, 'I can't think why they have given it to me.'

The treatments Alex endured for the disease were in themselves quite terrible. Once, when he went to the hospital to receive one of these, he discovered that 'a woman patient who was also suffering from Hodgkin's Disease had thrown herself down the lift-shaft rather than face the ordeal of the X-rays. Alex went on to his appointment.'

When these treatments had finished Alex returned to Portofino with his wife, improving a little. Unlike the character in the play he had planned with his friend Moorehead, however, he did not turn to debauchery; he did, though, turn to religion, going to Rome to investigate the possibility of becoming a Roman Catholic. When Alan asked him how this had gone Alex answered, 'It didn't work.'

In the end, the *Daily Mail* proved the greatest source of comfort and he did continue with his foreign correspondence – although it was more factual and less theoretical than before. 'Never at any stage now or later did he lose hope, and never in my presence did he give way to despair or even complaint.... None of his letters revealed the terrible crises in the night, the sweatings, the stricken breathlessness.'

The Mooreheads and the Cliffords decided to take a holiday together, and they met in Kitzbühel for a ski-trip. Alex seemed to be recovering, with only an occasional bad night. The four of them even attended a fancy-dress ball, travelling in a sleigh across the snow. The following morning, Alan and Alex went on the highest run of all, a dangerous slope of eight miles down.

It was a raw morning ... and even when we reached the heights the sun had not really broken through. Being one of the worst of skiers I balked a little at the ice and the steepness of the descent. But Alex, wrapped in a black jacket, his head in a bright woollen cap, spread his wings and flew. He skimmed away into the milky space like some great black bird on the wing, and when I rejoined him after several headlong falls at the bottom of the first run, he was grinning. I was breathless and dishevelled....

Then he was off again, gliding and swooping down the mountain, and I, gaining confidence, launched myself in pursuit. I caught him up presently, and now, when a little sunshine had broken through, we raced on together across enormous slopes. It was a wonderful thing: the sun shining, the crunch of the snow under the skis, and we two, moving in unison very fast with the wind rushing by. It really was like flying....

When we got down to the road in the valley we took off our skis and tramped heavily along to the station, half a mile away. We bought tickets to Kitzbühel and sat in the steamy little waiting room drinking hot wine laced with cinnamon. When the train came in a crowd of healthy young Austrians clattered on board with their skis, but we found seats on the opposite wooden benches. I looked across at Alex and saw that his face had gone a ghastly shade of whitish green. There was a little foam on his lip and he sat there absolutely still, looking out of the window but obviously seeing nothing, since his eyes were glazed and dull. So we sat for half an hour with the lively voices and the laughter of the young Austrians all about us, and when this eternity had gone by we found a sled at Kitzbühel station and rode in silence back to the hotel. That night he had a relapse.

Alex was rushed back to London and went into the hospital at once. There, he grew weaker and weaker. For six weeks he seemed convinced he would make a complete recovery. Then an overwhelming listlessness enveloped him and he lost all interest in what took place around him, failing to recognize any of his friends. It was apparent only the most extreme of treatments remained to be tried – and this was the mustard gas. In the night, Jennifer, Lucy and Alan decided that it would be cruel to prolong treatment and that the kindest course would be to allow him to die. But the specialist in the case would not permit this.

The morning after the mustard gas was applied Alex seemed to have recovered. The two women had gone out to lunch when he began speaking to Alan, his eyes feverish, with a bright light shining from them. 'You were quite wrong yesterday. They were absolutely right to give me the mustard gas. It's wonderful. Yes. It's wonderful. I see it all now. There are two sides, two levels. On one level I am vulgar ... disgusting. ... But on the other level ... clear ... beautiful.'

Alan saw that he was having a kind of vision that filled him with 'an inexpressible joy'. Although he said nothing more, Alan could see that he recognized him. A nurse entered the room and watched as Alex 'began to struggle for breath and there was a dry rattle in his throat'. The nurse left quickly and returned with an oxygen respirator, fixing it to Alex's mouth. 'Quite visibly,' Alan Moorehead wrote later, 'the grey paralysis of death was creeping over Alex's face.' The nurse told Alan that if he had anything to say, 'say it now'.

Alan said he loved him.

Then he stood by the bed until the two women returned and the three of them watched as his breathing slowly halted. At the time of his death, Alex was forty-two.

At about the same time that Clifford lay dying in hospital, Esmond Rothermere's divorce from Ann became final. The effect of this breakup upon the *Daily Mail*'s proprietor was to widen the gap between the two sides of his personality.

Esmond's relatives had always attributed his tendency to be at one moment remote and at the next gregarious, to his being a Gemini. It was one of those family jokes that held a kernel of truth. In fact, Esmond's eldest daughter Lorna remembered that he had always kept a carefully drawn line of demarcation between work and play. As a teenager she was accustomed to him participating with enthusiasm in the games of her schoolfriends and once, during a particularly competitive game of 'Sardines', her father had thrown a bucket of water over a bannister from the first floor down on Lorna and her guests on the ground floor.

But when she was about eighteen, she remembered, there had been an unexpectedly 'sticky weekend'. 'He asked some people down from the office, and my guests and I were supposed to be on our best behaviour and we got giggly and it was the only time he ever ticked me off – because the office staff were there. It was the only time I ever saw him get cross with one.'

Now, after his marriage to Ann ended, his demeanour towards his staff took on an aloof quality that made his distant manner into the stuff of legend. He withdrew into silence, and the rank and file who had been accustomed to seeing him now and then on the editorial floor grew used to Rothermere as a figure who ruled *in absentia* through his managers and editors. It was said more and more often that his opinions largely reflected those with whom he had most recently spoken. Altogether, he became a more remote character.

And yet, on the social level, he was as warm and as generous as ever. In this context his personality was a very strong one, exerted almost always on the side of geniality. Socially, he was a charming man, very well liked. One of his friends said, 'he was always sort of half smiling in a rather diffident way as if he was trying to convey to you, "Isn't this a ridiculous business, I don't know what I'm doing in it but it's rather fun, isn't it?"' His friends knew he was neither a schemer nor a manipulator like Beaverbrook; he was simply a very nice man.

Esmond's great friend Noel Barber once recorded his characteristic way of speaking in an incident that also told something of how Esmond treated his friends. In the early days in Monte Carlo, Barber had laid down £70 and won an astonishing £1500 at the betting tables. Flushed by his success – and by a glass of Moët et Chandon – he 'walked over to the [chemmy] table, looking for a vacant chair'.

> At that moment a hand touched my shoulder and all of Esmond's six feet four inches looked down on me. It is hard to describe his very special way of speaking, in which he accents words strongly, often lifting his voice a semitone at the same time, as when he says, 'Well, *really!*' or 'I *must* say'.
>
> 'Well, I *must* say,' he said now, 'that was quite a *coup*. I saw it *all*. It really *was*. But I do think you'd better be sensible. *Much* better, I assure you, if I take the money now.'
>
> Before I could say '*Banco*', he seized all my chips, and handed back a hundred pounds' worth with the remark, 'I'll give you the rest the day you leave. Then you'll be one of the few men who ever made a profit out of the Casino.'

Barber's wife Titina, whose friendship with Esmond was social rather than professional, remembered how surprising his generosity could be. Once, when she was a house guest, he had taken her shopping before she returned to her home in Switzerland. In one shop she had admired two porcelain zebras. But she decided to look over the rest of the wares before making a final decision.

When she returned to buy them, the zebras had already been sold. She was not to see them again – until she left Esmond's house. Then they were beautifully gift-wrapped and presented to her as a going-away gift. Another time she remembered having Christmas dinner at Warwick House, and she brought along her son and her niece. Titina and her niece both received gold bracelets as their Christmas gift, and her son received a leather wallet.

Dinner at Warwick House was a formal affair. The women wore evening dresses and fur coats, and Titina remembers a sense of great luxury and opulence, with a butler and several liveried servants seeing guests in. She remembered Esmond as being very lively socially, and it seemed that wherever he sat there would be a great deal of laughter and excitement.

For the many years she and her husband lived in Switzerland they were frequent weekend guests at Warwick House. Here it was customary for the women to have their breakfasts in bed, while the men assembled downstairs, eating in their dressing-gowns.

The maids unpacked everything, and Titina found her things put away in drawers and wardrobes, 'ironed perfectly'. 'In those days, all the women wore girdles. And mine was so tight I didn't wear underwear, and the maid turned to me in horror and said, "Your maid forgot to pack your underwear."

'"Oh, yes, silly girl," I answered, and I rushed out and bought underwear – just for the maid.'

Known for his relaxed sense of hospitality, Esmond could also be charming at work, as he was with Ted Pickering, the managing editor of the *Daily Mail* at the time Frank Owen was editor. Once it was decided Owen would go, Pickering had a long lunch with Rothermere in a private executive dining-room that had been set up in a building at the bottom of Carmelite Street. 'Esmond told me a long and fascinating story about his visit to Russia before the Revolution when he was a kid,' Pickering remembered, and Pickering had the opportunity to talk about where he believed the *Daily Mail* should go next. After this, he was fairly optimistic that he would become the next editor.

> Then, some weeks later, it was announced that Guy Schofield was to be editor. ... I'd seen Guy Schofield operating on the *Evening News*, which he edited, and I knew that the sort of paper he would want for the *Daily Mail* was not the sort of paper I thought it should be, that he would want to make it a very straight up and down paper, he wouldn't want any of the flashiness that is, correctly or incorrectly, associated with a big national newspaper.

Rothermere did offer Pickering the Manchester edition of the paper, but Pickering declined. Before two days had passed, Beaverbrook had got wind of what had happened and called Pickering to his house, where he offered him a position on the rival *Daily Express*. There, Pickering was destined to succeed the legendary Arthur Christiansen – who had also slipped through Esmond's fingers some twenty years earlier. Under Pickering's leadership the *Express* would reach 4.3 million circulation and he would edit the paper for seven years.

Back at the *Mail*, Guy Schofield was said to be 'a real gentleman'.

Distinguished, solemn and ascetic, Schofield was a figure of refinement. Under his leadership, so went the rumours, the *Mail* would be 'a different paper than it had been'. This turned out to be true. Within two weeks, Schofield called ten top sub-editors at the *Daily Mail* into his office and sacked them all. Said Tom Pocock, one of those spared,

> It was a clean sweep, it was terrible, a complete massacre. Not only senior people, others were just sent for and fired. One sub-editor, a very nice chap, witty, good at his job, was sent for and summarily fired. There was no compensation, you just got one month's money, and you were out, and everyone was shattered by it.

Schofield reduced the size of the headlines and began filling the *Mail* with more serious content. Immediately, the paper began to lose sales. But this didn't appear to dismay him at all.

One of those who escaped the knife was Arthur Wareham, who became assistant editor on day duty. For him the time logged under Schofield was 'the most frustrating of the whole twenty-five years I spent with the *Daily Mail*'. He submitted 'memorandum after memorandum to Schofield, but all were ignored'. Wareham made a note in his journal that Schofield

> favoured a paper more like the *Daily Telegraph*, even if this meant a circulation between a million and a million and a half. The *Daily Mail*, of course, was a popular newspaper and needed a circulation over two million to attract the advertising which makes it viable. How Schofield's policy ever came to be considered for a moment I shall never understand.

Wareham wasn't the only one with misgivings. But Schofield was firmly in charge and the *Mail* seemed destined to become a stodgy newspaper that reflected the conservative nature of its new editor. It was a far cry from the days of Frank Owen.

But despite this radical change it was a time for optimism on Fleet Street. To be on the Street was to be alive. The force of the competition between titles, the nation's survival and triumph in the war, the emerging affluence of the 1950s – all combined to make Fleet Street as colourful a place as it had ever been.

On the editorial floor of the *Mail* messengers scurried to and fro, running errands and carrying copy. Whenever a sub-editor needed a messenger he would lift up his hand and shout, 'Copy!' or 'Boy!' – although the men who ran the errands were usually ex-servicemen old enough to be the fathers of the young subs who barked out the orders. The messenger would pick up the copy and drop it into the vacuum tube system, where it sizzed along to the right destination.

In those days, the news-room was littered with papers, dirty china cups, typewriters clattering out a terrific amount of noise. The journalists stood in clusters, telling jokes and sharing gossip, many of them chewing cigars, the blue smoke making a light haze across the room. Virtually every office in Fleet Street employed a former sergeant-major whose job it was to supervise the porters. At the *Daily Mail* the porters wore dark-blue uniforms with red piping, lending an air of formality to the proceedings.

For a quick snack, porters and journalists alike might run over to Mick's Café, famous for being always open and particularly handy on a Sunday when the office canteen was closed.

Among the journalists, drinking bouts were epic. It wasn't uncommon, especially after an election or Budget Day, for men to drink the night through and afterwards turn up at the Smithfield Meat Market nearby and have breakfast alongside the market workers. Traditionally the journalists downed huge steak breakfasts, with beer, drinking whisky as a chaser. The Press Club stayed open until one in the morning and several of the pubs served all night if you knew which back rooms to go to.

It was the heyday of El Vino's, the Fleet Street bar. There, every day at a quarter past one,

> the swing doors would burst open and in would come a rather stocky man in a camel-hair coat, tie in a half knot, not quite like the old west, more like Al Capone. This would be Arthur Christiansen, the great editor of the *Daily Express*, followed by his top brass, and some of his columnists and correspondents who had been at the morning conference. And everyone would move up the bar a bit and they would take the place by the door and order double brandies, gins or whatever and stay there for half an hour, talking very loudly and roaring with laughter. Then they would all roar off to lunch. They would get back to the office about a quarter past three, having had gallons of wine but producing a terrific paper.

Each office had a pub it favoured. The *Mail* journalists gravitated to the Harrow and the White Swan, nicknamed the 'Mucky Duck' by the reporters who frequented it. The arguments and exchanges kept everyone informed, although it was very much a day-to-day existence. It was the nature of Fleet Street that if you left it for any time at all you were immediately forgotten.

The *Mail* was always housed in Northcliffe House. The *Daily Sketch*, also owned by Associated Newspapers, was partly in Old Carmelite House and partly in New Carmelite House. The *Evening News*, Northcliffe's first newspaper, was still part of Associated's group, and it had moved from a building called Harmsworth West into the first floor of Northcliffe House.

The *Mail* was on the second floor and the composing room was on the third. In the foundry, where the noise was deafening, the workmen stuffed paper into their ears, but if they decided in the late hours of the night or the early hours of the morning to go out for a drink they took out their earplugs, made them into tiny spitballs and flicked one into the huge spools of paper. If the spitball hit in precisely the right spot, the spool would split and it would have to be taken down and reloaded – a task carried out by the machine crew. This gave the printers a chance to pop out for a drink.

The run of the papers was on wooden blocks, so when it started up there was a deep rumble. Everyone in the building could hear the edition running, and it was at this point the older printers would cock their heads and say, 'Ah, they're on the woods.'

Upstairs, the electricians had a control room where they could look out on to the Embankment and could see the arrival of Lord Rothermere when he was chauffeured to the building. One of the electricians' helpers was a self-styled wit. When Ellison sighted the proprietor's Rolls-Royce, he would look out of the window and say, 'Oh, yes, here's Rothermere. It's Wednesday today. Sausages in the canteen. Lord Rothermere's fond of sausages.'

Ellison wasn't the only man on the staff with a sense of humour. Tom Pocock sometimes enjoyed the occasional lunch-time pub crawl. One day, he and his cronies passed a pet shop and Pocock spied a toad in a glass tank in the window. He rather liked it and decided to buy it to carry home to his parents in the country, where he would release it into the garden.

> So I bought this toad, put it in a paper bag and brought it back to the *Daily Mail*. We had a sort of partitioned room with about half a dozen of us and I put it on the desk and it was hopping about and then the telephone rang on the other side and I had to rush across and as I was talking on the telephone the toad crawled underneath and up into one of these huge 'sit-up-and-beg' typewriters.
>
> At that moment somebody who had got a big story from next door came rushing in and asked, 'Can I borrow your typewriter?'
>
> And I had that glorious moment of answering, 'No, I'm sorry you can't. There's a toad in it.'

Tom worked for a time with Humphrey Lyttelton, the jazz-band leader, Tom doing the letters to the editor and Humphrey illustrating them. Frank Owen had told Tom that the letters were dull and when Tom asked how he was to solve this Owen told him to make them up. This he did and the column, called 'The *Daily Mail* Bag' was a huge success. They ended up receiving thousands of letters of interest. Owen always advised Pocock that the English were more concerned with cruelty to animals than to children. So, during the period of meat rationing, Tom came up with a letter from 'London SW7' asking, 'I wonder how many others of your readers have tried the meat of the Shetland pony as a substitute for lamb?' The office was deluged with letters of protest. In another, regarding clothes rationing, Pocock suggested people share trousers, and Lyttelton duly drew a picture of two men wearing the same pair of trousers.

Then, one day, Lyttelton came in and announced to Tom that he was going on tour with his band for a month. 'What will I do for my illustrations?' Tom asked, with some alarm.

'Don't worry,' Humphrey replied, and he gave Tom a huge sheet of cardboard with thirty little illustrations, saying, 'You can write around these.' And Tom did that.

One drawing was of a man knitting his beard into a pair of socks. 'At a time of so many shortages,' Pocock wrote, 'it is scandalous that so much human hair is wasted on the floors of barber shops. Surely, this should be collected and woven into blankets for the needy.'

With the success of the column, Tom became so gung-ho that he wanted to emulate Frank Owen, becoming a first-class journalist. 'So I went out and bought myself a green eyeshade, as I had seen in the movie *The Front Page*. And Frank came in and said, "What in the hell are you doing, playing tennis?"'

Working for Schofield was somewhat different. Lyttelton by then had advanced to the strip cartoon. 'And I didn't get an awful lot of belly laughs from Mr Schofield....' Lyttelton remembered. 'Every now and then he looked at one and he didn't just say, "I don't understand it," he just used to hand it back. And without saying anything, I would take it back to my office and put it in the bin.'

Lyttelton's mentor was the great cartoonist Leslie Illingworth, who was something of a father figure 'with quite an element of Machiavelli'. He helped not only Lyttelton but also a host of young writers at the *Mail*. Many days at El Vino's it was not unusual to find Leslie Illingworth, 'holding court over some office drama or a girlfriend or whatever' and dishing out sensible advice. Illingworth had a kind of underslung jaw and tufted, huge, gingery eyebrows, and he was a brilliant artist of the very first cut. But he had no political views whatsoever, so it was not unusual for the editor to give him his idea. He would then go and illustrate it. At the time, the well-known leader writer George Murray and Illingworth worked well together, merging the political strength of

Murray's leaders with Illingworth's finely penned cartoons.

It was to Illingworth that Lyttelton now turned on the night his first wife had a baby. Humphrey had been up all night, 'and I was absolutely flaked out in the morning.' At the time, he was doing the strip cartoon and a record column.

And I called up Leslie and said, 'I have been unable to do this record column. I'm absolutely knackered and can't do it. What happens when I can't do it?'

And Illingworth said, 'It doesn't happen. If you're writing a column on a daily newspaper, it doesn't happen that you can't do it, it's just not conceivable.' So I put the phone down and was depressed for a couple of minutes and then wrote the piece. It was wonderful advice for a great many things.

Lyttelton learned a second lesson from Ted Pickering. Humphrey's record column was getting to be a bit lofty and specialized, and Pickering said, 'We don't want to have a "blank" column in the newspaper which is absolutely unreadable to people who haven't got a gramophone.' From that point on, Lyttelton made a point of making his column readable on the Underground or under the hairdrier.

Another cartoonist popular at the *Mail* was Wally Fawkes, or Trog, as he called himself. The pen-name was taken from the word 'troglodyte', because Wally found himself staying underground in basement flats a great deal in the early days in London when he had come down from Liverpool. Fawkes often played with Lyttelton's band at 100 Oxford Street, called simply the 100 Club, heady days just after the war when enthusiasm was so high nobody minded drinking Coca-Cola – all that was allowed in the club – all evening long.

In the spring of 1949 Esmond Rothermere returned from New York and summoned Fawkes to his office. He gave him a book he had picked up there that had originated from a carton strip popular in the United States. What Esmond wanted was for Fawkes to create a strip similar to 'Barnaby', a whimsical narrative about a little boy with a fairy godfather who had a touch of W. C. Fields. Esmond wanted Fawkes to do something like it and Fawkes in turn picked up a story lying about the office about a little boy with a friend who could change into other things. This was the original manuscript called 'Lefty and the Goop', by Douglas Mount. Fawkes changed the name first to 'Rufus and Flook' and from there simply to 'Flook', because that is what people who followed the strip tended to call it. In the first episode,

Rufus was having a nightmare that he was being chased by cavemen. He was in the Stone Age, and he had rescued this little woolly animal from the cavemen, and the cavemen chased them, and Rufus fell out of his dream, and the little animal fell out with him. And the little animal was named Flook. That all seemed very creditable at the time, if a little far-fetched.

A series of writers then wrote the script, first Douglas Mount, then Compton Mackenzie. Under each of them the strip tended to be whimsical. But when Humphrey Lyttelton took over, politics came into it for the first time.

It was in 1956 that George Melly was drafted in to write the strip. Destined to be the Flook's longest writer, logging in some fifteen years, Melly, as a well-known jazz pianist, had access to the royals, the débutantes, the world of art and of the theatre. Said Fawkes, 'All this went in, and the strip, already popular, became more popular still.'

Melly, who remained anonymous throughout the period he wrote it, said, 'It started as a kids' strip and it became more and more satirical, and it could be read on several levels, like *Gulliver's Travels.*'

Over the years, the strip would be censored only once. The incident would occur over a character based on Edward Heath, whose name was 'Fred Teeth'. Overnight, Fred Teeth disappeared from the script because, Melly and Fawkes speculated, the Conservative Party may have complained. Nevertheless, the pair felt they remained safe because, as Melly put it, 'we were once quoted in the House of Commons, and Harold Macmillan said it was the first thing he read in the morning, so we were on quite powerful ground. A lot of people said, "We only read the paper to read Flook." So it was quite successful.'

George tended to use too many words in his balloons, and Wally complained because of this and because George was often too esoteric. But on the whole, the two got along well, disagreeing seriously no more than a couple of times in the fifteen years the strip ran.

> We had regular characters, some already in existence, some we invented. One was a character called Bodger who was the villain. Wally had a passion to have a character called Lucretia Bodger, so we had a sister who was a South London witch, a transpontine, with a familiar called Gobstopper, who has a cat who could only make sounds like another creature, 'woof, woof,' and so on.

George Melly dealt with the sociological side of it. It was Wally Fawkes's job to get the clothes and the stance of the characters right. Unlike other strips, particularly those from America, the strip was never syndicated because it was too British. As Fawkes put it, 'It wouldn't syndicate abroad; it would hardly syndicate out of one or two postal districts in London.'

The strip covered the fashion scene, the crime world and, later on with the rise of rock and roll, the Beatles. The political front would also become an important focus.

One story, lightly concealed, dealt with the Profumo case and Christine Keeler. Flook was pulled up for wearing a clip-on bow tie, a scandal. In place of sleeping with Christine Keeler, he was tricked into wearing this bow tie, or he lent it to a member of the Government who wore it and then threw it all at Flook who got into trouble. It sort of paralleled the scandal as it was actually going on.

The world of the cartoonists was a fantastical one, imaginative and often whimsical. It attracted a kind of cult following of intellectuals and, in the case of 'Flook', of politically astute readers.

Another group at the *Daily Mail* were the gossip columnists, whose world is also fantastical, built on image, name and style. As often as not, they succeed in creating a sense of envy on the part of readers whose lives cannot compare with those featured heavily in their columns. But the most important function of the gossip columnist is to satisfy the curiosity of readers about what others are up to.

'The diarists can often live in a world of their own,' said one staff member whose impression was shared by many others. 'They are often dishing the dirt on people with whom they have to associate. And it's one of the reflections of society that there is always somebody willing to dish the dirt.'

In the heyday of the 1950s, these 'smooth diary chaps', as one sub-editor called them, were always coming in to the newspaper in the early hours of the morning handsomely attired in black tie. Said Neil Swindells, 'It was the London scene of débutantes with gallant boy-friends, shoes off in the morning mist to get a coffee at a stall on the Embankment, and read all about themselves in the early morning. That was the romantic press image that came right through from the thirties to the fifties.'

Donald Edgar was hired on to the *Daily Mail* diary by Guy Schofield, who had sacked most of the old guard to make room for his new approach. In fitting with Schofield's plan for the paper, Edgar had been hired from the 'Peterborough' column on the *Daily Telegraph*. His brief was very different from the traditional diarist's of dishing dirt. It was, said Edgar, 'to write about people who were doing something interesting in a lively way, and consequently to provoke an interest in the paper other than hard news'.

Edgar had worked under Bill Deedes, later Lord Deedes, and Schofield assured him he would have a free hand to make the column into what he felt was most effective. Pleased in the beginning by the 'gentlemanly feeling to the office', Edgar was given a free hand to select his assistants. One of them was Peter Black, who had an idea that television was going to be a big thing and who only wanted to write a column criticizing the new productions appearing on 'the box'. He was constantly at Schofield to buy him a television set and let him have a TV column. Eventually he would emerge as the major national critic of television. Edgar's sub-editor was David Attlee, who really wanted only to be a farmer. A former personal assistant to Rothermere, he was an 'able, pleasant chap, who had been to Eton.' 'We had an office to ourselves, four or five of us, and buzzing in and out was Duke Hussey, a junior management trainee, tall and quite modest. Why he used to pop in was because he had been in the Guards like Attlee.'

It wasn't very long, however, before Edgar began to see that Schofield's projection of a rather lofty column was opposed by 'certain nameless elements on the *Daily Mail* staff'. It seemed to Edgar that the newspaper itself didn't know where it was going. Looking back, he said,

> I did my best, but the framework wasn't easy. The *Mail* Group was falling behind the *Express* to such an extent that the powers that be were turning it into a competitor with the *Daily Telegraph* instead of the *Express*. . . . But other influences at work in the *Daily Mail* were pressing for a more gossipy column than I was willing to do.

Caught between these two schools of thought, Edgar wasn't enjoying his work. And he soon realized that Schofield himself didn't like the way his column was developing. Edgar believed that it was not so much his problem as the split personality at the heart of the *Daily Mail* itself. Were they going to try to compete with the popular *Express*, which was trouncing them on the circulation front? Or were they going to try to become a cheaper *Daily Telegraph*? Edgar didn't think the situation would get better, so he left for the greener pastures of the *Daily Express*.

There, Beaverbrook's flagship was soaring at a circulation of well over 4 million. Back at the *Mail*, the circulation was stuck at just above 2 million. For every *Mail* man on a story, so went the legend, four or five *Express* reporters were assigned. The *Mail* reporters felt like the poor relations of Fleet Street.

For his part, Rothermere had fallen into the very pattern that he had once warned his father to avoid: favouring management over editorial and changing editors frequently in an effort to find a quick fix for the growing headaches. So it came as no surprise when, in 1954, Schofield, who had sacked so many, was himself sacked. Arthur Wareham was accordingly summoned into Managing Director Stuart MacLean's office, where he was offered the position of acting editor. It seemed that Esmond no longer wanted to name a permanent editor for fear he wouldn't last long enough to warrant the title.

Rothermere, dynamic and energetic in the early 1930s, was now uncertain what to do next. The mantle of power he wore insured that few were aware his confidence was eroding. But Beaverbrook, who had vowed to destroy the *Daily Mail*, understood exactly what was happening. Some twenty-five years earlier he had told one of his confidants, 'I shall go back to New Brunswick and retire a failure if I don't succeed in killing the *Daily Mail*.'

At long last it looked as though his quarry was in sight.

5

The Snowmen Were
Abominable

The early years of the 1950s ushered in the age of the great adventurer-reporter, whose epic travels provided armchair entertainment for thousands of newspaper readers across England. The most famous of these was the *Daily Mail*'s Ralph Izzard. In the spring of 1953 Izzard caught the imagination of the reading public when he overshot the British Expedition of Everest at 18,000 feet by climbing up the mountain to the Khumbu glacier. Ignorant of the necessity for acclimatization, Izzard walked to the dizzying height in nineteen days with no ill effects.

There he waited for Hunt and Hillary, astounding the expedition's physiologist and getting the scoop of the decade. It was a record climb for a solo effort on Everest and along the way Izzard noted the 'clusters of orchids ... patches of violets ... and wild strawberries'. He also told of the sickening leeches infesting the lush vegetation that clung to a man by the dozen. He became aware of their presence, he said, by the 'tell-tale red patch on the shirt or the squelch of blood in one's boots'. From this point on, Izzard's adventures became the stuff of legend in Fleet Street.

Izzard was chosen for the assignment by Walter Farr, who had been one of the *Daily Mail*'s star war correspondents during World War II. Now the foreign editor, he and Guy Schofield decided that a *Mail* reporter should track the Hunt expedition.

Izzard had been chosen for the assignment because of a 400-mile trek he and his wife Molly had made in 1947 from northern India over the mountains and into Nepal. In those days Nepal dwelt in isolation, there were no tourist facilities and few outsiders ever went there. Walking 'over steep mountain paths', the couple made their way to Kathmandu, there to catch their first sight of Mount Everest – an unlikely spot to play such an important part in Izzard's life.

Izzard had had ample experience of dangerous assignments. He had worked in the Berlin Bureau as a young man, later becoming bureau chief, and watched with concern the increasing violence of Hitler's Nazi movement. He had escaped from Germany only thirty-six hours before war was declared.

After serving in the Navy during the war, he had returned to work at the *Mail* and was sent by the newspaper to India. From there, he was ordered to the eastern Mediterranean, where there were naval manoeuvres the newspaper wanted him to cover. During the two weeks the manoeuvres lasted the partitioning of India began, along with terrible rioting and bloodshed. Izzard had with him a very large trunk and because of this he did not fly home by aeroplane but instead took a train from Bombay, 'which came up through Karachi, made its way across Pakistan and then turned down towards Delhi'.

The train was carrying fleeing Hindus and it crossed with another train that was carrying fleeing Muslims; one of the trains came in one way, the other the opposite and there was a fight on the platform.

> Looking out of the train window, as the train was just starting to glide out, I saw a Sikh rush forward and decapitate some women who were just – it was blood everywhere. I watched the whole thing, it was very bad, long swords – they were just slaughtering them with long swords. They took the bodies off the train in Delhi station; they piled them on to the luggage trucks. They came on to the train and slaughtered them.
>
> I was obviously a white man; it was the best colour of skin to have. I was in the first-class carriage, I had a sleeper. And I met a young RAF officer on the platform, he hadn't booked a sleeper, and I invited him to share mine with me. He wasn't travelling first class and I said, 'Don't worry, I'll pay the ticket.' The guy had a machine pistol that offered us some protection. They were Muslims looking for Hindus. They killed people all up and down the aisles.

When Izzard disembarked in Delhi, the entire town seemed to be ablaze. He made his way home, slept a couple of hours, then began typing. Shortly thereafter, when the riots in Calcutta started, Izzard was sent there. It was in this way he gained his reputation as an adventurer who could be sent into any part of the world and emerge with a story.

Perhaps as a reward for the difficult posting he had had in India, Izzard was sent, along with his family, to Washington, D.C. For Izzard, it turned out to be a sterile assignment, his main job simply a matter of going daily to Capitol Hill and getting a hand-out. Izzard quickly became restless. During the war, he had briefly worked with Ian Fleming at the Naval Division of Intelligence and in 1948 he heard that Fleming was in New York. So he travelled up there to try to see him. Fleming at that time was foreign manager of the Kemsley Group, and Izzard was hoping to leave the *Mail* and get a position with Fleming.

But when Ralph arrived he found Ian with the wife of the proprietor of the *Daily Mail* in what was certainly an intimate relationship of long duration. The situation seemed unduly complicated to Izzard. He rightly thought 'this wasn't the moment' and returned to Washington empty-handed. Soon thereafter, he received a visit from one of Ann Rother-mere's minions on the newspaper, asking if there was something Izzard wanted. Izzard said he found the posting too tame, and lo and behold, he was transferred to Egypt.

Izzard was still there when, in 1952 in Kenya, a secret indigenous organization fomented a blood-bath known as the Mau Mau Uprising. The British declared a State of Emergency as white colonists and native Kenyans alike were murdered in the direst of conditions. Izzard went to Nairobi to cover the story and over the next few years he went in three or four times to report on the bloody guerrilla war.

James Cameron from the *Express*, Bert Hardy from *Picture Post* and Ralph Izzard often met up in far-away places like this one, sharing facilities. On his first trip to Kenya Izzard was sharing a jeep with these two veteran reporters when they received a tip-off that a terrorist attack had taken place at an outlying farm.

On their way back, as it was growing darker, they were travelling down into a valley on a winding road and the jeep began to skid.

> It slid down the road and got stuck over the edge ... and the villagers saw that the jeep was hooked and they start climbing up. Bert Hardy said, 'We'd better start walking.'
>
> We left the jeep and started walking until we finally came to a cross-roads. A local police officer was at the cross-roads, trying to reach a British army post. But he didn't know which road to take either. A nasty situation and we more or less had to toss a coin. We chose one road and we were overtaken by a British army truck. Eventually, we made it back to the British army camp.... I didn't write a dispatch on this. It was really nasty, I really thought that I would have to get off the road and find a strong point at the top of the hill and stay there for the night.

Izzard sought danger and, by request, did three reporting tours during the Korean War. But he was best known for his 'stunt' journalism and, by 1954, he and his editors were creating adventures. The best-known of them all was the search for the Abominable Snowman, or the Yeti, as it came to be called. His search, which caught the imagination of every civilized nation, became a rage with children and the image of an Abominable Snowman – and the question of whether or not it existed – appeared in news-reels, comics and magazines throughout the world.

According to an expert on the animal whom Izzard consulted, the Yeti was a beast

about the size of a 14-year-old boy, of the same build as a man, covered with light reddish hair, a little lighter on the chest and with the hair longest about the head and waist.

The head is strikingly pointed. It has a loud, wailing yelping call, and when heard near at hand often makes a chattering noise.

It normally walks on two legs like a man, but when in a hurry or when going through deep snow it drops on all fours.... It is not thought to be particularly aggressive towards man, but it is very shy and very intelligent.

The 'discovery' of the Yeti's 'footprint' at the point of Izzard's departure, accompanied by nine Westerners and 300 sherpas to carry the expedition's gear, lent an air of anticipation to the great adventure.

On his famous search, Izzard encountered a Himalayan golden eagle's nest as the team chugged through waist-deep drifts of snow. By early March the team was convinced it was following reasonably fresh footprints higher and higher into the Himalayas, and reports from the natives indicated that they had actually 'seen' the rare creature 'some days previously'. Aware of two Yetis tantalizingly close, Izzard and one of his team thought perhaps there was 'a third Abominable Snowman in the vicinity of this frozen lake, nearly 17,000 feet above the sea'.

From the imprints left in the snow which Izzard and his party traversed he became convinced one of the three creatures was a tobogganing Yeti. Though the animal stayed well out of sight, 'at least we have confounded the theory that the Yeti cannot exist because no life is supportable at high altitude in winter. In fact, we have found that wild life abounds as high as we have been able to climb – that is, certainly to 20,000 feet.'

Further evidence unearthed by Izzard was a piece of Yeti skin. The skin, 'three inches long by an inch and a half wide and covered with reddish-black hair, has been presented to our Expedition by a senior lama of Thyanboch Monastery'. It was then sent to Britain, where Izzard was hopeful experts could determine 'to which class of animal it belongs'. In the meantime, he speculated about various characteristics of the strange creature.

An 'oddity' which Sherpas will ascribe to the Yeti ... is that it walks with its toes turned back to front 'to enable it to climb hills more easily'.

There could be a simple and logical explanation for this phenomenon – namely that, like the large apes, the Yeti might walk on the backs of its hands, in which case its fingers would be turned to the rear.

In the three months of his search, Izzard and his party walked right through the Himalayas. But alas, after all was said and done, although they encountered the Prime Minister of Nepal they came across no Abominable Snowman. Promising he would he back, Izzard wrote to his public back home that he had the uncanny feeling all along that a Yeti 'watched us from the surrounding rocks' as the expedition made its progress. 'If so, he must have felt contemptuous of our speed and supremely confident of his ability to evade us. Certainly we never saw him.'

A second great operator, also known as 'the last of the champagne and caviare foreign correspondents', was Noel Barber – an adventurer who was knifed in Algiers, shot in Budapest and managed to make it to both the North and South Poles, to the chagrin of his rivals. Barber had a great sense of epic style and of the importance of the narrator. It was personified in the lead that typified his writing: 'As we banked over Delhi, I turned to Pandit Nehru and said....'

Noel Barber was the editor of the *Continental Daily Mail* for eight years, from 1945 to 1953. Whether he had got the job because of his great friendship with Esmond Rothermere, or whether his work led to friendship with the *Mail* proprietor is unknown, but their long-term camaraderie was based on love of tennis. Throughout the war Barber was often a guest of Esmond at Monte Carlo, where they were seen together on the courts.

Because of his closeness to Rothermere and perhaps because of his flamboyant style of reporting, Barber was subjected constantly to ribald criticism from his rivals. In one version of a story, Barber and Rothermere won the amateur championship game at Monte Carlo; in another Barber bought the game for the pair. In a third, Barber arranged for Esmond to meet Marilyn Monroe; in yet another, he offered Monroe money for the meeting (it fell through because she asked too much, so went the tale). The story showed the kind of ambivalence typical of fame on Fleet Street, when truth gives way almost entirely to the fanciful speculations of rivals. For it was not Barber who tried to set up Monroe with Rothermere, but Spyros Skouras, the president of 20th Century Fox, who knew Esmond through his holdings in *Movietone News*. Esmond rejected Skouras's offer but it was Barber to whom was attributed the dubious honour in the lore of Fleet Street.

Envy and rumour followed the buoyant Barber throughout his career, but at all times he ignored his competitors and their innuendoes, remaining cool and dapper – and astonishingly successful. In later years when he was honoured on the successful television show *This Is Your Life*, he looked up at a gathering of journalists in the front row, eyes sparkling with mischief, and said, 'Oh, I thought you all hated me. But you're all clapping.'

Soon after the *Continental Daily Mail* folded, Barber became the chief foreign correspondent of the *Daily Mail* in London. Rivals insisted Barber was 'up to every trick'. If he weren't allowed into a country where an important news event was taking place he would fly in, so went the story, in the airliner of some little air company, get out of the plane and stand on the airfield, just so he could get the all-important dateline 'Inside Tibet'. 'Questionable ethics', his enemies called it; 'enterprising', his friends preferred.

It was true Barber enjoyed a privileged position. When he married his Italian wife, the Countess de Feo of Florence, Rothermere gave them a wedding luncheon at Warwick House and then Titina and Noel spent their honeymoon with Esmond at Villa Fleuri in Monte Carlo. His wife, herself quite colourful, remembered how it was.

> It was a ghastly time on my honeymoon. I had to look at a game of tennis every single day. So I bought a big straw bag and I put a book inside. 'Oh, well done, oh, good shot,' I would say. It was the most boring honeymoon I ever had.
>
> When we got married I think Noel was going to China. Esmond was very shy. At the door he said, 'Goodbye, bless you,' and he gave an envelope to Noel. And he said, 'Buy something intelligent with this.' Noel bought us this Ming vase as a present from Esmond for our wedding. He always bought intelligent things.

Always on the lookout for an angle, Noel once asked Rothermere, 'You know so much about the stock market, Esmond, tell me what shares I should buy.'

Esmond responded, 'Stick to what you know. Write, and buy pictures, but don't start investing.'

As the *Daily Mail's* chief foreign correspondent, it quickly became obvious that Barber had a penchant for making headlines for himself. In Casablanca during the French–Algerian war, Barber, the *Mail* reported, was 'murderously attacked'. Barber wrote the story of how it happened himself:

> For three or four long and very lonely minutes late last night I fought for my life with a Moroccan terrorist in a deserted street almost at the centre of Casablanca.
>
> I received one fairly deep wound in the forearm with which I was protecting my chest, five super slashes – one 8 in. long – on my left arm, shoulder and back as we fought on the ground. By the luckiest chance, only one wound was deep. The bruises from kicks in the stomach hurt more.

Thus was the legend born.

Probably the most famous Barber tale concerns his being shot twice in the head in Budapest during the Hungarian uprising in October 1956 when Red Army tanks invaded the city, killing as many as 30,000.

Barber, who lived with his wife Titina in Switzerland for tax reasons, had been to London to see the *Daily Mail* editorial staff and to buy baby clothes at Harrods for their daughter. In sudden inspiration, the *Daily Mail* foreign news editor, Peter Hope, called Imre Nagy, the Hungarian premier, and actually succeeded in reaching him to ask for a visa for one of the *Mail* reporters. The visa was granted to Noel Barber and he, baby clothes and all, diverted to Hungary, where he was met by Jeffrey Blyth. Blyth had been in Cairo when it dawned on him that the Soviets were pouring into Budapest. After he telexed the desk back in London to ask what he should do the message came back, 'You Budapestwards to upmeet Barber Vienna airport soonest.'

> We met at the airport and I'd been told, I think I'd got there first, to lay on two cars, rent them. They wouldn't rent them to me ... I had to buy two cars, £800 apiece.
>
> Noel came back the next night ... and he gave me this story and I filed it for him.
>
> In the Foreign Room in the *Daily Mail* office everyone took turns taking down a sentence or two at a time. The time was about 10 p.m. when I started dictating. I was still dictating an hour later when someone broke in to read me the front-page headline – and the start of the story I was dictating ... a Fleet Street triumph.

Noel's report was seventeen pages long and was accompanied by sixty photographs. It led, 'At least one thousand people have been killed in the most ghastly massacre, the most cold-blooded murder. I saw tanks and artillery mow down cheering crowds.'

The next night Barber himself was shot. He was travelling through the streets of Budapest by car, accompanied by his famed rival from the *Express*, the colourful Sefton Delmer. The pair of them had been trying to turn away from streets that had Red Army tanks on them and had just found their way

> gingerly through the tangle of pulled-down tram wire and overturned tramcars and broken glass by Karl Marx Square when, rat-a-tat-rat-a-tat, the whole car became a chaos of flying glass and tommy-gun bullets.
>
> *Barber stood on the brakes and collapsed against me. Out of the darkness came a frightened little Red Army man with an automatic. I explained to him as best I could in primitive Russian that we were British newspapermen....*
>
> 'Get me to a doctor, quick,' said Barber....
>
> *'See that the office gets the story,' Barber kept saying. 'Gosh, what a headache I have got.'*

Barber was hit twice and had to have sixty-two stitches. 'There was cut-out, burned and shattered flesh where the bullet had passed through just above his left ear ... a very wonderful escape,' the surgeon said.

Jeffrey Blyth, who was Barber's contact back in Vienna, rushed to Budapest, and 'there's Noel in bandages and all the rest of it, I took a picture actually'. The photo Blyth snapped was on the front pages of the *Daily Mail* the next morning.

Then Blyth travelled back and forth between Budapest and Vienna until he and most of the journalists got stuck in a small Hungarian town mid-way between Budapest and the Austrian border. He had gone there by car, having drained the petrol from Noel's vehicle, since it was obvious he couldn't travel. The car was the one Barber and Sefton Delmer had been travelling in and it had a shattered windshield and bullets had riddled the side.

A few days after Blyth, Noel and Sefton Delmer made their escape. Finding that their car had no fuel, Barber traded the baby clothes he had kept with him for petrol. He was still in his pyjamas, and bandaged and wrapped in a large blanket, when the pair drove through what they later discovered was a minefield, making it miraculously to the Austrian border.

Upon seeing Blyth, the first thing Noel said was, 'Who took my bloody petrol?' He then collapsed into Blyth's arms and Blyth in turn negotiated his return to his wife in Switzerland, a difficult task since most airlines refused to carry him for fear he would die in transit; eventually Swissair obliged.

Back in the office, so went the legend, word was quickly flashed from sub-editor to sub-editor: 'Noel Barber's been shot!'

'Is it serious?' asked one.

'No,' came the answer. 'It's only in the head.'

Barber not only survived; he prospered. And his fame made him the logical man to cover the Transantarctic Expedition of Dr Vivian Fuchs in the winter of 1957–8. By now Arthur Wareham was editor of the *Daily Mail* and, having learned of the plan to go to the South Pole early, he offered £24,000 for the newspaper rights to the story. But the Expedition Committee decided in favour of *The Times*, regardless of the fact it had offered £4000 less.

Wareham was so disappointed he made an uncharacteristic boast. 'All right,' he told Admiral Parry, who was in charge of headquarters administration for the project. '*The Times* may have bought the story but the *Daily Mail* will get it.'

... we succeeded beyond my wildest dreams. Noel Barber spent a month at the South Pole reporting the progress of the expedition – Sir Edmund Hillary's unscheduled dash to the Pole, the arrival of Dr Fuchs and the race against time to complete the journey before the full rigours of winter set in. The rest of Fleet Street and the world's press were nowhere.

Special permission from Washington had to be granted to the *Mail* and once he started, Barber took an American Air Force plane from New Zealand, where he had been waiting for clearance, to McMurdo Sound. In his cable from there he wrote, 'I am 800 miles from the Pole and with luck I should be there by Christmas. This is a beautiful world where night and day are friends, a continent that has 84 per cent of all the ice on earth, and where all men are equal in face of dangers like the dreaded white-out which obliterates everything to the human eye.'

Only four days later, on 16 December 1957, Barber filed the most famous of all his dispatches – 'I AM AT THE POLE'.

From Noel Barber: At the South Pole, Sunday
I have reached the South Pole. I am the sixth Briton in history to do so, the first for 45 years since Scott's party of five reached here in 1912, only to perish on the return journey. It took me eight hours to fly from McMurdo Sound base.

At this time Fuchs, having travelled fewer than twenty miles per day on caterpillar-tracked vehicles, was still some 550 miles away and Sir Edmund Hillary 470 miles away from the South Pole, waiting for Fuchs to catch up. When Hillary clapped eyes on Barber actually waiting for him, he was nonplussed: 'I wondered if you would be here to greet us. Wherever I go it is either you or Izzard.'

It was a great victory in the *Daily Mail* camp back in London, but a little-known fact was that Barber managed to get his private parts stuck on a freezing toilet seat in an outdoor loo at the South Pole and the American medical staff had to rescue him. After the triumph of his dash across the world, it was something of an embarrassment, even to a man as outgoing and assured as he was.

There was also the question of morale. Even Noel Barber could have his spirits dampened by being away from his family during the Christmas season. The staff back in London never fully took in the fact that he was to spend Christmas at the Pole among American servicemen who were complete strangers to him. But in the end they went out of their way to make him feel at home.

One of them wrote later, 'It was 60 below zero and the air force was making an airdrop with parachutes, supplies and Christmas parcels.' There were none, however, for Barber.

On Christmas day Noel was sitting in the back of the mess hall looking a little disgruntled but one of our men was dressed as Santa Claus and he came forward with Christmas gifts and so forth and much to Noel's astonishment suddenly his name was called out, not once but again and again, about 18 times in all. The fact was Noel's name was transferred to a number of the parcels, each of us had given up one. Noel was delighted. You should have seen the expression on his face.

After that, all went well and back in London Rothermere gave a dinner at the Savoy Hotel for the entire editorial staff.

Two years later, in November of 1959, the *Daily Mail* decided on a return venture, this time with Barber going to the North Pole. Once again he succeeded in gaining access to a hostile environment, thus capturing the headlines back home and indeed the imagination of the nation. But this time he managed to get home for Christmas, making a quick detour to Hawaii first.

An irrepressible character, Noel Barber once got himself into hot water when he was sent to cover the escape of the Dalai Lama from Tibet as the Chinese troops filtered in and occupied the country. The foreign press corps were based in Calcutta, they had an aeroplane, they flew off and, once off the ground, Barber said to them, 'I hope you chaps don't mind, but I've already filed my story.' Unfortunately for him, the plane never arrived at its destination.

His lead began:

> Today I flew over the monastery of Towang as the Dalai Lama and his followers rested there under a strong guard of Assamese riflemen and hundreds of shaven-headed Buddhist monks.
> The high walls of the magnificent monastery ... [etc., etc.]

Legend has it that the press corps, especially the Americans who were so shocked by such an act that they refused to fly with Barber, insisted he be grounded for the rest of the assignment.

Whether that was true or not, the pursuit of the Dalai Lama resulted in one of the great *Daily Mail* 'moments', passed down from editor to editor through the decades. It happened to Laurie Turner, who was an Australian heading the news desk at the time. Turner and the staff were trying to fix up a telephone link from the news-room to Delhi in order to speak to the Dalai Lama direct, when the phone rang and Turner picked it up.

All around the news-room people were shouting, 'For Heaven's sake, keep quiet, this is an unreliable line and Laurie's got to speak!' At that very moment Turner spoke into the phone, ''Allo, 'allo, 'allo, is that the Dalai Lama? This is the *Daily Mail*.'

Although Esmond remained a remote figure, anyone he knew and liked prospered on the newspaper – whether by his intervention or by the eagerness of his underlings to please. Among those favoured was Iris Ashley, charming, capable and, as described by a smitten sub-editor on the newspaper, 'extremely dainty'. Iris became the fashion editor of the *Daily Mail* in 1949.

As for Esmond, after his divorce from Ann in 1952 he was never very long without attention from the opposite sex. Esmond was a catch in any woman's estimation. That he lacked confidence seemed only to enhance his appeal.

It was unlikely, however, that women interested in him could compete with Iris Ashley once she set her sights on a man. When her husband died in 1953, Iris was a very stylish and slim forty-four. Esmond, who was involved with another woman at the time, lost no time in becoming close friends with the self-possessed fashion editor.

Iris Ashley was a woman with 'a past'. That is, for one so well-born it was inappropriate that as a young girl she had sung in cabaret. Early in 1932 she had been praised for her talent in the *Daily Mail*'s gossip column. A short piece entitled 'A Peer's Niece' pointed out that she was the niece of the Earl of Iddesleigh and that at the age of only twenty-two she was 'remarkably pretty and attractive'.

> She has the perfect cabaret manner, and her songs which she writes herself to the music of her partner, are catchy.
>
> That her turn is going to make a hit in the West End is obvious for she has been encored nine times in two nights, and is already drawing crowds.

According to family lore, Iris got her start at the Café de Paris when she was sitting in the audience and turned to her companion to say, 'Oh, I could sing better than that.'

The owner was sitting nearby and leaned forward to say, 'Well, why don't you?' She did, and after a season there, she discovered in herself theatrical ambitions.

A spate of publicity stories about the aspiring young performer followed in various newspapers. In one, she was leaving cabaret for 'the legitimate stage'; in another she saved a young child from being run over by a lorry in Oakley Street, Chelsea. A complete apologia for her unusual desire to be an actress appeared in 1936, when the theatre correspondent of the *Star* explained that

> A well-known Society girl who lost a fortune 'playing the markets' when in her teens, has by her own courage and hard work, paid back every penny she owed.
>
> Her name – or the name she uses professionally – is Iris Ashley, and by sheer grit and a good deal of talent she has not only paid her debts of honour, but has 'got somewhere' in the process.

None of this bumf seems to have taken, although Iris did have the requisite number of profiles allotted to a young starlet. But she had fallen in love and, just before the war, had left the stage to marry a diplomat, Stanley Knowles. Afterwards she followed her husband to Washington, where he was attached to the British Embassy.

She was a singular woman. It was like her to meet a journalist at a party and end up writing something for his newspaper. In fact, she did meet a *Washington Post* editor and tried her hand at becoming an agony aunt for his newspaper. But when a woman wrote asking for advice, and Iris sent back a common-sense answer, Iris was shocked to receive a return letter from the woman saying that Iris had changed her life. She immediately resigned from the job, appalled by her own influence. In this case it had turned out all right, but what if things had gone wrong?

Fashion was a different matter. Iris's daughter Penny Knowles, who became for a time a fashion model and writer, before leaving the industry to become a psychoanalyst, said, 'I wouldn't say that she was interested in fashion, I would say that that was what you were told to write about because it was a woman's subject. . . . I think she then enjoyed the life and she was very concerned about looks, about how she looked, she always looked very good, it was very, very important to her.'

But Iris Ashley was not only good-looking. She was also very ambitious and, unexpectedly, extremely bright. She had been at Lady Margaret Hall at Oxford and though she didn't stay for her degree there was no question but that she was very intelligent. She appeared on the radio show *The Brain of Britain* and won it several times.

At the *Mail*, Ashley soon managed what the other fashion editors had not – to have her own office and her own secretary. She no doubt used her looks and femininity to get what she wanted and it was rumoured she had a relationship with Guy Schofield. If men did adore her she didn't hesitate to take advantage of their admiration. She soon cut a swath through the male-dominated newspaper world and, together with her illustrator Penny Marshall, Iris was determined to set the fashion world on fire.

It was 'Turnip Winter', 1954, one of the coldest in the history of the country. Luxury goods were still in very short supply when Vivian Hislop, a newly hired fashion illustrator on the *Evening News*, was assigned to go to Paris to cover the first Chanel show since the war:

We had to go on the night boat and that night there was a ferry lost (the *Princess Victoria* that was going to Ireland) and we tossed around all night. 'Thank heavens we're nearly there,' we said to one another. And the next morning we were still in Dover harbour, and then we had to get on a boat to Boulogne, and the train took hours and hours.

The streets of Paris were almost empty, almost like Siberia. There was a desperately cold, piercing wind. It was so cold we couldn't wear ear-rings and our ears and nose felt like bits of cold meat.

In those days we did not have lovely leather boots, just after the war. I had a pair of white button-up rubber shoes to put over my high heels, and when I at last got off the streets and into the cab I almost cried from pain when the feeling came back.

It was typical of Iris Ashley that even as these young women made their way to the Paris show by boat and train she had contrived to fly. And at the all-powerful Chambre Syndicale de la Couture she managed to get good seats.

This was no mean feat. Fashion spies were everywhere, so a record was kept of everyone authorized to get into the shows. Every fashion correspondent had to be registered with the Syndicale. Otherwise they would issue no press card and there would be no admission to any of the collections. Photographs were not permitted and artists were not allowed to draw during the shows. This meant they either remembered the new lines, or they drew small hieroglyphics on the edge of their programmes.

When the show was over the artists would rush to Keystone, the photographic agency in rue Royale, where the pictures were put on the wire and sent to their newspapers abroad. The artists, allowed to show no detail, would try to carry the idea of a new hat or dress with a simple line, printing a short caption at the bottom. In this world Iris Ashley was known for her intuition 'to pin-point' what was going to be important that year. She also had the ability to give a sense of excitement and anticipation to her readers, becoming in a sense the fashion guru of the newspaper world.

Somehow, Iris always managed to be treated like royalty. When she went to Paris she insisted on staying at the Ritz Hotel and she always had the same taxi driver. He would pick her up at the airport and would turn up at the Ritz every morning with his beret on, and drive her to all the collections. Her daughter later remembered what she was like.

My mother had a quality that was both infuriating and endearing, which was that she expected the best, so she wasn't going to be put into a little hotel in the backstreets. It actually gave the *Daily Mail* a good image as well. She was jolly well going to stay at the Ritz, which is where she felt she ought to stay if she went to Paris, and she wasn't going to stand in the rain and wait for a taxi. She expected people to treat her as though she was somebody special and so while she was in that job they did.

It was impossible not to. In the office, and among the men who dominated the business, she was known for her style and *savoir-faire*. Once, at a party, as Iris was recounting an anecdote her underwear dropped down around her ankles. Said Donald Todhunter, who was the news editor at the *Daily Mail* and was at the time standing beside her, 'Iris, without showing any signs of interruption in what she was saying, sort of stepped out of them, picked up her knickers, put them in her handbag and carried on with the conversation. That's style, isn't it?'

Iris Ashley had a house in Chapel Street just off Grosvenor Place and also a cottage in Sussex. And of course she knew, as her male colleagues acknowledged, 'all the right people'.

Iris Ashley's attraction for Esmond became well known throughout the *Daily Mail* building. The press lord's weakness for intelligent women made Iris practically irresistible and the pair were seen together to the extent that, among staff members, it was thought they were involved. If they had decided to marry it would have surprised no one.

Whenever Iris travelled to Monte Carlo she joined the ranks of the rich in their sumptuous tents along the rocky beach. Three rows of the tents were placed on specially built terraces, and in these hired, colourful 'accommodations' were the well-connected and the wealthy, chatting with and visiting one another as they bathed in the Mediterranean. The tents and space rented for a great deal of money, and Iris would say that she got a special price because of the *Daily Mail*.

Next to the pool was a stylish restaurant where the rich and powerful went to lunch. It was extremely difficult to get a table here. But whenever Esmond appeared there was no difficulty at all. No matter how large his party, somehow they got seated, and seated quickly. Iris took her daughter along and Esmond was always very happy to include the children of any woman he was seeing in the festivities of the day. Thus, it was in Monte Carlo that Penny Knowles, who was then a teenager, first met the awesome press lord. 'He was a powerful man; they behave in a particular way. He was very charming. He was at ease with his manner of being powerful.'

Given her connection with Rothermere, and her privileged position, it would be easy to conclude Iris Ashley coasted in her job. But nothing could have been further from the truth. Through her very light, very direct and descriptive prose, her readers lived vicariously as Iris cut a stylish figure among the fashionable set. Here is Iris Ashley at Ascot –

giving a day-by-day diary of the clothes she wore, what worked and what didn't:

Thursday, Gold Cup Day

Convention says the sun *must* shine today (only the sun doesn't always know this). A dress of pure white silk printed in black with a pattern of precious stones – seemed a lovely idea in the warmth of the dressmaker's salon!

The pleated skirt again is the result of a lesson well learnt. I went to Ascot in a slim white skirt once. You have to walk *miles* between Enclosure and Paddock, and in a tight skirt – you can't.

What about that hat? A large hat, moddom, is so correct for Ascot ... and 'so' romantic.... But what if I have to clutch the darn thing on my head all day? How will I be able to write my notes – let alone look romantic?

Or the slender Iris Ashley on dieting:

Beans look fine on a plate, but I think they look depressing walking about.

No, the idea of getting rid of overweight is to give you back the bounce and brightness, the easy movements of youth. And to control your proportions.

Or the buoyant Iris Ashley on exercise:

Incidentally, a normal weight is no promise of a good figure. Proportions are what we're after. Measure yourself here and now. Over an uplift brassière is all right and over your girdle too ... that's the way you look most of the time! Got it?

Now the waist: 8 to 10 inches less than the bust is elegant. Six is so-so. Five to four, we hate to tell you, is a middle not a waist. Hips that are 2 inches more than the bust are still slim; 3 inches is average, 4 inches is full: after that ... let's talk of something else!

Iris Ashley on the Queen's Coronation gown:

Norman Hartwell has made it of white satin and embroidered it with the emblems of Great Britain and the Commonwealth. The embroidery is not as we expected, all in gold, but in lovely and delicate colourings.

In addition to the golden crystals, diamonds and pearls, soft-toned silks are used to embroider pale green leaves, mauve thistles, and the pink Tudor Rose.

Down to earth, comfortable, energetic – her prose set a model of intimacy with her readers. And the readers believed she was the perfect model of the perfect fashion editor. On the *Daily Mail* she was something more than a star: she was a compass to the values of women of the age.

As the epitome of the ideal woman of the 1950s Iris Ashley set the tone. The day *she* left the *Mail* it would be a sign that times had changed, that women had changed; it would mark the beginning of an entirely new era.

6

The Sons of Great Men

The first public insult dealt to Esmond by Randolph Churchill, son of Winston, occurred in September 1953 at a rather innocuous literary luncheon given by Christina Foyle at the Dorchester Hotel. 'I have known Lord Rothermere all my life,' Churchill said to the gathering, 'but I can only confess myself baffled that so rich and cultivated a man should hire people to prostitute newspapers in this way – it must be a case of pornography for pornography's sake. He has no need to do it to earn a living....'

This stinging blow was delivered because the *Sunday Dispatch*, where Randolph had for a time worked as a political correspondent, had serialized the sensational historical novel *Forever Amber* by Kathleen Winsor, which had leaped to the bestseller list in the United States.

The controversial book had been selected for serialization in the *Dispatch* by its editor, Charles Eades, in an attempt to keep up with Beaverbrook's *Sunday Express*, and in fact, when the *Dispatch* put on 400,000 circulation as a result of its apparent success Eades, encouraged by an over-eager circulation manager, began to publish more of the same kind of material.

Esmond was not at the luncheon at the Dorchester and the *Manchester Guardian* was the only newspaper that mentioned his name in reporting the attack. Undeterred, Randolph Churchill decided to have another go and a week later he fired off another volley:

Let me assure you: there is no sinister motive on my part. I am pursuing no vendetta against any individual, nor am I working off any private spite.... As one who has worked all his life in the profession of journalism I feel that every member of our profession has a responsibility to make it respected and honoured. It would be an affectation to pretend that this is the case today, and this is where the Dog Don't Eat Dog rule is so pernicious.... [Lord Rothermere] desires, not only what his father was accused of by the late Lord Baldwin – 'power without responsibility, the prerogative of the harlot throughout the ages' – but the cash that comes from the sale of pornography without the shame attaching to this squalid way of life.

The *Sunday Dispatch* wasn't the only newspaper to blame, Churchill continued. He named the *Sunday Pictorial*, the *Daily Mirror*, the *Daily Sketch*, the *Weekly Overseas Mail* and *Reveille* as well. But if these papers were also purveyors of pornography, Esmond Rothermere, with his shameless editors, was the 'Pornographer Royal'.

As if this charge weren't enough, a good friend of Churchill's remembered seeing Randolph attack Esmond face to face at an assembly. 'How can you make so much rotten money on appealing to the basest instincts in the human race?' Randolph asked Esmond. And when the 'horrified' Esmond could not answer, Randolph continued, 'Why do you just stand there like a flogged jellyfish? ... I hate flogging jellyfish.'

Like his father before him, Randolph Churchill was given his start in journalism by the Harmsworths. When he was only twenty, Randolph began writing for Harold Rothermere. At his twenty-first birthday, 16 June 1932, there was a grand party for Randolph at Claridge's, attended by eighty of England's good and great. They included Lords Camrose, Beaverbrook and Rothermere, as well as Lloyd George and many others. And especially the press lords, ever mindful of his father Winston's great power and prestige, actively supported Randolph's career as a political pundit, offering him choice positions on their newspapers.

Randolph had also been supported in his political aspirations. The *Mail* proprietor had contributed heavily to his various campaigns for office, giving him editorial support as well. So was Randolph's attack upon Harold's son Esmond just another version of the old adage, 'No good deed ever goes unpunished'? Or were Randolph's criticisms motivated by a sincere sense of outrage at the direction of the modern press?

Or could there have been yet another motive?

Randolph was a great friend of Beaverbrook, who, like Harold, had been an instrumental force in furthering Randolph's career and, in making his accusations against Rothermere, Randolph had been scrupulous in avoiding mention of any of the newspapers owned by Beaverbrook, for whom he sometimes wrote. When Randolph quoted Baldwin's famous phrase, accusing Esmond of wanting 'power without responsibility, the prerogative of the harlot', Randolph had omitted mention of the fact that Baldwin's charge had been levelled *not only* at Harold Rothermere but also at his best friend Max Beaverbrook.

For his part, Beaverbrook must have been delighted to sit back and watch his greatest rival, the proprietor of the *Daily Mail*, hurriedly begin cleaning up his newspapers. In his zeal, Esmond fired both the editors of the *Sunday Dispatch* and the *Daily Sketch*. Was Beaverbrook behind Randolph Churchill's attack? Most probably he was.

Seeing he was on a winner, Randolph held on to the 'pornography question' and continued hectoring Esmond for several years. Eventually, the *Sunday Dispatch* began to lose money, a lot of it – some £600,000 a year – a drain that forced Esmond at last to fold the newspaper. Significantly, he sold the title to the *Sunday Express*, a signal victory for Beaverbrook's camp. On that occasion Randolph was quick to put salt on the wound and on 12 June 1961 he wired Esmond:

> So glad you have at last taken my advice and got rid of that disreputable rag the *Sunday Dispatch* stop why is the *Daily Mail* trying to ruin Mrs Kennedys Greek holiday? How would you like it if you were chased around the Riviera by the gutter press? Try and be a better boy stop Chuck it Esmond chuck it warmest regards – Randolph

In the unrelenting competition between the *Express* and the *Mail*, Beaverbrook was clearly winning. And it was not only because of tricks like Randolph's.

Inside the *Daily Mail*, morale was low. The staff perceived – and it became common lore to impart to any new reporters – that no expense was too great for the *Express* in beating the *Mail*. 'Four against our one' became the battle cry. But Esmond's swinging-door policy on editors also contributed to the sagging morale.

There was, in addition, a perceived 'three-months' policy that bothered staff: that is, it seemed to many of the beleaguered reporters that they were in good stead on the newspaper for just about three months. Then, without any warning, or any seeming dereliction of duty, they would suddenly be out of favour and for three months or so they would be unable to get anything into the paper.

At the sub-editor level morale was down as well. One young sub-editor at the time, Brian James, found himself travelling home in the wee hours of the morning alongside the printers from the *Mail* and the *Express*. The *Express* printers were full of beans: 'Christ, did we get a scoop today!' they would boast. The *Mail* printers simply didn't have the same pride in their newspaper. Listening to the *Express* printers, James would get a sinking feeling – even though he defended the day's headline in the *Mail* as best he could.

Low morale was not just a figment of the imagination of a few disgruntled employees. The advertising figures reflected the terrible truth. By 1957 the *Express* could comfortably charge £5000 for a full-page advertisement; the *Mail* was down to £3250.

As if this weren't enough, there were also the union problems that hit the *Daily Mail* full force in the mid-1950s. It was the general belief among the management that these woes stemmed from the paternalistic attitude of the press lords themselves – all rich men who took the view that anyone who had fought in the war should have the right to return to full employment. So the soldiers came flooding back in to print a paper that was, since rationing was still in force, only eight pages. Even when the pagination did move up it stuck at sixteen pages. There were simply too many workers for a newspaper of that size.

Bolstering the trend was the tough-guy stance of the union leaders. In this arena Esmond shone. He stood up to leaders with a thug's mentality without giving it a second thought. A young manager, Marmaduke Hussey, watched transfixed, as Esmond dressed down 'a most terrifying union leader, a man who was nothing short of a crook':

> I saw him reduce this man to an absolute pygmy by just going at it like this – 'What do you mean? I'm not accepting that. Do you mean the one thing, or do you mean the other? I want an answer! Don't just sit there. Don't blather at me! Are you a man of power or are you not? If you're not a man of power, get out of the room and bring back someone who is.'

Usually less aggressive, Esmond brought himself to dress down the man, no doubt, because he felt particularly ill used by the truculent unions. His great-uncle Northcliffe had helped the unions get their start in Fleet Street, because he believed in the working man's right to representation – even against his employer, *even* if the employer were himself. Their aggressive new attitude smacked of disloyalty to the press baron. Most important, just after the war, in 1945, Esmond had started a non-contributory pension scheme and later made it into the contributory scheme that saw his employees safely into old age. Now, witnessing the new aggression of the unions he had sought to bolster, it wasn't very likely he would succumb to their threats.

It was with a sense of real misgiving that he witnessed the first major newspaper strike after the war. It lasted from 26 March to 20 April 1955. When the *Daily Mail* at last returned to the news venders' kiosks, the front page greeted its readers with the admission: 'Strike action has done what Hitler's bombs never succeeded in doing – stopped your *Daily Mail* for nearly a month. . . .'

Although the firm appeared to be made of money, and its early attitude of *laissez-faire* towards the unions did nothing to dispel that belief, Esmond had, from the time he took over the company, overcome several challenges, some of them a clear threat to its survival.

When his father died in 1940, for example, Esmond had had to deal with enormous duties on Harold's estate; he told his friend Aidan Crawley they amounted to £36 million – an unheard-of sum at the time. Even if the amount were exaggerated, as it no doubt was, Esmond found himself deeply submerged in very hot water. He was in the position of having to make a number of ruthless decisions, among them the selling of his two sisters' waterfront properties in Bermuda that Harold had left them, correctly believing the land would be worth a fortune in later years. But such sacrifices were unavoidable. Then, too, Harold had made a few decisions himself that had been less than sensible.

He had been downright cavalier about selling *The Times* immediately after his brother Northcliffe's death. Well, *The Times* always *had* been a drain on the company's resources – although Northcliffe had gone a long way towards restoring it to a position of fiscal responsibility. But when, in 1931, Rothermere let drop the *Mirror* and the *Sunday Pictorial* a cash cow dropped out of the control of Associated Newspapers, one that others were more than happy to milk.

Within three years editorial control was in the hands of Harry Guy Bartholomew ('Bart'), 'the *enfant terrible* of Fleet Street', as he was known, and the very man destined to carry the *Mirror* to great success as a popular tabloid. In describing Bart, Cecil King, who would succeed him, said he 'was short and square, very good-looking, with a shock of white hair, and with features and mannerisms not unlike Northcliffe, whose illegitimate son he was quite erroneously supposed to have been'. With little formal education but a great aptitude for newspaper work, Bart had begun at the *Daily Mirror* in 1913 as manager of the process-engraving department. Together with Arkas Sapt he had helped make it into a great illustrated newspaper, after it failed as Northcliffe's first (and last) newspaper for, of and by women.

Bart's genius in the newspaper industry led him in 1944 to become chairman of the companies that owned the *Daily Mirror* and *Sunday Pictorial*. But through company intrigue Cecil King managed to unseat him and get the coveted job for himself. Bart unwittingly aided King in the take-over by drinking entirely too much and by acting like a despot, but not before Bartholomew did Esmond a singular favour – and one that did little to endear him to Cecil King.

He aided Esmond in securing control of Daily Mail & General Trust. When Harold had secretly in the early 1930s sold off his interests in the *Daily Mirror* and the *Sunday Pictorial*, even his son had not been fully informed of this move. Later on, Esmond began, just as secretly, to accumulate *Daily Mirror* shares. This was after he became chairman of the Daily Mail & General Trust in 1937. Most especially, after the palace coup that nearly saw him removed from power in 1944, Esmond saw the necessity of gaining unassailable control of his own company.

On 17 February 1947 Esmond explained his position over the previous decade in a letter to one of the directors of the Daily Mail & General Trust, Sir S. Hardman Lever:

The whole motive of the transaction is to terminate once and for all the inter-company finance which has been an unwholesome feature of some phases of our past history which in all other respects has been so successful and of which we are all proud. The situation was not of my making but fell into my lap on my father's death in 1940. When I made a careful study of the position I found that the Harmsworth newspaper Empire had become extremely mixed up.

My father had sold all his interest in the Daily Mirror and Sunday Pictorial companies, but had left a large residue of interest in the Daily Mail Trust Limited and Associated Newspapers in the care of these companies. Whilst the late John Cowley was alive he gave me an undertaking that those shares would not be used antagonistically but could not bind his successors.

But just in case 'the directors of the *Daily Mirror* and the *Sunday Pictorial* become antagonistic', Esmond had begun to accumulate *Daily Mirror* shares on Cowley's advice. To this end, he told Hardman, he accumulated *Mirror* shares – 'for this purpose and this purpose only'.

On the death of John Cowley, the policy of the *Mirror* and *Pictorial* newspapers not only continued their divergence from the policy of the Mail Group but became completely opposite. These inter-company holdings, fully justified on my part by the position I had been left in, could obviously not endure indefinitely.

Whilst remaining secret they could do no harm but if forced into the open could give rise to misunderstandings. The purely company view would have been unimportant in comparison to the political view when newspapers are being subjected to scrutiny by the appointment of a Royal Commission. In any case the Companies Bill would have the effect of full disclosure.

The proposed transaction would have been impossible had I not held a sub-stantial block of Daily Mirrors and should I have not held them their disclosure of the holding of Daily Mail Trust Limited and Associated by the Mirror would have forced the directors of that Company to interfere politically with the political control of the Mail Group.

It was Bartholomew who aided Esmond in his goal, exchanging all the Mirror Group shares he had accumulated with all the Mail Group shares Bartholomew held. Thus the pair thwarted Cecil King's plans eventually to control the Mail Group. It had been a carefully finessed exercise, and one that showed that Esmond was capable of watching and waiting, in the tradition of his great-uncle, Northcliffe, and his father, Harold.

But though Esmond succeeded, the result had grim consequences. For one thing, it gave Cecil King the impetus to stage his own palace coup and oust Bartholomew. It also thwarted the clever King, who had always hoped for and planned the take-over of the Daily Mail Group as well. As a result, when Bartholomew died, King refused to give him a service at

St Bride's in Fleet Street – an unheard-of omission for someone as prominent as Bartholomew had been in the publishing world. Esmond took the unprecedented step of telephoning King to ask him if he wouldn't after all give Bartholomew the service he deserved. But King refused: 'Absolutely not! Don't believe in services,' he answered. King's fury with Bartholomew pursued him even after death.

What did Cecil King have against Esmond? They were first cousins. King's mother Geraldine had been the sister of Northcliffe and Harold Rothermere, a very bright woman with a great deal of spark; King's father was a gifted linguist. Cecil was given his start by Esmond's father, Harold, and he appeared never to have forgiven his uncle for doing so, for he never missed a chance of putting down the family of which he was a part. Certainly, he bore an unaccountable grudge against his own forebears, most especially his grandparents whom he denigrated along with Northcliffe and Rothermere more and more publicly as time passed. This truly was the no-good-deed-ever-remains-unpunished principle at work, and it was an attitude that continued to puzzle the family.

King was enjoying an illustrious career in the publishing business. He was respected and admired. But he apparently wanted more – control of Associated Newspapers and the Daily Mail & General Trust. And when, by 1961, it became obvious King would not succeed in gaining control of Esmond's company, he determined to get even – with Esmond, with *everybody*, by 'going public'. But this was still to come.

It did not escape Esmond's attention, nevertheless, that King wished him less than well. King was certainly a Harmsworth, though he had never borne the name, and his savage attacks on the Harmsworth clan seemed rooted in jealousy, but also in self-hatred. And this, too, was a recognizable strain in the family – a dislike of self so strong it caused self-destructive behaviour. Eventually, and in as bizarre an episode as Fleet Street has ever witnessed, King would annihilate himself.

But for now, so far as the *Daily Mail* was concerned, King was neutralized. This in itself gave little reason for celebration, for at every level in Fleet Street the highly competitive atmosphere was palpable.

The 1950s were a transition period. They represented a time when conservative thinking still reigned. But beneath the surface a surge of energy was building up across a newly optimistic nation. What it meant to Esmond was pressure – from his competitors, his relatives, the unions, the editors of his newspapers, the managers. Among all these, the shareholders were not an inconsiderable force, exerting pressure upon the chairman of the Daily Mail & General Trust.

The company had, under the leadership of Esmond and his managing director, Stuart MacLean, made what in retrospect has been recognized as one of the shrewdest decisions in the media business – to invest in commercial television. At the time of the investment, however, the full potential of ITV, as it was called, was only a gleam in the eye of the investors.

Three companies joined together to apply for a licence to transmit – Associated Newspapers, the Rediffusion Company and British Electric Traction (BET). The resultant company was named Associated Rediffusion, with Associated Newspapers owning a fifty per cent share and each of the other two companies taking a twenty-five per cent share. When the newly formed company won the London weekday television franchise, it seemed as if it had gained a licence to print money.

The idea was to sell on-air advertisements that would cover the operating expenses and eventually lead to hefty profits for the investors. But by the day of the launch, 22 September 1955, of the four million sets licensed to receive commercial television only 188,000 had been converted to do so. The 'set count' was to commercial television as circulation was to newspapers. Advertisers could be persuaded to buy time only if the set count was sufficiently high. And the set count continued to be low.

The following year, at the July AGM, the stockholders in Associated Newspapers were exerting subtle pressure on Esmond to re-evaluate the investment, making certain it was viable. If expectations were high, so were suspicions.

'How are you getting on with the ITV?' one of the stockholders asked; it was a man named Nichols.

ESMOND   With what?

NICHOLS   With the ITV.

ESMOND   How do you mean – how are we getting on?

NICHOLS   You forecast that for the first three years there would be a loss.

ESMOND   It is still making a loss.

NICHOLS   Is it making progress?

ESMOND   It is making progress but it is still making a loss.

HALL (*stockholder*)   You are satisfied with your investment?

ESMOND   I am never satisfied with anything.

NICHOLS   You are a wise man! It is not too bad, is it?

ESMOND   It is not too bad but it is still running at a loss.

NICHOLS   You said that for the first three years there would be a loss.

ESMOND   Owing to the fact mainly, of course, that the 'credit squeeze' has not exactly helped matters ... Hire purchase and the credit squeeze have greatly reduced the volume of people buying new sets, and so on. It would have been two or three times what it is but for the advent of that situation. It has fallen off but that is nothing that we can help.

NICHOLS   You could not budget for it, could you?

ESMOND   We could not budget for that, no. . . .

Whether he had budgeted for losses or not, there was no end to the losses Esmond privately envisaged. Neither through sales of sets, nor from conversion could Esmond see a way through these accumulating losses. He could borrow, but the idea was repellent to him. He could stay the course, but he risked fiscal oblivion.

Between these two undesirable outcomes he could envisage no alternatives. Esmond had inherited the great Harmsworth publishing dynasty; his responsibility weighed heavily upon him. The huge profits that the franchise would begin to produce, only a month after Esmond's deliberations took place, were beyond his imaginings. Esmond dithered. He took advice from family members, all of whom gave differing counsels, but he still could not decide.

Casting a shadow over the proceedings was the terminal illness of Stuart MacLean, Esmond's brilliant managing director, who had been diagnosed as having thyroid cancer. MacLean's illness took the wind out of Esmond, although, practically with his dying breath, MacLean had counselled the press baron to stay the course with the franchise.

Esmond could not. He sold his holdings in Associated Rediffusion, squandering his firm's early advantage in the fledgeling television industry.

It was the biggest mistake of his career.

In the City Esmond's decision was quickly labelled 'Rothermere's folly', and derision and ridicule marked the aftermath when profits for the franchise started to climb towards the astronomical figures they would eventually achieve. It was thought that the set count – the vital guide to potential advertising revenue – was incorrect, causing Esmond's withdrawal.

But generally speaking, Esmond had been a dupe to his own expectations of propriety and good conduct. His reliance upon the integrity of business associates sprang from Esmond's strict public-school upbringing. He was cautious and perhaps even naïve, especially since, some years later, one of his own top executives would admit to having resorted to 'industrial espionage' to stay abreast of events in the fast-moving world of television. 'He should have had more business spies,' was the cynical but no doubt realistic view of another of his executives of the day. If the books had inaccuracies at one level or another, it was Esmond's responsibility to have found that out.

But it was not in his nature. Raised by his father to be a gentleman whose conduct was exemplary, equally at home in palace or boardroom, Esmond lacked the ruthlessness that was an integral part of being a successful business magnate. Both Northcliffe and Rothermere had had it, and they had earned the dislike and even hatred of their rivals, whom they so often bested.

This Esmond understood from a young age. In the early 1920s, as the youngest MP in Parliament, Esmond had written to his father, 'At present you are naturally hated by all three parties, Conservatives, naturally, Labour naturally, but also the Liberals, I am afraid.' Dislike of the Harmsworths was a foregone fact in the family. They could refer to it among themselves in an almost jocular tone, although in the final instance it did have the power to rankle.

It was ironic that Esmond was, if it were possible, even more reviled than his great-uncle or his father, despite the fact that he inevitably tried to please much more than either of them. He was subject to a bombardment of hostility. Why?

Part of it was political. In the polarized political spectrum of the day, and continuing on into the present, the left and the right could brook no compromise. Many of the journalists were liberals, many left-wing, and yet they worked for conservative owners, a strange anomaly. Harold's right-wing views, seen as eccentric by some, extremist by others, alarmist by still others, had sharpened the divide between the left and right in the country. The left-wing hated him; the right-wing were suspicious of him. Both groups envied his power and wealth.

Like his father, Esmond was conservative, but, unlike his father, his views were moderate. He was the very picture of a moderate man. Nevertheless, Esmond invoked the dislike common to the Harmsworth family. Beaverbrook, on the other hand, was much more extreme in his views than Esmond, but he suffered not half the contempt and ridicule that Esmond did.

Part of it *was* political spill-over and part of it did stem from envy. It was true that many felt that the position occupied by the Harmsworth family would be better occupied by a more established lineage. But some of the hostility resulted from Esmond's personality.

He was shy and this made him seem a distant figure, difficult to talk to, difficult to approach. At one moment he was conciliatory and in this guise he was considered a patsy. At the next he was remote and in this he was considered a threat. In social situations, especially when it was his responsibility to do the entertaining, his natural diffidence became an asset, something that made him human, approachable, comfortable and charming.

But within the firm, 'an interview with Lord Rothermere was not an occasion which most people in Northcliffe House regarded with relish'; this according to his editor, Arthur Wareham. And in the aftermath of the calamitous decision to sell his holdings in Associated Rediffusion Esmond receded more, becoming increasingly remote.

He did host lunches and dinners for the journalists on his staff. At these affairs he was said to be elegantly mannered and he entertained beautifully. But even setting aside the problem that he was growing deaf, making communication difficult, the staff members invited along thought of him only as 'a polite and courteous man with whom we would manufacture conversation rather than have it just flow'.

More often, the words 'intimidating' and 'forbidding' crept into the vocabularies of journalists who met him face to face. Donald Todhunter, then assistant editor on the *Daily Mail*, was one of those who found Rothermere 'a very intimidating chap'.

> Most people found great difficulty in communicating with him. He rang me up once and said I would like you to come to lunch with me. I did my best to pre-equip myself with something to talk about. I got there and was shown in. His Lordship came in, and I had a dry martini followed by another dry martini, in a dining-room large enough for twenty or thirty people. I tried my best but the prolonged silences were very uncomfortable.

There is no doubt Rothermere could be discomfiting to his staff, so when he summoned a journalist to his office to congratulate him or her on a job well done, to the resourceful reporter it became a challenge to withstand the interview.

When Louis Kirby made his first visit to Rothermere's office, a march that seemed 'like about ten miles' to the young reporter, Rothermere simply 'turned his icy blue eyes on me for about twenty minutes'. At the end of that time,

> Rothermere just nodded and said something like, 'Right Kirby, well done,' and I went out.
>
> But by the next time I had read a bit about him and discovered he was a great devotee of Clive of India, and I went to Powis Castle in Montgomeryshire in Wales, near my sister's home, which is the ancestral home of Clive of India. So when Rothermere sent for me a second time I allowed about a minute and a half of silence to lapse before I told him where I had been and went on at great length about a Gainsborough painting of Clive, and he was fascinated, and I spent an hour there and I spoke of Clive and the memorabilia. Rothermere sent for tea,

and we discussed not only Clive of India but also everything about the newspaper and also the stories that we should have discussed before.

One legendary story grew up around a visit by the brilliant newspaper technician Howard Keeble. In 1952 Associated Newspapers had taken over the *Daily Graphic*, formerly known as the *Daily Sketch*, in an attempt to improve its declining fortunes. The name was duly changed back to the *Daily Sketch* and Keeble was hired to redesign the newspaper.

Now Keeble was a legendary drinker and because of this he did the unthinkable: he turned up too late for dinner at Esmond's opulent country home in the Cotswolds – Daylesford. The next morning, still hungover, Keeble and Rothermere were in the library, looking over Keeble's designs. But Esmond had misplaced his glasses and, unable to make out what Keeble had drawn, finally called it a day. The two men had lunch and made an appointment for another time. It was not until he was on the train back to London that Keeble discovered he was the culprit who had accidentally picked up Rothermere's glasses and put them in his own case. Not exactly sure how he could ever explain himself to the press lord, he opened up the train window and threw the glasses out. It was a classic Howard Keeble story.

But for the more purposive journalist there was a serious side to a visit to Esmond. Wally Hayes, who had been assistant editor on the *Daily Sketch* and eventually became editor of the *Sunday Dispatch*, usually lunched with Rothermere on Sundays. Often, the lunch took place at Warwick House and Hayes would sit at the opposite end of the very long table from Rothermere.

> And we would discuss affairs and the paper in general and I would keep trying to point out the complications of trying to run a small paper and how I thought they should invest in the *Dispatch*, and Rothermere would say to me, 'I don't know why you go on in this way. Your business is to run the editorial and not to worry about the management of the paper.'

Hayes was frustrated by this point of view. He believed that unless he understood the strategy of the newspaper, editing it would be a much harder job. Hayes was the kind of talent that Esmond had trouble managing: lively, mischievous, energetic and with a mind of his own. Not at all politically cautious, Hayes made no secret of openly disagreeing with company policy when he believed that policy was wrong. But this approach bore little fruit with Rothermere, and eventually Hayes resigned, rethought his future and, to the surprise of everyone on Fleet Street, went to Ford Motors, where he carved out a successful career for himself away from the newspaper world.

But if the energetic Hayes couldn't please Rothermere, neither could Arthur Wareham, who styled himself 'The Quiet Man of Fleet Street'. Stable, hard-working and conservative Wareham should have been the ideal editor for Rothermere, who eschewed flamboyance. He had been with the firm since the mid-thirties, working his way up by means of cautious and sensible craftsmanship. He was loyal and, in return, his subordinates were loyal to him. Nevertheless, on 15 December 1959, after nearly six years in the editor's chair, the unsuspecting Wareham received a call from Queenie Davis, Rothermere's secretary, telling him to come to Warwick House for a meeting at 6.15 p.m.

Between editor and proprietor there had been no disagreement, except a long-standing one about the size of the newspaper – which could vary daily from six to eighteen pages. This was dictated to Wareham by the management on the basis of advertising content – to any editor's mind an impossible situation. However, it wasn't a hanging offence, or never would have seemed so.

Nor, probably, was it the reason for Wareham's dismissal – although the editor was never to find out what actually was. For all Esmond told him was that he had 'decided to make a change in the editorship of the *Daily Mail*'. The dismissal was strangely cordial, and the negotiations that followed, conducted by the then managing director, Bobby Redhead, were very civilized as well – a series of lunches at the Savoy Grill filled with gossip and good humour, and a few hard-line negotiations. At the end, Wareham made a little note in his diary marking how generous Esmond always was 'from the money point of view'.

But he doubted that Rothermere understood how important it was to a journalist 'that some appreciation, support and encouragement should be mingled with the kicks. This was perhaps because he was essentially a shy man,' Wareham philosophized.

In his room at Northcliffe House hung portraits of his two elder brothers killed in the First World War. It is said that these two sons were the favourites of the first Lord Rothermere and that Esmond, who was to inherit the newspaper empire, received little encouragement and sympathy from his father. Perhaps this helps to explain the mixture of diffidence and hardness in the character of the second Lord Rothermere. Wealthy, powerful, one of the handsomest men in the country with his slim height and noble head, he ... failed to make the mark on the country's affairs which might have been expected of him.

The quizzical sacking of Arthur Wareham was characteristic of Esmond's way of dealing with underlings during this critical period in the firm's history. In turn, Wareham's gentle assessment of his former proprietor's failings showed that regardless of the sudden ending of his term of employment with Associated Newspapers he still rather liked Rothermere, although he always remained a mystery to him.

By the time he sacked Wareham, Esmond had been in the firm nearly thirty years, and he had been chairman of the Daily Mail & General Trust for over twenty. He was over sixty years old, although it was almost impossible to believe it, since he had a youthful appearance that suggested he was a decade younger. He was for all purposes the living emblem of the firm. Others came and went. Their influence waxed and waned. But Rothermere endured.

Here, then, was a man who had survived the changing conditions of three fraught decades in his company's history. He had, as well, been an important inside player in the nation's history since he had served as ADC to Lloyd George at Versailles in 1919. He had watched the comings and goings of no fewer than nine prime ministers. He had been a close friend of the king who abdicated. Those who believed they understood him had actually known Esmond only briefly in the course of his leadership of the company. And because of his vast symbolic importance it was beyond their capacity to imagine him as an ordinary mortal who himself had to deal with the challenges of living.

Truly, the 1950s were the cruellest decade for Rothermere. The glamorous life he shared with his wife Ann very publicly dissolved, she going off to pursue a complicated and shadowy relationship with Ian Fleming, while he suffered the public humiliation of her conduct. Again, he received a grave public attack as a *pornographer*, no less – an absurd accusation when all was said and done, but one that society enjoyed taking seriously. In his business dealings his disastrous sell-off of his shares in Associated Rediffusion again subjected him to general ridicule.

To one observer, evenly weighing Esmond's performance from the beginning of the 1950s, it seemed 'that he simply didn't know what to do'. But in this Rothermere was not alone.

The 1950s were a strangely confusing and contradictory period. The generation still struggling through rationing at the beginning of the decade was, by its end, being told that they had 'never had it so good'. It was a false era, when deep corruption was glossed over in icy glamour. Hypocrisy and a willingness to pay lip service to the *status quo* led to institutionalized mediocrity, and not rocking the boat was thought to be the path to success. On the surface everyone was following the rules; beneath it, the same ruthlessness that had informed every other age reigned supreme.

Complicated though he was, Rothermere was unequipped to deal with the reality. Over and over again, in his private and professional life, he took what he saw at face value, trying to react unexceptionally to exceptional events.

The ideal man of the fifties was reflective, stable, intelligent and cautious. If ever anyone fitted an ideal, Esmond Rothermere was that man.

So, why wasn't it paying off?

7

The Invisible Man

Esmond Rothermere's son Vere was so good-looking it was actually an impediment to his being taken seriously. A photograph taken when he was twenty-one years old showed a dark and handsome young man with curly hair, high cheek-bones, heavy eyebrows and a cleft chin. He was also very tall, almost as tall as his father who was six feet four inches. In later years, Vere would describe his early appearance as being like an 'Italian gigolo'. But that self-assessment was based on the exaggeration of humour. What the young Harmsworth actually looked like was a Hollywood film star *playing the part* of an Italian gigolo.

Besides these lush good looks, Vere was further handicapped by coming from the shy side of the Harmsworth family. Practically tongue-tied from his youth, he was reminiscent of the early Harold who stood near the doorway whenever he and his brothers attended dances, asking how soon they could go home. Vere could dance, and would dance, but his conversation remained distinctly limited. From an early age his taciturn manner led others to underestimate him. His whimsical sense of humour was yet another reason people found for dealing him out.

It was shocking to realize how little Vere's own family knew about him. His sister Esme, who had been evacuated with Vere to the United States during the early part of the war, did not know that, in returning home to Britain, he had followed her earlier route via Estoril. The city, centre of espionage in neutral Portugal, had nevertheless remained a colourful interval in the teenage boy's life. For there, he had enjoyed several weeks of watching the suspicious and nocturnal characters who peopled it during the war – spies, gamblers, mysterious women, secret agents from both extremes of the political spectrum. He later said he learned to gamble in the famous casino there. So far as Vere's family knew the episode never happened.

After he returned to school in England, Vere remained as non-communicative as ever. Said Esme later:

My father had an enormous black horse, over seventeen hands high. I used to ride this horse all the way through Windsor Park, down through Windsor, through the high street and then to Eton College. Then I'd stop and say hello to my brother. There was a famous tea shop there, Miss Master's, and we'd go and have tea. Miss Master's had cakes even in the war, chocolate and marmalade cakes. They were really gooey and not iced, because icing sugar was rationed, but whatever they were made of was wonderful. My brother must have been fifteen or sixteen at the time. He was very quiet in those days. He didn't say much. He didn't talk about himself really. He was very silent.

A psychoanalyst might have speculated that Vere's withdrawn manner stemmed from the bitter divorce of his parents. And indeed, when he later spoke of their breakup he would sometimes say, 'When my father divorced *us* ...' He also remembered times when it was impossible not to fail one parent or the other. There was an occasion in particular when both his mother and father met him at a railway station, demanding he choose which one he would go with. He decided to ride in his mother's car to his father's house, but the fairness of his choice didn't do him any good: his father resented his decision and never forgave him.

At another time Vere felt the full trauma of his parents' very different methods of child rearing. He was about nine years old, and he had accompanied his father and sisters to Kitzbühel. Esmond had the habit of walking up the smaller mountains and skiing down, but Vere, being nine, couldn't keep up, so he would be left behind to find his own way back, sometimes in the dark. On one of these forays Vere reached the top of the mountain to find the inn where the family had lunched closed.

He was so thirsty, he ate the snow, not realizing it had absorbed the bacteria from the ploughed fields several feet beneath. He was quite ill when, almost miraculously, his mother appeared from St Moritz where she had been vacationing. She had had premonitions that Vere was ill and travelled to him immediately. In fact, she was right; he had con-tracted hepatitis. 'I nearly snuffed it then actually,' he said later. He remained strangely non-judgemental in what was clearly a central event of his youth.

The youngest of his parents' three children, Vere was the one most affected by their divorce and, because he was the only boy in a family that relied wholly upon primogeniture, he was under the most pressure. Passivity appeared to be one of his defences against the powerful forces of his parents' personalities.

But beneath his mild manner, Vere seemed to have inherited the very strong character of both his parents. His father was secretive and intelligent; his mother strong-willed and gutsy – to say she was not lacking in courage would have been an understatement. And although Vere was frequently subject to the strong cross-winds that blew between them, what worked against him in that instance manifested itself to advantage when it came to his own personality.

Another familiar trait in Vere was his tendency to follow his thoughts for what could seem a very long time, creating long silences that made others feel uncomfortable. It was this kind of mental 'knitting' that many members of the Harmsworth family shared: as if the person they were with were not present. In Vere, it seemed particularly pronounced. Another contributing factor to Vere's dreamy manner might have been the strange duality characteristic of so many of the family.

The young Northcliffe had been energetic and optimistic, but after periods of great activity he could suffer one of his 'nervous attacks' and simply collapse, subsiding into hypochondria and becoming reclusive and withdrawn. His brother Harold, the first Viscount Rothermere, alternated between periods of great optimism and debilitating pessimism. His confidence could be shattered by minor crises.

In the case of young Vere, warring factions vied within his breast and these seemed to express themselves in mutually contradictory motives. He wanted to win, but he wasn't ruthless. He enjoyed getting the better of an opponent, but there wasn't anything personal in it. The sort of competition that suited him best was boxing and indeed, he won the boxing championship when he was at Eton.

Not at all vituperative himself, he remained unsurprised by the lengths to which people would go to get what they wanted. He was particularly fascinated by the story that his great-uncle Northcliffe kept an aquarium in his bathroom in which two fighting fish were separated by a movable pane of glass. According to legend, Northcliffe would lift the glass from time to time to 'study the results'. Such results were of some interest to Vere as well.

If the young Vere had a besetting fault it was that he was lazy. He slept late as often as he could get away with it, which was fairly often. In his world, he could effect change as easily by inaction as by action, since many were ready to do his bidding, to act on his behalf, to get him whatever he wanted – even before he himself might know what that was. This led him to adopt a singular style involving economy of motion. Unconsciously, Vere cultivated the skill of getting the most done with the least amount of effort. In this sense he was something of a minimalist.

This may have been a contributory factor to his remaining in the ranks during the war, when he was stationed in North Africa. A more obvious cause was that he contracted an African strain of glandular fever which, inaccurately diagnosed, worsened, nearly killing him. A beautiful young Chinese doctor, a woman, put him in an ear, eye, nose and throat hospital where he lay slowly dying. Eventually, a surgeon making his rounds recognized the illness, sending Vere to the intensive care unit, where he was injected with the new wonder drug penicillin every two hours, thus saving his life. He convalesced in Alexandria.

Until this point Vere had lived a rarified life of privilege and advantage. The friendships he made now among the rank-and-file soldiers in Africa gave him his first glimpse of how the rest of the world lived. He was surprisingly comfortable with the ordinary soldiers. It led to an egalitarianism that would later embarrass some of his more uptight, middle-class, upwardly mobile executives who wanted to put all that was common as far behind them as possible.

From his two brushes with death Vere learned a lesson, albeit on an unconscious level: if he was ill, someone would take care of him; if he were dying, he would be saved. It was okay to be weak in some instances; it was okay to have faith in Providence. What, after all, were the alternatives? This downward path to wisdom may have been how the young Vere Harmsworth learned to trust his own vulnerability – but it was dangerous knowledge in the hands of any member of the Harmsworth family.

He emerged from these days of his youth better equipped than those around him might have thought as heir apparent to the Harmsworth publishing dynasty; more so, no doubt, than he himself imagined. Now began his actual training in the firm.

He spent a couple of years working for the Anglo-Canadian Paper Mills which Harold had founded in Quebec. He chose the location over Grand Falls because he thought the isolation of the Newfoundland paper mill would be unbearable. When he returned to London he began at Associated in 'Postal Bargains', a division of advertising made up of small advertisers and bargain offers. He then took a turn as a sales rep, travelling around the countryside and spending a great deal of time in pubs, where he entertained the clients with whom he would have to develop personal relationships if he were to make a sale.

Then, for a while, he became a circulation representative in Devon, ensuring delivery of copies and negotiating returns with wholesalers. It was there that he met Bert Irvine, who would later become one of Associated Newspapers' top executives but who was now established in the region surrounding Exeter as a circulation representative for the *Daily Mail*.

The pair met at the Clarence Hotel in Exeter and Irvine found him 'a very likeable young man indeed'. Vere told Irvine he should not be buying him a drink, but he was reassured when Irvine explained to him that his father would end up paying in the end. Irvine said later,

I remember he made a great impression on my wife when he came home to tea.

Not only was he handsome, but so polite. He rose to his feet every time she entered our small 12 × 10 sitting room, and made small talk with my five-year-old son and three-year-old daughter – even taking her on his knee. We spent a few days touring the seaside and the country checking availability of the paper, putting up posters outside newsagents' shops, and I introduced him to agents and wholesalers.

His return to London would initiate him into the political exigencies of the work place. On one level it was a benign system of apprenticeship. On another it amounted to training in a more cynical reality. Before he reached the age of twenty-five a cabal approached Vere, trying to enlist his help in overturning his father by offering to put him in his place. Vere thought over his actions very carefully before proceeding. At last, he went to the very man he suspected of secretly fomenting the plot and, placing the incriminating documents on his desk, told him of the cabal's perfidy. In this way he put an end to it. He absorbed such intrigue as a matter of course. 'I was born to it, you know,' he would say.

For his part, Esmond could behave with profound warmth and benevolence towards his son. His counsel on Vere's stock portfolio proved to be first rate and, at least in this regard, Esmond was a most capable businessman whose advice was almost prophetic. Another act of kindness came when Esmond invited his son to join the Beefsteak Club. His father told Vere he would arrange it, asking Boofy Gore, Lord Arran, an executive in the company and a well-known columnist on the *Evening News*, to nominate his son. Vere then wrote to Lord Hartwell, who was head of the *Telegraph*, asking him to second him. But by the time Hartwell had replied that he would be delighted, Esmond had undergone one of his wholly characteristic changes of mind, deciding he wasn't ready for Vere to become a member. Boofy duly explained to Vere Esmond's change of heart, and the to-ing and fro-ing continued until Hartwell, furious at the delay, put a stop to it by writing to Esmond directly and telling him to get on with it – which a somewhat abashed Esmond did.

As the son of the boss, the heir apparent, Vere was exposed to this kind of ambivalence from his father and also from staff members. In the latter case it could amount to passive aggression that was very difficult to combat. If it was true, as was often said by those who worked for him, that his father Esmond 'couldn't find the light switches on the wall', then his son Vere 'couldn't tie his own shoelaces'. Vere's office mates often secretly resented his wealth and security. One bitterly complained of his success with women. He stated it outright; if he had had the power and money of the young Harmsworth, he too would have women clustering round him.

It was true that many of the young women in the office swooned whenever Harmsworth came round. One executive noted that when Vere was on the *Evening News* all the telly ad girls thought he was the most eligible bachelor of all time. They seemed to be abuzz whenever he entered the room.

But if Vere was aware of the commotion his presence aroused he never admitted to it. He learned to be self-directed, to be his own man; there was actually no other option in an environment where his very existence roused such ambivalence.

By 1956 Bert Irvine had become deputy circulation manager of the *Daily Sketch* and Vere was assistant general manager to George Abel.

> This was a lively year for the *Sketch* – probably the best of its life: before the release of newsprint controls enabled the *Mirror* to sail away. We had a great team. Bert Gunn, the editor, Duke Hussey, the circulation manager, Vere and George Abel. David English was features editor ... I think it was during this period that Vere really became a newspaperman. He was very close to Bert Gunn – one of Fleet Street's greatest editors: and there is no doubt George Abel was a great entrepreneurial manager. Two good tutors. Certainly Vere's close attachment to the *Sketch* began at this time...

Vere went into promotions on the *Daily Sketch* and oversaw his own project – 'Win a Pub'. Although it succeeded, putting sales of the paper up about 200,000 to one and a half million and making a profit of some £400,000, it went largely unacknowledged within the firm. By common consensus it had been decided Vere had no business head and so, when he succeeded at business, his success had to be disregarded. In some ways he was the invisible man.

It was about this time that Vere met an eager new features editor on the *Sketch* – David English. A great deal of importance has been attached to this early meeting, because it seemed in retrospect to portend great things.

English, twenty-five years old, was at the beginning of a great career. One of his colleagues described him at this time as 'very flash, quite loud, very young, he did a lot of shouting. More astonishing than that was the speed at which he ran around. He was always on the dash, always papers and writing schemes and writing material himself. You couldn't help being aware of his being there.' Harmsworth, by contrast, was quiet and self-effacing. You could hardly help being *un*aware of his being there. The two men's personalities complemented one another and they liked each other. And their meeting amounted to a modest achievement – they met and found they worked together compatibly. Maybe they would meet again.

Two years after he met David English, in 1957, Vere married. His bride was a Rank film starlet whose stage name was 'Beverley Brooks'. She had been married and had a baby daughter, Sarah, by her first husband, Christopher Brooks, a former Coldstream guards officer and a racing enthusiast.

Her maiden name was Patricia Matthews and she was the daughter of a successful architect. Although she had loved him, she had married her first husband reluctantly. She was a rare beauty and knew it. She was also energetic, theatrical and full of life. She loved the theatre and theatre people, and her enthusiasm was effervescent. She told Christopher Brooks she wanted to become an actress and he agreed. So she set out to attend a drama school near their house in Chelsea. Almost immediately she was spotted by a talent scout, who signed her up for a seven-year contract as a Rank 'starlet'.

From there, she was chosen for small parts in several British films. She was pregnant when she had her chance at what would turn out to be the best role of her career – playing the girlfriend of the famous fighter pilot Douglas Bader who lost his legs before the war. In *Reach for the Sky* Patricia played the feckless girlfriend who left him while he was recuperating in hospital. Rather plump for the role, she later told her daughter Sarah how the wardrobe mistress had helped her disguise her widening girth. The story was typical of Patricia. She made events that were dull seem exciting; those that were dramatic in and of themselves she made more lively in the telling. Patricia was, in the parlance of the time, a live wire.

One of her favourite stories was that she had to choose between Vere and Hollywood. It was said that Darryl Zanuck of 20th Century-Fox invited her to work for him in Hollywood at about the time Vere had proposed. If her looks were anything to go by the story may have been true.

Named by society photographer Baron as one of the ten most beautiful women in Britain, Patricia was more than just another pretty face. She was a colourful personality and her fanciful versions of reality usually stuck. In her version of how she met Vere, he and her husband nearly came to fisticuffs over her. The duller and more prosaic truth was that the two men had known one another ever since they attended Eton together. Vere had met Patricia at a party soon after her breakup from her husband, and he and her husband did not fight over the pretty young actress. But Patricia liked embellishments and, as she got older, these would grow more fanciful. One of her favourite stories was that

Vere's father, when she married Vere, had told her she was marrying more than a man, she was marrying an empire.

Whether those were his exact words or not, Patricia *was* marrying an empire. She would one day be a viscountess, her entertainments would become legendary, she would be the centre of a great deal of attention. But her marriage to Vere Harmsworth would also put her at the centre of intrigue – a place she would come to enjoy. There would be flattery, sycophancy, downright obeisance – and she became one of those rare women who could have whatever she wanted in the world. Was that lucky? Was her position enviable? Time would tell. For now, Patricia quickly developed a following and, like Vere, a style of conduct that was characteristically her own.

Vere Harmsworth's young wife had a photographic memory and the random chatter that often accompanies it. Her tongue could be very sharp and if she decided to cut someone down, it was done with such acuity that they would find themselves in pieces before she had done. She didn't mean anything by it. It was really only a style of attack and defence, even if the person under scrutiny was left reeling. She did not intend to cause lasting hurt, it was a momentary temper and Patricia was so lovely, nobody seemed to mind.

It was generally credited that Vere's gregarious wife helped him overcome an early confidence problem. Typical of each of them, Patricia was happy enough to take the credit, Vere happy enough to let her have it.

If Vere did have 'a confidence problem', he had a compensatory characteristic: he was very emotionally stable and herein he differed from Northcliffe as well as the first Viscount Rothermere, and even Vere's own father. Vere took his time in deciding a thing, but once it was done he stood by his decision. He valued loyalty above all things, and he himself was loyal to his loved ones and business associates, indeed sometimes in the face of their own disloyalty.

Vere Harmsworth was steady. In the face of panic and chaos he stood firm. But what value this trait could possibly have in the running of a newspaper was very difficult to discern – at least in these, his early days.

David English was in the mid-1950s an unimpeded man of action. He swept through his early career with the exuberance of a young man who knows he will win, one way or another. The mature David English also covered vast tracts of ground, but he no longer wondered what form his success would take. Thus, by 1995, still a magician, English had developed into a marvellous raconteur whose distinctive imprimatur informed the stories of his youth. One of his favourites was about his coverage of the death of Errol Flynn.

By now, English would explain, he had advanced to the position of assistant editor in charge of features on the *Daily Sketch*. It was 1959 and a married couple who were American literary agents in Hollywood arrived in England with a copy of Errol Flynn's memoirs to hawk around Fleet Street. When they telephoned English to offer him the manuscript, he was less than impressed. 'Please,' he said, 'Errol Flynn. It's 1959, he hasn't made a film for ten years, who cares?

> I mean, I wasn't rude to them particularly, but I made it absolutely clear we were not interested. Nobody knew where Errol Flynn was, or anything. The manuscript was only three-quarters complete and nobody was interested. Literally within twenty-four hours of their traipsing round Fleet Street the news came through that Errol Flynn had died in Vancouver and that he'd been doing a variety song-and-dance act and that his girlfriend who appeared with him whom he announced he was going to marry was in fact only seventeen years old, and her name was Beverly Aadland, and she'd been taken into care.

Instantly, all Fleet Street, including David English, began ringing the Dorchester where the couple were staying. There was of course no way to get through, so English hopped over to the hotel where he discovered that the memoirs had already gone to the *People* for a rumoured £50,000, a gigantic sum of money for the day.

> So this couple, who were very Hollywood, a very tough wife – younger wife, older man – were very dismissive of me. So anyway I said to them, 'Okay, all right, you've made a lot of money but what about the girl's story? I think I'll go for the girl's story.' And they instantly said, I can see their faces, 'We've got the rights there.' So I said, 'Okay, let's negotiate now.'
>
> Well, they didn't have the rights, they only had the rights to Errol Flynn's manuscript. Anyway, they pretended they owned the rights and so I said, 'Well, you've got to prove to me you own the rights.'

The couple telephoned America, only to discover that Beverly Aadland had been returned by the Canadian police to her mother in America, who had engaged a lawyer to protect any rights she might have to the Flynn estate. 'This', said David English,

> had been done in twenty-four hours actually. So they get hold of the lawyer and in front of me on the phone, they do a deal with the lawyer that they will act as agents for the lawyer and they have a verbal agreement to act as agents for the lawyer who was acting for the girl, Miss Aadland. The lawyer's name was Melvin Belli, one of the most famous lawyers in America, and he said, 'Sure, yeah, well, you fly to San Francisco, I'll have my office meet you, you bring a banker's draft, and as soon as I've got that, I'll produce the girl.'

English rushed back to the office to report that he had struck a deal for £25,000 – if they moved fast – telling the editor of the *Daily Sketch*, the rather notorious Bert Gunn, that they wanted the money in cash and it had to be in dollars in case sterling was devalued. Gunn told English to get on the plane 'because it was a hell of a long way in those days, you changed in New York', and he would sort out the money.

But when English rang back from New York, he found Gunn and the two agents had become involved in a row because they couldn't get enough dollars to close the deal. Coutts had put in their whole supply of dollars, which wasn't enough. So they had got the rest in travellers cheques, arguing the whole time.

> So while I'm in the air, the editor and his managing editor and this couple who are in Coutts Bank, they're counting out the lot of it in small bills – it goes on for hours – anyway, finally it's done and they sign the agreement and they walk off into Fleet Street and they hail a cab and as they get in the cab the guy has a heart attack and dies on the spot. I swear it's true, he certainly died.
>
> I then appear in San Francisco and I am not met by anybody which I think is odd. I'm absolutely exhausted, I go to the hotel, there's no messages, so I ring up Melvin Belli's office and I'm told he's not there and I say, 'I phoned to see him and someone was going to meet me and he's not there.'

English was informed that the lawyer was at a law conference at a Texas university where he was giving a lecture. English telephoned him in his hotel room, by now 'panicking badly'. And when he finally reached Belli, the lawyer said to English,

> 'Oh, yeah, sure, you were coming, yes, well I'm here doing this for two days and I'm too busy to see you and, in any case, the money is not enough for my client, and you might like to talk to your principals about that and if you've got the rest of the money and you've agreed to that and you've got a banker's draft, come and see me next week and we'll do the deal.'
>
> So I said, 'You don't understand, I mean, this deal becomes less possible as every day goes by. British papers deal in immediacy and Errol Flynn died three days ago and every day the body gets colder and the story gets colder.'
>
> He said, 'It's $150,000 or forget it.'

By now, English was in 'an incredible sort of panic'. He had one last thing he could do and that was to fall back on his routine reportorial skills. He rushed to Belli's house on Telegraph Hill, found it empty, so went from house to house to see whether Belli had a country house. But nobody knew or would tell, so English went to the local paper, the *San Francisco Chronicle*, where he found a formidable stack of cuttings and, most pertinent, he discovered that Belli's current wife – there had been others before – was just then being painted by a famous local artist who lived in the Valley.

I got the address of the painter, hired a car, drove out there, rang the bell, hoping the wife might be there, hoping for anything really, and the door was opened by Beverly Aadland, whom I recognized, and Mrs Belli was having her picture painted. So I instantly said, 'Hello, I'm David English and I've come to interview you.'

She said, 'You shouldn't be here, I don't know what you're doing here,' and Belli's wife came to the door and she was tough as old nails, she was an ex-Flying Tiger air hostess Belli'd met on a trip to the Far East, a real bottle blonde, and she said, 'What the hell are you doing? It's all been put off.'

I said, 'No, it hasn't. Why do you think I'm here? I'm here because I spoke to your husband and we've got a deal.'

She said, 'I've got to ring my husband.' Fortunately she rang this university, she got the office, they couldn't find him, he'd gone.

I started to get very stroppy and said, 'Look, if you want this deal to go down, Mrs Belli, you've got to be responsible. I don't know what your husband is going to say to you. I don't know what Beverly Aadland's mother is going to say to you, but I've got $150,000 to go in the bank and if she doesn't start talking to me right now, you don't get it.'

So she says, 'Okay, sure, have a drink, let's all settle down,' which we did. And I just worked like crazy to get as much as I could. I just got absolutely as much as I could. I think it took two hours and then they had to go back to San Francisco but I had an amazing amount in my book, because I was desperate, but I was high on adrenalin, I knew I'd defeated these people who were trying to thwart me and double-cross me. I was elated as I drove back. I got into the hotel room and I rang London and I told them what had happened and I began to write.

The next day, the circulation of the *Sketch* started to climb and the day after, sales went even higher. By then, Belli had got wind of what English had done, and he rang him and accused him of being a liar and a cheat. To this, English countered that Belli knew nothing about the immediacy required by British newspapers. Belli replied that English knew nothing about the law in California, that he had defrauded a minor and, under California law, which was based not on English law like the rest of the country, but on Spanish law, this gave Belli the right, the *responsibility* to 'put you in jail'.

And I was really quite scared, and he meant it. So I rang up London and said, 'God, he's going to do this.' He had demanded that I appear at his office, threatening to send police or bailiffs to come and arrest me if I didn't.

I said, 'What am I going to do?'

Gunn said, 'I'll tell you what to do, you've got to call his bluff. The fact is he can't sell this story to anybody else now because we've already run 5000 words of it. Second, he broke the deal and, third, his eyes will light up with money. Go to the bank. We'll make all the arrangements with the bank, buy a suitcase, get $75,000 in bills and when you get to his office, just open it up and say, "Okay, what do you want to do? Put me in jail or take this money?"'

Which I did.

At this moment, so goes his story, English looked at Belli, and Belli looked at English, and 'we had instant recognition that we were two of a kind'! And it appeared to English that the Aadland girl wouldn't have minded if he had gone to jail. She asked the lawyer, 'What do you want me to do?' Belli answered, 'Sweetheart, just tell him what he wants to know.'

In the end, English chalked up his success to his persistence and his luck. But that was not what set the young English apart from his rivals on Fleet Street. In terms of determination and persistence, most of his fellow reporters would have the story one way or another; that was the brief. What made David English special was his delight in the pursuit. And in the telling and retelling of the adventure, he emerged in his own narrative as a personality, a character. His excitement was contagious and others couldn't help joining in. He took childlike pleasure in the chase, in winning, in meeting the fascinating characters his job threw in his path. He carried with him this sense of event, and he had the crucial ability to swing others aloft with it.

A colleague of his remembered working alongside the young reporter on the *Sketch*, and when one of English's scoops was actually in print, he held the newspaper up in his hands, reading it, then turned to his friend and exclaimed, 'Christ, I love this business!'

That was English and that was why he would win.

David English's father had died when David was only nine months old and, because of this, he was raised partly by his maternal grandparents, who doted on him and saw no limits to what he would be able to accomplish in his lifetime. He was an only child, and the poignancy of losing his father made the child all the more precious to the ageing couple.

According to family legend, David's father had, as a teenager, caught a chill after a football game. The illness developed into rheumatic fever, damaging his health permanently and eventually contributing to his death at the relatively young age of thirty-one. He had been an accountant in a bank, but when it became clear he would not be able to continue in such a demanding position, he and David's mother Kathleen moved into the country, where they managed a pub.

After her husband's death, his mother had bought a seaside boarding-house at Broadstairs in Kent, and David split his time between his doting grandparents and his mother. She was forceful and fiercely ambitious for her son. His grandfather spent valuable time with the boy, teaching him everything he knew.

Alfred Brazenor had owned a saddle shop in Wimbledon at the turn of the century, a big shop that had been in the family for three generations, and he had been forced to close it as the motor car reduced the number of horses used for transportation on the road. Then, in order to earn a living, Brazenor had become a tram driver and a conductor, eventually becoming a leader in the Transport and General Workers Union before he retired.

A Methodist and a Socialist, he was also an avid reader who had three newspapers delivered every day – the *Daily Herald*, the *News Chronicle* and the *Daily Mail*. Together, he and his grandson pored over these three papers, one Socialist, one Liberal and one Tory, and David's grandfather would talk about politics, while David absorbed whatever he could. He later remembered,

> I was an avid newspaper reader from a very young age. I was fascinated by the look of them. When the war came, you read them avidly, the maps and vivid battle accounts. It was fascinating for me to see three papers and how they dealt with different stories. I used to keep the papers, I always used to go back and look at them, I had masses of papers I kept under my bed.

In the mid-1930s, David's mother Kitty sold her boarding-house and his grandparents sold their house, and they all went in together on a hotel in Bournemouth. There, David had an almost idyllic childhood, playing with the children whose parents were guests in the hotel.

The evenings were spent with his grandfather, either reading the newspaper, or talking, or listening to the radio. They always tuned in for *In Town Tonight*, a celebrity programme; *Monday Night at Eight O'clock*, a variety programme; and *Inspector Hornby Investigates*, a whodunit. David and his grandfather played football and cricket, and his grandfather made many of his toys. He remembered that during the war, when there were no footballs, his grandfather became a local hero because, as a former saddler, he could make them. David remembered the deputy headmaster coming to his house to thank his grandfather for keeping the school supplied right through the war.

David's mother read popular fiction, and one of David's jobs was to go to the library to return books she had read and check out new ones.

His own favourites were the *Just William* stories by Richmal Crompton, and he read himself into the character of William. 'I know that when I was about eight or nine I was recapitulating William Brown's gang in my own life. My mother used to laugh because small boys came to the door and said, "Is William in?" I had taken the part of William Brown and I had a friend called Ginger and we all played and acted out these roles.'

At the onset of the war, David's mother sold the hotel, and she and David's grandparents bought a smaller house together. She went to work as secretary to the postmaster and eventually became PA to the town clerk, who ran the town.

David never felt any sense of deprivation during the war, but after it ended he went on holiday with his mother to Switzerland, and there, amid the chocolate bars and sweets and bananas and cakes, he realized with a shock what he had missed. Yet he had never felt it at the time. All around Bournemouth the beaches were mined, with barbed wire curling across them, but the swimming pools were open, the cinemas were open and he had no sense of missing anything during the actual war years.

His grandparents and his mother were 'fanatical movie buffs', going to the cinema two or three times a week.

> I do remember, after Dunkirk and all the defeated soldiers coming back, they put them in the schools. And everyone thought the Germans were going to be on their heels and I remember my mother saying, 'If the Germans are coming we've got to go and see these films quickly before they get here and shut the cinemas.' She took us off every day! That was a tremendous sort of week, we went about twice a day that week!

Some of the films were about American journalists, 'trench-coat reporters', and they inspired the young teenager. Then, too, his mother had once worked in an office in Fleet Street and she told stories about the reporters, which had a great influence on David.

This no doubt contributed to David English's plan to become an editor himself and he decided to practise by making his own version of a boys' comic. There was a newspaper shortage during the war, and the wonderful D. C. Thomson comics became more and more scarce. So David set to work on his own version, using the same copy and layout as D. C. Thomson, and he would write the stories himself. He then lent the one original copy out at a ha'penny a time. 'I was really doing it, not for the money, but for the sheer pleasure. One of the main stories was called, "The March of the Z-Men", about robots taking over the world.'

At about the same time, David became fascinated by gambling, thanks to reading *The Three Musketeers* at school:

> So I set up a complete gambling system in the school. At that point, a boy had about six pence pocket money and anyway if you put six pence in the bank, you could get five hundred *livre* in Monopoly notes. Then I realized that boys were bringing monopoly money in that wasn't official, and I had to get a rubber stamp made and stamp our monopoly money with the official stamp of my bank. Otherwise the whole currency was going to be devalued!

The gambling became so popular that David set up a second plan – a huge insurance system in the school. He had been in a very well-behaved class, but occasionally one of the pupils would get Saturday morning detention, or would have to write lines, or even get caned. David devised an insurance system whereby participating boys could pay tuppence a week with the idea that if they were assigned lines, they could have them written by smaller boys. If they got detention they received a six-pence payment; if caned, they were paid a shilling.

David made a profit for several weeks,

> but then bolder spirits began looking for trouble in order to get into detention to make money. Eventually, from being the best-behaved class in school, it became the worst! And I was paying out a huge sum of money, I had to get money from my mother and my grandfather to pay these kids because they threatened to beat me up severely if I didn't pay! I realized I had to pay them all and cancel the scheme and pay back my mother and grandfather and this came to the headmaster's attention, who was not unamused by it, I think, but I got the cane for it none the less.

By the time he was a teenager, David realized that he possessed not only organizational abilities but also leadership qualities. And if he were sometimes too enthusiastic, he found he could take the heat necessary to get the job done. With this in mind, he decided to quit school and get a job.

In the centre of Bournemouth, the local evening paper, the *Bournemouth Echo*, occupied a building, opened in 1934, that was the British version of art deco, known as Odeon Architecture. English fell in love with it and determined he would work in this magnificent structure. His determination was cemented by the fact that an older boy he had known and admired at school had gone to work there. David was much impressed by the smart suit he wore and 'sort of hero-worshipped him a bit'.

> My mother was absolutely furious. She wanted me to go to university. She

changed all her stories about Fleet Street and then it was all, you know, doom and gloom and Fleet Street was nothing but full of drunks and ne'er-do-wells and people in deep debt. But I was encouraged by my grandfather, who felt that I should write and do what I wanted to do. My grandfather was very courteous, he would never fight with my mother, he would be magisterial with his lovely mane of white hair. He would say, 'I think the boy should do what he wants. Let the boy do what he wants.'

So it was that David wrote to the editor of the newspaper and was called in to meet a Mr William Saltmarsh, the chief sub-editor. He was elderly, slightly bald and always wore spats, striped trousers and a black coat, a winged collar and bow tie. He peered through his glasses at the young boy and told him he had to learn to type and take shorthand. When he had learned that, he was to come back.

For the next year, David attended the Bournemouth Municipal College, the only male in a class of girls – 'I had a wonderful time there!' And when he returned to ask Mr Saltmarsh for a job he was put in charge of placing the PA tapes in order of priority. Then Saltmarsh sent him out, editing the copy himself, and generally gave him first-hand experience of how a newspaper worked. It wasn't long before David saw he would benefit by working on a weekly, so he went to work on the *Christchurch Times*. He was the youngest of three reporters, but on a Friday he also got to do sub-editing, and 'I became amazingly interested in typography ... I loved the smell of ink and lead, and I really did think I had a vision for laying out pages as well as writing them.'

But the *Christchurch Times* was poor, and they had no italic type. Undeterred, David travelled over to the compositors on the *Bournemouth Echo*, friends of his from when he had worked there, and he would write the headlines, then talk the compositors into setting them up for him. Then he would come back on the bus, happily carrying the purloined headlines with him to be printed up at his own paper.

He loved the work. On a small newspaper, he said later,

I learned how a community works, its finances, how it is policed. I learned about its history, architecture, art, everything. The first thing I had to do as a trainee reporter was to write about dead people.

Of course, I had no knowledge of dead people. I was young and I can remember being sent out. I went to the deceased's house and spoke to his widow and his children, I learned how to relate to people in grief. I was surprised that people were so grateful. But I learned how to handle difficult circumstances. It's a wonderful sort of grooming school, finishing school really, how to relate to people.

Soon David moved to the *Portsmouth Evening News* and there, he finished his apprenticeship in the provinces. His first job on Fleet Street was on the *Daily Mirror* and as he left his interview for that job, the managing editor, Cyril Morton, yelled down the stairs after him, 'Are there any more like you where you come from?'

To which David yelled back, 'Yes!'

English went back to the *Portsmouth Evening News* and told his buddies how he had quadrupled his salary and what a fine guy Cyril Morton seemed to be and how they should all apply to work for him. This, four of them did with alacrity, and actually got jobs with the *Mirror*. 'The *Portsmouth Evening News* then went absolutely mad and they sued the *Mirror* and tried to sue me for Enticement! So I was swathed in controversy before I even arrived in Fleet Street! There was an out-of-court settlement, but I was certainly in trouble before I began.'

There were other difficulties in store. Because English was young and flippant, the news editor at the *Mirror* took an instant dislike to him and began to get at him for minor infractions of the rules. So when a certain project came up, the news editor, perhaps anticipating disaster, made sure David English got the assignment. It was the idea of the chairman of the company, Guy Bartholomew,

a tough, brawling, drunken guy. In those days he was coming to the end of his life but he was quite bizarre and he'd got a lot of money and he had a magnificent yacht, which he kept up on the east coast. He also had a totally mad obsession: he was enormously into power-boat racing, hydroplanes really.

But Bartholomew believed that you could introduce this sport to Britain and it would be as popular as horse racing. The short of the thing was that Bartholomew decided that the *Mirror* would spend vast amounts of money on making power-boat racing the great national sport of Britain and he put thousands and thousands and thousands of pounds aside and he got boat yards and he wanted someone who would mastermind it.

Bartholomew said to English, 'I want you to go round the country and give demonstrations in your speedboat, hold public meetings, see if you can start a club.' English did this and had a wonderful summer, until the fateful moment when someone suggested they get women involved in the project.

At this time, there was an American ice show in London and English enlisted them to drive the power boats, with the boast that if American women could do it, why couldn't the backward British women do likewise? There was only one problem: the American women couldn't do it. After they made their try, two boats caught fire, there was a crash and 'it was a total disaster'.

English managed to gloss it over in the coverage, but eventually the truth got out and British women who had actually been watching the débâcle unfold became angry over the approach of the story and complained to the chairman.

That was the end of English's assignment. Back on more routine beats, the news editor hounded him. At the time, he habitually wore white socks to work and the man subjected English to ritual humiliation over this.

'I won't have reporters wearing white socks, go home and change.' He used to put on the notice board things like, 'For the second time this week, a reporter has been sent home because he was not dressed to represent the *Daily Mirror*. Any more sartorial aberrations by this man will result in dismissal and anyone else who indulges in sartorial aberrations will be fired as well.'

This continued until English felt himself compelled to leave. He had believed he would get another job with ease, but instead he was forced to free-lance to earn his crust. 'It took the wind out of my sails. I had been very well paid on the *Mirror*. I had a car, girlfriends, stacks of money. Free-lancing was hard.'

At last, English landed an interview with the news editor at the *Daily Express*, who said he didn't have anything at the moment, but if he got something he would let him know. When English told Cyril Morton this, Morton suggested he write direct to Beaverbrook something to the effect that he was a talented young journalist, that he wanted to write for the *Express* and that he had been thwarted by a fool, 'your news editor'. In English's own words, it was an 'enormously presumptuous letter'.

The reply he received was not from Beaverbrook but from the news editor, Morley Richards, himself. He wrote that he was about to offer English a job but, after what he had said in his 'disgraceful letter', he just wanted English to know he would never work for the *Daily Express* for the rest of his life.

Thus David English's first two adventures on Fleet Street were shining examples of failure – but failure of a certain kind. For he had no stop mechanism, absolutely no desire or ability to halt once he had set a thing in motion. In these early days the trait would get him into trouble, but later on it would develop into a great asset in the highly competitive environment of Fleet Street.

Nobody could stop this oncoming train.

8

'Popcorn and Pasta'

Cecil King was on the move.

Having ousted Harry Bartholomew and assumed control of the company that owned the *Daily Mirror*, King found himself in the sanguine position of controlling a going concern in Canada as well. Located in Quebec City, the Anglo-Canadian Pulp and Paper Company had been founded in 1930 by none other than King's uncle, Harold Rothermere. That its governance was now in the hands of Cecil King was one of the great ironies of the Harmsworth dynasty. For King had begun to see himself as the natural heir of Northcliffe. All he had to do to inherit the mantle was to dislodge his cousin, Harold's son, Esmond Rothermere.

In a circuitous way, Anglo-Canadian was the result of a quarrel between Harold and Alfred, back in the early days when the two brothers worked hand in glove. Alfred had wanted his own paper mill and he chose a site in the interior of the poorest British colony, Newfoundland. The Grand Falls mill would meet the newsprint needs for his newspapers while at the same time bringing a measure of prosperity to Newfoundland.

Harold was dead set against it, predicting disaster from the ice-locked location of the shipping port that serviced Grand Falls. Alfred nevertheless prevailed and, in 1905, he founded the Anglo-Newfoundland Development Company. From the start, shipping difficulties plagued the company during the winter months and decades later the AND, as it was called, was continuing to make losses. It was only saved from liquidation because of the 'Buchans Find' of 1927 – a rich vein of zinc ore that the company arranged to exploit.

Three years later, as if to drive home his point, Harold had founded the Anglo-Canadian Pulp and Paper Company in Quebec City, a concern that manufactured newsprint for many major newspapers in Canada and the United States. It was tied to the Mirror company and when Harold divested himself of control of the *Mirror* and its subsidiaries he gave up control of the Anglo-Canadian Pulp and Paper Company as well.

This stake in the New World, brought about by Alfred's idealism and

Harold's shrewdness, gave both Cecil King and Esmond Rothermere a second string to their bows, with King at something of an advantage over his cousin because of the prosperity of the Anglo-Canadian Pulp and Paper Company. But a New York sales organization, ably managed, had brought the companies into close parity by selling the newsprint of both around the world. By 1960 both paper mills were 'oversold', a highly desirable situation.

King now sought to regain his advantage by giving Esmond an ultimatum. Rothermere was to merge his Anglo-Newfoundland Development Company with Anglo-Canadian, or, said King, 'My sales organization in New York will stop selling your company's newsprint.' So it was that in the last lingering days of the summer of 1960, Esmond Rothermere organized a 'War Council' to plot a defence against King, inviting all the principal players from Canada and Newfoundland to come to his country estate at Daylesford.

Left behind in Montreal was a fresh young lawyer by the name of Robert Morrow, who had been a director on the board of the AND since 1954.

One of Bob Morrow's favourite watering holes was Ruby Foos Restaurant, located north of Montreal near the golf clubs frequented by the shakers and movers of that city's powerful financial community. What attracted Morrow to Ruby Foos was of course the good food but, more important, the extensive bar where, after a game of golf, he would repair for a drink with a friend. At about the same time that Esmond's War Council was assembling in the Cotswolds, Morrow was having a drink at Ruby Foos with his good friend, Alan Gordon, president of Royal Securities and a director at Price Brothers & Co.

Morrow was aware of two facts pertinent to the present crisis at Anglo-Newfoundland caused by King's ultimatum – first, that one half of the sales organization King chose to claim as his own was actually owned by Anglo-Newfoundland (which was in turn controlled by Esmond Rothermere). The second was that Price Brothers, also a paper mill, was undersold and running only four days a week. The company would greatly benefit from representation by a top-class sales organization such as the one owned by King and Rothermere in New York.

Standing at the bar, Morrow decided to confide in his friend, and he told him the story of Cecil King and his threats to Esmond and Associated Newspapers. He then said to the financier, 'Alan, why do we not form a sales agreement such as Anglo-Newfoundland Development Company has had with Anglo-Canadian?'

Gordon said, 'Bob, why bother with a sales agreement? Let us merge Anglo-Newfoundland Development Company and Price Brothers.'

As a result of this conversation, on 2 September 1960, Morrow wrote the following letter to Esmond in London:

I have some information which if not already known to you I am sure will be of interest. Alan Gordon, the President of Royal Securities, who as you know is a close personal friend of mine, has a very active interest in Price Brothers ... They look with considerable envy at Anglo-Newfoundland Development both from the point of view of management and sales ...

They have apparently considered that ... the possibility exists of Anglo-Newfoundland becoming freed of any association with Anglo-Canadian and they would view with considerable favour a proposal to merge Anglo-Newfoundland and Price Brothers. I do not know whether such an idea would have any appeal whatsoever, but superficially there would appear to be benefits to be gained from such a merger.

The benefits of such a deal were more than 'superficial', for what Bob Morrow had in mind was what is known as a 'reverse take-over'; that is, the accumulation of sufficient stock to give Anglo-Newfoundland a controlling interest in Price Brothers. The advantage to Esmond Rothermere was immense; it amounted to a stronghold in the Canadian paper industry, one that reduced Cecil King's position at the same time as it strengthened that of Esmond. But in this effort Morrow was very much opposed by a prominent Canadian financier, E. P. Taylor, who controlled Domtar, another company involved in the manufacture of newsprint and, more pertinently, Beaverbrook, who owned considerable shares in Price Brothers.

At first delighted, Esmond was, in the next instance, worried and upset. This response was not atypical of the press baron. He did not want to contravene the wishes of his father's old friend Max and cabled Morrow accordingly: 'Will not enter into fight with Max nor deal with Taylor stop do not intend press on with merger if that is the price stop.' Was this an example of Esmond's wavering? If so, it was wasted on Morrow.

Morrow was a man of strict priorities. Having set these priorities and once engaged in action, Bob Morrow did not deviate from them. It was an old habit from his youth, when he had been given command of the first Canadian Fighter Wing by the commander-in-chief of the Royal Canadian Air Force in England.

In fact, Bob's absolute homing instinct had saved his life more than once, but most dramatically in 1942 just after he had completed a month's leave in Canada. He was flying a twin-engine Boston, a light daylight bomber built by Douglas Aircraft.

One of the problems with crossing the North Atlantic in a Boston was not only the limited range of the aircraft, but also the absence of de-icing equipment on the wing. In the freezing flying conditions of Newfoundland, Greenland and Iceland, the Boston could be treacherous. The night before Morrow was due to make a trip to Greenland and Iceland, he had drinks with another pilot who was also flying a Boston. The two men speculated on what they would do if their wings froze. Bob's friend said he would ditch the plane. Bob said he would try to fly her in.

The next day, on the first leg of his trip, Bob encountered a layered cloud formation and he followed the standard procedure of trying to fly on the layers. This worked, but unfortunately it caused ice to form on the wings of the aircraft. As he began picking up ice, he watched as two other Boston aircraft 'went into the drink of the North Atlantic'. He sent an SOS of their position back to base and carried on.

> Finally, as I recollect, at an indicated speed of about 180 mph, the aircraft spun, meaning it was completely out of control and I assumed that's what happened to the other two Bostons. I decided to correct the spin which I managed to do and then to stay in a dive which was very steep and I think, somewhat inverted, and try to get to a lower altitude where I might get warmer weather and perhaps get rid of the ice. Finally at a very high speed, it was indicating some 400 mph, I decided it was now or never so I pulled the aircraft out of the dive and as I did so I did hit warmer air close to the sea and the ice came off in great sheets about 6 feet long and I very nearly, because of the angle of attack and the dive, dove into the sea and I made a last-minute wrench and just missed the top of the ocean waves.

At last, Bob headed for the Atlantic coast of Labrador, climbed through a hole in the clouds and, miraculously seeing the coastline, managed to get radio contact with Goose Bay, who informed Bob that they were 'zero in fog'.

Goose Bay suggested to Morrow that he fly on the radio range, and he and his crew should bail out and they would try to pick them up. 'Well,' as Bob put it later, 'being picked up in the snow in the wintertime in Goose Bay didn't have much appeal,' so, being familiar with the area, he decided to try to bring the plane down at Conche Harbour, on some pasture ground up behind the town.

> I then made another run or two over the ground where I intended to land and came in wheels up at about 110 mph indicated, landed on this pasture land which was very, very rough land, broke up the aeroplane, it was badly broken up, both wing roots were broken off, tail plane was badly damaged, the nose was completely shattered and so we came to rest.

Shrewd and pugnacious, Morrow believed that had he deviated from a strict adherence to his own sense of priorities at the time of that crisis, he would not now be working on behalf of Esmond Rothermere: he would be dead. And sadly, the pilot Bob had shared a few drinks with the night before he made his crash landing had ended his days then and there in the North Atlantic.

The Bob Morrow who was putting together the reverse take-over of Price Brothers by Anglo-Newfoundland Company used essentially the same reasoning in the situation now before him, with the change 'of a few particulars'. And not even his boss, Esmond Rothermere, was capable of blurring Morrow's priorities and preventing him from reaching his goal if he could.

Duly noting Esmond's reluctance to proceed, then, Morrow proceeded. Eventually, on a trip to Monte Carlo to visit Rothermere, he came face to face with Beaverbrook who, as Esmond had warned Morrow he would, sought to make his dissatisfaction with Bob and his take-over project known.

Beaverbrook began his assault on Morrow by saying, 'Mr Morrow, I understand you are an optimist.' Without thinking, Morrow answered, 'Lord Beaverbrook, only an optimist would fly those aeroplanes you built during the war.'

Thus was Beaverbrook silenced, Cecil King foiled, and the Daily Mail & General Trust thrust into the enviable position of becoming a major player in the paper manufacturing industry in Canada. AND gained a twenty per cent shareholding in the Price Company and, 'with a few squabbles', succeeded in taking over the board of directors.

But this was only the beginning of the mega-deals that would emanate out of Canada, most of them brokered by the maverick Morrow. Rothermere's Daily Mail & General Trust would one day find itself embroiled in a make-it-or-break-it deal that would come to be known as the largest take-over in the history of Canada.

Whether through ignorance or arrogance, or perhaps a mixture of the two, the journalists on the *Daily Mail* and its sister publications saw themselves as the only true centre of the Harmsworth publishing dynasty. Because they were high profile, it never occurred to them that the company might be involved in dramatic business dealings abroad. What they judged by was the response of the reading public in London itself. And by this reasoning the most important event of 1960 and the following year was not the take-over of Price Brothers in Canada, which indeed was not highly publicized, but the merger into the *Daily Mail* of the *News Chronicle*, and into the *Evening News* of the *Star*.

The *News Chronicle* was itself the result of the merger in 1928 of two Liberal newspapers – the *Daily News* with the *Gazette* and, later, in 1930, with still another Liberal newspaper, the *Daily Chronicle*. Eventually, the trustees who administered the new newspaper gave way to its most powerful member and Laurence Cadbury, the chocolate magnate, more or less assumed full control of the *News Chronicle*. The most important single fact about the newspaper was that it embodied the Liberal ideals of three separate publications, all of which had been serious Liberal mouthpieces.

For it to fall into Tory hands was therefore thought by its reading constituency to be nothing short of abhorrent. As one of its better-connected readers, Lady Violet Bonham-Carter, put it in a letter to one of the newspaper's management team, the 'tragedy' of the *News Chronicle* falling into Harmsworth hands brought untold 'pain and utter bewil-derment . . . to those who have given it their unswerving love and loyalty for countless years'.

But if indeed the readers *had* given the paper 'their unswerving love and loyalty', the merger would never have happened. In the decade before the *Daily Mail* took over the *News Chronicle*, the paper's circulation had dropped from 1,534,000 to 1,162,000 and its financial losses were in six figures. Its decline was chalked down to uninspired management and perhaps even laziness on the part of the editorial team. By 1960, it had weakened to the point that no fewer than three press barons – Lord Beaverbrook, Cecil King and Roy Thomson – had shown a serious interest in taking it over.

If any of those who had been interested had got the Liberal newspaper, the end result would have been, as one journalist put it, 'a mixture of popcorn and pasta'. That it was the Tory *Daily Mail* that in the end won the day was actually neither here nor there; there was no one with the appropriate political credentials waiting in the wings to rescue the declining paper.

The brutality of the take-over, its speed and secrecy also took a serious toll. Ted Jeffery, one of the key members of the backbench on the *Daily Mail*, recalled:

> We announced at six at night, virtually the *Mail* taking over completely and yes, people were surprised. At the *News Chronicle* they were called to a meeting by an editor after they had actually started work on that night's paper. They were informed their effort would not be necessary. Obviously, the *Mail* didn't need any printing staff, only a few editorial people.

It was the evening of Monday, 17 October 1960, when the staff of the *News Chronicle* was dismissed; the readers discovered the change when the *Daily Mail* came through their letter-box the next morning. This is the way of newspaper mergers and closures. For a variety of business reasons they must be clouded in secrecy. But for Rothermere and the management of the *Daily Mail* it amounted to another well-publicized error of judgement, based, in the popular perception, upon financial strong-arming and political rivalry.

As for the *Mail*, the assumption that the newspaper could retain most of the readership of the *News Chronicle*, raising the circulation of the *Daily Mail* from 1.5 to 2.25 million, was a faulty one. In the coming weeks and months it would become painfully apparent that it wasn't possible 'to buy circulation'. The Liberal readers of the *News Chronicle* refused to accept the *Mail* and fell away in droves.

The editor during the merger was William Hardcastle, who, in December 1959, had succeeded Arthur Wareham in the job. Never were two men less alike. Wareham was, by his own reckoning, 'quiet'; indeed, his survival for over twenty years in the *Daily Mail* news-room probably stemmed in part from his ability to blend in with his surroundings. Mature, hard-working and sensible, Wareham was reflective by nature, with a great deal of respect for matters intellectual. Like most editors on the Street, Wareham had worked up from the backbench, meaning he had been a sub-editor and he came from that tradition.

Hardcastle, on the other hand, had emerged from the reporting side of print journalism, with fast-breaking news as his speciality. As a young man he had planned to become a doctor and had studied Greek and Latin seriously in preparation. But he had never made it to university because he developed a rare illness that had to do with the bone marrow. Cured after painful operations that left deep scars on his legs, he never went back to finish his education, instead joining Fleet Street as a reporter.

Eventually, his career carried him to Washington D.C., where he reported for Reuters and, while he was there, he had been offered a job as a news editor on an American newspaper – a job he turned down reluctantly. He had taken to the American experience with gusto, finding their treatment of the news more to his liking than that of his countrymen. Macho and tough to the point of ruthlessness, he was what the Americans called 'a news junkie'. The *Mail's* television reviewer, the late Peter Black, recalled that when Hardcastle heard via the paper's New York correspondent about the confrontation between JFK and Khrushchev over the Cuban missile crisis, he 'put down the phone and rubbed his hands. "Oh boy!" he said. "This could be the Big Bang!"'

Hardcastle was round-faced and overweight – about seventeen stone on the frame of a man of average height. The day he took over the paper his first words were, 'I want this paper to run scared.' What he meant, and everyone on his reporting staff understood him, was that he wanted 'a good, hot, newsy paper'. Hardcastle would stalk the news-room, smoking heavily, with his shirt-sleeves rolled up, looking every inch the stereotype of the hard-boiled editor. As such, he was very popular with reporting staff. But the management at Associated Newspapers viewed him with suspicion. And indeed, even his best friends on the paper would say that in some of the essentials Hardcastle did not 'shine' as an editor. His 'quick-takes' could and sometimes did get the *Daily Mail* into trouble.

An example of this occurred when the *Mail* sustained an attack on their gossip column, 'Paul Tanfield', so named in the tradition of the 'William Hickey' column in the *Daily Express* that had in turn taken its name from a well-known seventeenth-century gossip. In her article published in *Queen*, entitled 'The Friendless Ones', Penelope Gilliatt blasted the *Daily Mail* in particular for its irresponsible reporting of marriage breakups, job losses and various falls from grace.

She said that 'Mr Tanfield projects a disagreeable character: he can stomach a more disagreeable story than anyone else in the field ...' As for the other purveyors of unpleasantries in Fleet Street, Gilliatt wrote, 'They go where they are not asked; they live in a world which exists only in their fertile imaginations; they are supplied with information by your friends; they have a language, a code, an attitude as unreal as the news they deal in. They are the gossip columnists.'

She singled out one of them for special criticism. Of the editor of the *Mail* she wrote, 'Hardcastle is an out and out title snob, and doesn't pretend to be anything else.'

The other media in London jumped on the article and especially on television Gilliatt's accusations got heavy play. Ill advisedly, Hardcastle agreed to appear on a television programme, and when the researcher asked him 'how he could countenance editing a newspaper that published this kind of material', Hardcastle crumpled abruptly. He blurted out an answer he made up on the spot, saying that, as a matter of fact, he had decided to abolish the diary column. And he went back to the office, killed Tanfield and put a rather prosaic column in its place, one that heavily featured buildings and good works.

Another area where Hardcastle was undeniably weak was in administration. He disliked paperwork and his in-tray piled up, while his out-tray remained empty. Moreover, he was reluctant to see the many people who had lined up outside his office and, as one of his colleagues put it, 'People do want to see the editor.'

What really happened to Hardcastle? One of his friends, Alan Brien, speculated later:

> Lethargy attacked him, he used to sit in his office as things piled up on his desk...
>
> Later I said to him, 'What happened to you?'
>
> He said, 'I don't know, I just got into a situation where nothing seemed of any importance.' He asked me, 'Why does everybody think that fat men are cheerful?'
>
> I said, 'Well, you're a fat man, you always look as though you're cheerful.'
>
> He said, 'I'm not cheerful. I'm not cheerful at all. I have to be cheerful because everybody expects fat men to be cheerful.'

Oddly enough, for all his popularity, Hardcastle had not improved the image or the circulation of the *Daily Mail* during his tenure. And his particular brand of journalism – the hard-bitten, news-orientated approach – while sexy and masculine, was no longer what the *Daily Mail* reader was looking for. The new affluence was changing the lives of the middle classes in Britain, making them look outwards. In a way, the readers were looking for a new identity. Had Northcliffe chosen the early 1960s to return to life, he would have found a fertile field. But for the moment no Northcliffe was in sight.

And as the *Mail* struggled to find the right image for the changing times, one based on social issues, consumer concerns, human interest and women's matters, so William Hardcastle was casting about for a new direction in his own life, although, had you asked him, he would not have put it that way. An assistant editor from the *News Chronicle*, Mike Randall, one of the few journalists to make the jump from the Liberal newspaper to the *Daily Mail* during the ill-fated merger, had ideas radically different from his hard-nosed editor. He managed to capture the ear of Esmond Rothermere, thus sealing the fate of William Hardcastle.

Rothermere sent the editor on a fact-finding mission to the United States, a soft way of sidelining him while giving him the impression he remained of importance to the *Daily Mail*.

For Hardcastle, the parting was painful but in the long run beneficial. A year later Andrew Boyle, a producer at the BBC, conceived an innovative news programme, *The World at One*, and decided Bill Hardcastle was his man. He asked the former editor to become his presenter. In this world of fast-breaking news, Hardcastle found his *métier*. He became one of the best-known newsmen in Britain, along with Boyle, improvising and inventing an entirely new concept in radio news reporting. If ever there was a right man for a job, Hardcastle was that man and from this point in his career, his success was assured.

As for the *Daily Mail*, Hardcastle was the newspaper's sixth editor since

Esmond Rothermere had become the chairman of Daily Mail & General Trust in 1937. Esmond's changing of editors, his search for a 'quick fix' in the manner of his father, actually fomented instability at the paper. All kinds of people were waiting for the moment of the *Daily Mail's* demise to jeer, he had written to his father thirty years before. But then he had been an idealist. Now, with circulation on the slide and the newspaper's lack of a coherent editorial policy, what Esmond had feared as a young man was upon him – and he no longer seemed to care.

When a friend at the Beefsteak Club said to him, 'Oh, I see you've changed editors,' he gave an answer that was to follow him to the end of his career. It would be used by his critics to show his growing cynicism, by his advocates to show his ready wit.

He replied, 'I tried a short, fat one, and that didn't work. So now I'm having a long, thin one.'

At the same time that Rothermere countenanced a revolving-door policy for editors of the *Daily Mail*, he gave his City editor a sense of security much envied at the other newspapers of the day. A personal friend of Esmond's and, more important according to some, a tennis partner, Patrick Sergeant brought a shrewdness and creativity to the job that no other City editor on the Street could emulate.

The charismatic Sergeant, tall and handsome – it was said he began his career as an Arthur Murray dance instructor – wrote his column for ordinary folk, but it was also read with enthusiasm by people in the City. His contacts were at the highest level, probably because of his personal charm and undeniable intelligence.

Christopher Fildes later estimated that during Sergeant's thirty years as City editor of the *Daily Mail*, many competitors came and went. 'Patrick saw off rival City editors literally by the dozen,' said Fildes.

One of Sergeant's ideas, 'Money Mail', might have come about as a result of the accusation by a competing publication that the City office of the *Daily Mail* was overstaffed. The staff put their heads together to save their jobs, it was said, and came up with the weekly insert on money and personal finance. Branded 'Sergeant's Folly' in the beginning, it featured stories that gave sensible financial advice to the emerging affluent middle classes. It became so popular that the circulation bumped up on a Wednesday when it appeared. This was in 1966. Soon afterwards, the very newspapers that had ridiculed the idea were imitating it in their own pages. Not only did it appeal to the readership, it also brought in a great deal of advertising revenue from banks, building societies and various investment vehicles.

The biggest asset in 'Money Mail', however, was Patrick Sergeant himself, as one of Sergeant's colleagues, Brian Henry, explained:

> When we were launching 'Money Mail', we had to back up our assertions with quantified research and one of the questions which we asked banks was what was the influence of City editors. The sample we took was a sample of brokers, investment analysts, financial advisers, merchant bankers and other journalists ... What came out was that the only journalist ... who, because of his status, was able to influence the price of shares in the market was Patrick Sergeant.

A man about town, Sergeant was 'never a man who was short of lunch'. Tea was another matter. It was said he did all his sacking over tea at the Ritz.

But Sergeant made another contribution to Associated Newspapers: the magazine *Euromoney*. His brain-child came to him when he was in New York and it was said Esmond Rothermere agreed to float the financial magazine for some £6000 while sitting with Sergeant on a park bench in Central Park. This was in the 1960s. By the mid-1980s, when it was floated as a separate company, its value had risen to £92.5 million.

Another well-known and popular byline in the *Daily Mail* at the time was that of Anne Scott-James, who wrote a weekly column of general interest. Scott-James came to the *Mail* from Beaverbrook's *Sunday Express*, which she left because Walter Hayes, who was an assistant editor, and Bill Hardcastle promised her a chance to get away from 'women's topics' and write on subjects of general interest. 'We all had lunch,' said Anne,

> and cooked up a feature of five articles about going on safari in Africa. I think the lunch was at the Ritz. Walter said he had a great admiration for my work on the *Express*. Bill wasn't interested in women's features, but he did say he was interested in acquiring me. In general, we decided there was a great feeling at the time for wildlife and how about going to Africa and looking around the animal world? And so it started.

The three of them came up with the idea as a kind of flyer, but it established Scott-James as one of the brightest writers on the *Daily Mail*. Her articles on Africa were serialized around the world, not least because it put a new slant on the killing of animals for profit. Later, she looked back on what she had seen in Africa with distaste.

> To be honest, the safari wasn't very pleasant. The animals weren't genuinely tracked down, they were produced for the great hunter and he was allowed then to shoot. If you don't shoot an animal properly, it can be pretty terrible. And with these rather amateurish shots, the 'experts' had to follow the animals into the bush and finish them off.
>
> I remember a buffalo, in the course of the safari, that had to be done in this

way. On safari, you were supposed to be able to shoot an elephant, a buffalo, a leopard if you were lucky. Then the hunters would take them back and hang them on the wall at home.

Scott-James signalled the changing attitude towards the wildlife of Africa. Until then, Africa was to a large degree considered by Westerners as a theme park for those wealthy enough to hunt big game. But she brought a sense of 'this jungle business' to the attention of the average reader. 'As the animals die, murdered by the million,' one of the sub-heads for her article read, 'shrewder Africans take a second look at their heritage. And they see MONEY!'

She led with the idea that if someone 'wanted to smash up the Parthenon or drive a bypass through Westminster Abbey', an outcry would be heard around the world. But the animals of Africa, one of 'the wonders of the world', were in terrible danger of extinction and no one seemed to care.

While Anne Scott-James's companions on the safari, a cola manufacturer from the United States and his wife, hunted down the animals, sometimes making a mess of their killing, Scott-James went on the first 'camera safari', taking her shots on film. In thirty years' time, her way would be the only way to go on a safari in Kenya, but for now, her ground-breaking article only suggested a need for change.

The safari series paved the way for Scott-James's acceptance among the male-dominated news-room at the *Daily Mail*. She didn't leave until she personally saw her column on the stone, thus earning the respect of her male colleagues. One of the sub-editors, Neil Swindells, said,

It was the 1960s, a carry-over from the wild and woolier times. There was hard drinking and hard smoking and not many women in the office. The last woman would go through the door about six in the evening, with the exception of the big-name columnists, like Anne Scott-James. The subs loved her. So did the compositors. She always cut her own copy. Having written it, having subbed it, this elegant lady, who went on to marry Osbert Lancaster of the *Express* and become an actual 'Lady', was one of the few women who would be tolerated in the very male *Mail* offices.

At about the same time that Anne Scott-James was forging a sense of responsibility towards the wildlife of Africa, the giant continent was undergoing massive upheaval as Britain and other European countries granted independence to their colonies. The tribal struggles, often bitter and bloody, became the focus for the news as different factions vied for power.

To the reporters who covered Africa, the heart of darkness could be very dark indeed. The Congo became independent on 30 June 1960 and, by 5 July, a mutiny against Belgian officers brought about a flight of Belgian civilians, causing essential services to collapse. In the wake of this, premier Tshombe of Katanga, a province of the Congo, declared his country independent, and both the United Nations and Belgium flew in troops to try to restore order in the region. Leaders of various tribes began building up their own forces and a state of anarchy prevailed. As if this weren't enough, the region became subject to manipulation from the superpowers as the Cold War was exported to the Congo.

The reporter for the *Daily Mail* during this time of dangerous upheaval was a South African, Peter Younghusband. One of his stories of the time was a strange one that included an unlikely protagonist.

Some time before the Congo rebellion of early 1963 broke out, a music critic for the *Baltimore Sun* by the name of Weldon Wallace had been more or less exiled from his newspaper for a while. President Harry S. Truman's daughter Margaret was a singer, and she had given a recital in Baltimore which Wallace attended and panned, to great public furore. The President became very angry, causing tremendous upset at the newspaper and as a result Weldon Wallace was transferred to the Rome Bureau, where he was assigned to cover opera and similar subjects, a job that had lasted some years.

When the rebellion broke out in the Congo the *Baltimore Sun* wanted urgently to cover the story, since a great battle was about to take place. The newspaper found that the only correspondent they could get in place in time was Weldon Wallace, because there happened to be a direct flight from Rome to Salisbury Airport in Rhodesia. From there, it was fairly easy to travel by road into the disputed area.

Wallace was in his mid-fifties, a music critic and he had never covered a war in his life. At the border, he asked Peter Younghusband to take him in on his next trip and Younghusband said to him,

'Look, you're American and you don't have a visa. You're going to have a lot of problems because they are only allowing British journalists in.' At the time the United Nations, which had the backing of America and various other nationals, was very unpopular because they were fighting the Tshombe regime which in turn was supported by mercenary troops. I said to Wallace, 'It's suicidal at the moment for an American journalist to try and cross that border.' Wallace said, no, he was definitely going to go in.

I said, 'Well, we can't help.'

So Wallace decided, very courageously, that he was going to go in and the way to get in was to take them a great gift. He'd heard that there were refugees camped around the immigration post and he took them a sack of flour, and he took with him in his car two other desperados, one was Lionel Fleming of the BBC, who was also having difficulty getting in, because he had an Irish passport and there were Irish troops fighting for the United Nations. They also had with them a CBS cameraman who was an American too.

As it happened, the three reporters got past customs with the sack of flour, as far as the immigration post, where they had the misfortune to meet Tshombe's army in full retreat. The mercenaries were drunk and dangerous. They pulled the three correspondents, including Wallace, out of the car and, finding the sack of flour, ripped it open, whereupon the refugees, who were starving, began fighting for it.

When Younghusband approached the immigration post about an hour later the first thing he saw was 'a nebulous great white cloud rising over the post'. Younghusband, who was well known to the immigration officers there, asked what was happening, and an officer answered that they were arresting some spies and they had them in a shed. Younghusband walked over and saw 'a small galvanized-iron shed the size of a garage'.

> I went over and looked through the window, and there they had Weldon Wallace and these two other guys lying on the ground, and they were kicking them and hitting them with rifle butts. I had in my possession a Tshombe press card that was issued to favoured journalists by President Tshombe himself and signed by him personally, and these things always worked miraculously. People always dropped on their knees when you presented it.
>
> I went round to the doors of the shed and pushed my way in and went up to the officer in charge and I said in my very bad French, 'I'm a member of the Katanga press corps. Here is my press card signed by your president. I want you to release these prisoners. They are not spies, they are journalists.'

The officer, his eyes red-rimmed and puffy, immediately knocked the press card out of Younghusband's hand, slapped him across the face and threw him to the ground. And they began to beat him along with the three others.

> Meanwhile, my colleague, John Monks of the *Daily Express*, came and looked through the window and he saw what was happening and he ran back and jumped in his car and he raced back to the British border. We were both incidentally good friends with Sir Roy Welensky, who was then the Prime Minister of the Rhodesian Federation and he prevailed upon the immigration authorities to give him a telephone and then he telephoned Welensky and he said, 'Look, there are four journalists including Peter Younghusband who are under arrest and I think they are going to execute them.'

Welensky immediately sent for a company of his troops nearby and ordered them, in what could have been a serious diplomatic incident, to cross the border and rescue Younghusband, Wallace and the others.

Back in the shed, we'd undergone quite a tough time because at one stage they brought in a sten gun and they set the thing up on its tripod at one end of the shack. One of these drunken troops got behind it and took off the safety catch and put a round on the barrel. He sighted it on us and we thought we were going to be killed on the spot. People were hanging through the windows and urging the troops on and drawing their fingers across their throats. We thought, when this guy got behind the machine-gun, 'This is it.' Then he rolled over on his back and burst out laughing.

I remember Lionel Fleming was extremely stoic under all this. Weldon Wallace was amazing, kept amazingly calm. The CBS man started to crack up, and I kept saying to him, 'Don't show any fear, if you show any fear it makes it worse.'

Now the immigration officer came to the shed showing the drunken officer Peter Younghusband's British passport. So he was allowed to leave. Once outside, he told the immigration officer he couldn't leave without his colleagues.

He said, 'Look, I've saved your life, I can't save the others. There's my car and my driver. Get into the car and drive to the border, take my advice and just go.' I did as I was told and on my way, I came across the troops Welensky had sent.

Younghusband told them what had happened and they went to see what they could do. Two long hours Younghusband waited and then, at last, a flat-bed truck appeared with the three reporters on the back of it. The officer had found them in a glade, stripped, their clothes and belongings stolen, about to be executed.

The men were in very bad shape and, after being taken to a hotel, Weldon Wallace was given an injection, but just before he passed out he said he wanted to write his story. So, after a few drinks of whisky, all the men sat down and wrote their stories and sent them.

And we then suffered a sort of reflex that you get after a thing like that. We went on a real high and then we suddenly looked at Weldon Wallace lying totally asleep on the bed. We decided we'd write his story for him. We wrote the story. I remember the opening phrase which was the one I thought up and I wrote down as the lead, 'My American passport almost cost me my life today.'

We wrote the story in a rather jazzy Fleet Street journalist's style. The *Baltimore Sun* was rather a staid newspaper. We sent this story off under Weldon Wallace's name and perhaps if we hadn't been slightly high at the time and thought a bit more, we wouldn't have done it. But the way we sent it off under Weldon Wallace's name, the story landed. The *Baltimore Sun* splashed it word for word.

It was picked up by agencies all round the world. Wallace woke up the next morning to a tremendous congratulatory cable from his editor and said, 'But I don't remember writing the story.'

We said, 'Weldon, you wrote the story, it was the sedatives the doctor gave you, you don't remember writing it but you did.'

The next thing the four correspondents knew, the *Baltimore Sun* wired Weldon Wallace congratulating him again and saying they were nominating him for the Pulitzer Prize.

Wallace made short shrift of this, however, when he couldn't find his 'black', that is, the carbon journalists made in those days of their stories. He withdrew the story, which always seemed to the high-spirited Younghusband a great shame, because he was convinced it would surely have won the Pulitzer.

9

'A Wind of Change'

There was a standard joke about Esmond that made the rounds among the journalists on the *Daily Mail*. In it, Esmond rings up the editor every afternoon between 4.30 and 5.30 – whether from Monte Carlo or Daylesford or Warwick House – and he asks, 'What's the news?'

And the editor answers, 'Well, the Queen has broken her leg.' And Esmond responds with silence. 'And 250 people have just been killed at London Airport.' More silence. 'And there's been a pit explosion and 600 coal miners are trapped below ground.' Still more silence.

And then, at last, Esmond enquires, 'And what about the *weather*?'

Not since Northcliffe, the journalists opined, had any proprietor been so obsessed with the weather. So this interest in its turn spawned a whole string of weather jokes. In one of them, Esmond has called the editor, asking about worthwhile stories. And the editor goes down the list, getting only the most bored of responses from his proprietor. At last, he falls back on the one subject he knows will interest Esmond. 'Look, it really has been a pretty dreadful day. It's been pouring with rain since early morning.' Silence. 'It seems to have stopped for now, but the forecast is not good.'

Then this voice at the other end says, 'I'm sitting just across the road in my office looking at the same damn weather as you are. So what are you going on about?'

At last, the quintessential weather joke about Esmond was told by Gordon MacKenzie, deputy editor on the *Daily Mail*, a position he shared at the time with Australian Bruce Rothwell:

One Sunday night in 1960 Esmond called up. This was when Harold Macmillan was Prime Minister and he was in Capetown making a now quite famous speech about a wind of change sweeping across South Africa. He was talking about the inevitable end of apartheid in South Africa – 'there's a wind of change blowing across the Southern African continent'. This Sunday night, Rothermere, having missed his five o'clock call, rang at about seven and everybody had gone down to the pub for a drink, and he'd asked for the editor. He wasn't there, Rothwell wasn't there, I wasn't there, so finally they put him through to the news editor, but he'd gone out too. But a junior reporter was sitting there and he had to take the call.

'Well, what's happening?' Rothermere's voice booms over the line.

'Oh, it's very quiet, very quiet, Sir.'

'Well, what's the leader about?'

So this reporter grabs the paper, madly reading. 'This wind of change, Sir ... it's about the weather.'

By now, Esmond had been the proprietor of the *Daily Mail* for over twenty years and his past life was unknown to the present generation of journalists. At sixty-two, he had become an austere figure of authority, and stories about him took on the mythic qualities befitting some distant and powerful potentate of yore. Though at the heart of him was a somewhat simple man of elegant tastes and good humour, within the office his every action took on a symbolic significance.

Thus when Esmond summoned Peter Younghusband peremptorily to London, Younghusband felt that his colleagues on the *Daily Mail* were eyeing him suspiciously, in the belief that he was soon to be offered an executive position on the paper. Younghusband was in the Congo on an assignment when he received the cable from the *Daily Mail* foreign desk telling him to fly to London urgently because Lord Rothermere wished to see him. Bewildered, Younghusband caught the next plane, arriving in London in freezing mid-winter in a tropical suit. Rushed to Moss Brothers for heavier clothing, Younghusband found himself immediately afterwards packed on to the train to Daylesford by Rothermere's secretary, who told him that if he was sent back by the Rolls-Royce he was to return the unused portion of the ticket.

Meanwhile, Younghusband prepared himself for the possibility of promotion, demotion – or worse. With some trepidation he entered the grounds of beautiful Daylesford, only to find that Esmond had his grandchildren at home from Eton and elsewhere for a long weekend. What he wanted was for Younghusband to tell them stories about Africa. So the journalist had been brought back as a story-teller. As to Esmond, Younghusband said:

he was a difficult man to judge. He kept on firing questions at me about investments in South Africa and I'm no financial person at all. He seemed to know quite a lot about South African financial affairs too. He asked me if there were any good publications for sale in South Africa. I told him about a newspaper which was for sale and he said no, he didn't want that newspaper. I said there was a string of trade publications for sale, but he said no, he wasn't interested in those. So I remember that long discussion as we walked.

We walked through a copse and he kept on reaching up and breaking down pieces of dead wood from the trees above his head. He was a tall man and I remember him at one stage reaching, he just managed to touch a dry branch, he couldn't quite reach it and I was taller than him and I reached up for him and got it down for him. 'No, no,' he said. 'Leave it there,' he said. 'I'll do it the next time I come around.' I remember swimming in the indoor swimming pool, watching movies in the indoor cinema.

He prided himself greatly on making Martinis. The first evening I got there, when I'd changed for dinner and come downstairs, he was mixing Martinis. I didn't like Martinis and he said, 'Have a Martini,' and I said, 'No, thank you, I'll have a Vermouth or something,' and I chose something else and he didn't say anything, he went on finishing the mixing of the Martini. When he'd mixed it, he held one out to me so I said, 'No, no, I prefer something else,' and he took my hand and he closed my fingers around the glass and he said, 'You'll have a Martini.'

History had shown that those whom Esmond favoured drank Martinis. So when Younghusband refused a Martini, Esmond, who obviously liked him, forced it on him so he would not join the list of outcasts who had been foolish enough not to drink up. An act of generosity signified friendship with Esmond, and those whom he favoured were expected to accept his largesse.

And Esmond did have his favourites, among them Robert Morrow, who had masterminded the reverse take-over of Price Brothers by the Anglo-Newfoundland Development Company in Canada. The business deal had led to a long and loyal friendship, with many acts of generosity on the part of Esmond and numerous business activities over the years.

One morning just after breakfast, when Morrow was staying at Warwick House, Esmond said to him, 'Bob, this morning we're going to go out and get some new shoes.' So the pair of them walked over to Lobb's Shoemakers, the finest in the world. And Esmond said to the shopkeeper, 'Measure Mr Morrow for a pair of shoes.'

So they sat me down in a chair and this man came over and took all sorts of measurements of my foot for new shoes and he said, 'Mr Morrow, the shoes will be ready in two months.' I gave him the address and this was all fine with me because Esmond was paying for the shoes. But they were so comfortable and they lasted so long that I got used to wearing them.

Then a couple of years ago I hadn't ordered any shoes for a long time so I very offhandedly wrote a note to Lobb's and said, 'Please make me a pair of black shoes and a pair of brown shoes.' So a month or so went by and I got a note from them saying the shoes would be ready and they'd be prepared to ship them and please would I look after the enclosed invoice and there was the invoice, $3000 a pair!

On another visit, Morrow was travelling over with a close friend and he asked Esmond if he could bring him along to a dinner. And Esmond replied without pause, 'You're not going to bring him over for dinner. We'll have a cocktail party for him.' That was Esmond all over again, Morrow said.

On another occasion Esmond invited Morrow to stay at Warwick House, and he also asked his daughter Esme and her husband Rowley Cromer, the governor of the Bank of England, to the dinner.

> So there were four of us. Esme was across the table from me and her lovely face was playing in the candlelight, and dinner had already started and there was a terrible 'thwap'. Rothermere had rapped me on my knuckles with the handle of a spoon and he said, 'For God sake's, Bob, stop staring at Esme and pay attention to what I'm telling you!'

This was the private Esmond, charming, graceful and really very mischievous. In his strangely civilized world, one lunched with friends who had just been sacked by one of one's editors. This happened to Quentin Crewe, who had taken over from Bill Hardcastle, the 'short, fat one'. Why, Quentin Crewe asked thoughtfully, was the *Daily Mail* so gloomy?

'My father was a gloomy man,' Esmond responded. 'I think that's the reason.'

But regardless of this sad assessment of Harold, in a lot of ways Esmond still lived in the shadow of his father, now many years dead. Despite the fact that Beaverbrook and his *Daily Express* had soared ahead of the *Daily Mail*, Esmond honoured the old man almost as if he were his own father. On Beaverbrook's eighty-third birthday, Esmond gave him a party at Warwick House attended by Sir Winston Churchill, as well as all the leading newspaper proprietors. It was an opulent affair, with a birthday cake made by the fashionable Madame Floris, with a music box and skating rink on top.

As to the setting, according to one rather florid account,

> The great crystal chandelier in the superb first-floor Grinling Gibbons drawing-room of Lord Rothermere's home shone down as he received his guests and a special place was found for Churchill as soon as he arrived ... Lord Rothermere had his guests group themselves round the settee on which sat Lord Beaverbrook flanked by Sir Winston and Mr Macmillan. The highlight of the party was the presentation to Lord Beaverbrook of a two-foot-wide solid silver gallery tea tray, engraved with the signature of every guest ... [Sir Winston] sat on Beaverbrook's right, turned up his hearing aid to make sure that he did not miss one word of the conversation ...

In return, Beaverbrook wrote a note to Esmond, thanking him for a party 'exceeding in glory all my many birthdays'.

Esmond Rothermere's son Vere. He was so good-looking, it
was thought to be an impediment to his being taken seriously.

Left A self-portrait of Humphrey Lyttelton, the jazz-band leader, who was also an illustrator and columnist on the *Mail*.

Above Flook. The cult cartoon strip had a series of writers, including Douglas Mount, Compton Mackenzie, Humphrey Lyttelton, George Melly and Barry Norman. Wally Fawkes was the artist throughout.

Left Iris Ashley as a young actress. During the 1950s, she would become the most famous fashion editor on Fleet Street. Ashley soon caught Rothermere's eye, and the pair had a romance that lasted many years.

Right Anne Scott-James in Kenya. Her series on killing animals for profit in Africa was serialized around the world.

Three editors of the *Daily Mail*; three styles of editing. William Hardcastle (top) stalked the newsroom, smoking heavily. He later became the famous presenter of the BBC's 'World at One'. Mike Randall (left) was a kind of symbol for the changing times. He wanted the *Mail* to reflect higher values. Arthur Brittenden (far left) was Esmond's last editor. He found Esmond amiable but no longer willing to promote the *Daily Mail*.

Left Paul Bewsher, one of Fleet Street's great characters. A contemporary of the great Northcliffe, he outlasted 28 news editors.

Below The master of the incongruous, the famous columnist Vincent Mulchrone. The column for this photograph began, 'Two hundred and fifty miles north of the Arctic Circle, 80 in the shade and, just along the beach, a bronzed, flaxen-haired beauty stark naked … I tell you, it's hell up here.'

The *Daily Sketch* editor, Howard French. Crusty and colourful, French voluntarily stepped aside to give a young editor the chance to change the fortunes of the dying *Sketch*.

The editor who took over the *Daily Sketch*, David English. English was thought among staffers to represent the new journalism.

Anthea Disney. David English read the American book *Black Like Me* and came up with the idea of having Disney dye her skin and experience prejudice first-hand.

Daily Sketch

EXCLUSIVE: The most significant social experiment ever conducted by a newspaper in Britain

WHY DOCTORS TURNED THIS WHITE GIRL'S SKIN BLACK

How I crossed the race barrier

TODAY Daily Sketch reporter Anthea Disney begins the full story of how she became the first woman in Britain to change the colour of her skin in an experiment to discover how coloured people really feel and live.

The publication of this story—which the Daily Sketch believes is the most significant experiment in human relations ever conducted in this country—has aroused world-wide interest.

TV and radio reporters have interviewed Miss Disney. Foreign newspapers and agencies are competing to publish it.

They will do so after it has appeared in the Daily Sketch.

VERY SERIOUS

The story begins in the clinic of Dr. Lawrence Fleischer, one of America's leading dermatologists.

After exhaustive tests Dr. Fleischer agreed to administer the drug which temporarily changes the skin's pigmentation.

"You are setting out to achieve something that can be achieved in no other way," he said. "I believe it to be a very serious project."

Three weeks later Anthea Disney took a train to Birmingham.

There she met an amazing mixture of reactions—ranging from rejection and aloofness to a warmth and kindliness which confounds many of the criticisms of British people's attitudes to coloured immigrants.

Anthea Disney after three weeks of treatment by Dr. Fleischer

SEE CENTRE PAGES

Robert Morrow, mastermind of the reverse takeover of the Canadian paper-milling firm Price Brothers by Rothermere's Anglo-Newfoundland company. Lord Beaverbrook confronted the young lawyer with the words, 'Mr Morrow, I understand you are an optimist.' Morrow answered, 'Lord Beaverbrook, only an optimist would fly those aeroplanes you built during the war.'

Left Peter Younghusband, the *Daily Mail*'s colourful African correspondent. He survived the Congo rebellion of 1963.

Opposite Rothermere with his third wife, Mary Murchison Orhstrom. The mother of six boys by her former husband, Mary became pregnant within a year of marrying Esmond, and in June 1967, had a son, Esmond, named after his father.

Vere and Patricia Harmsworth at their son's christening. The mother of three girls, Vere's wife Patricia had been warned not to have another child for health reasons. But when she found out Mary had become pregnant, she tried again. Jonathan was born in December 1967.

The Harmsworth children. Sarah, Jonathan, Camilla and Geraldine.

Norman Heath, Mick Shields, Bert Irvine and John Winnington-Ingram. Each of them played an important part in Vere Harmsworth's flash-point reorganisation of Associated Newspapers.

U.K PRES GAZETT

The cover of the U.K. Press Gazette for May 10, 1971; Mick Shields, Vere Harmsworth and David English at the launch of the new *Daily Mail*. The new editor, David English, is still in his shirt-sleeves; it was a hard day's night.

On the button, the new Daily Mail signs on

Dead on time, chairman Vere Harmsworth pressed the button which ended the four months of dreams and schemes which went into the devising of the Harmsworth pioneer for "a new generation of newspapers."

ABOVE: Too late now for a re-think; too early for a verdict. But a new national newspaper which cradles the hopes of a few thousand people is an event to be autographed. Vere Harmsworth, centre, signs a copy for Teddy O'Brien of Natsopa machine section (with glasses). Shirtsleeved editor David English and managing director M. J. (Mick) Shields complete the foursome as their anxious first week began. For comment, see page 3 and Dog Watches Dog.

Daily

Curb on car HP is to be lifted	

SPY SCA IN BRIT DEFENC

Child die in M1 pile-up

Ministers demand pay rise from Heath

HE GUA
WINS T

PAGES C

Esmond identified with his father's generation almost more than his own and certainly he honoured them. At the same time he took up the role of philanthropist, treating it very seriously. He had become in 1959 the Chancellor of Memorial University of Newfoundland and his Rothermere Trust sponsored graduates of Memorial University, a sponsorship that continues to this day.

His staff was keenly aware that, again somewhat reminiscent of Northcliffe, he took a special interest in competitions. One in particular, the Garden Flowers Competition near Daylesford, always attracted his attention. And each year the *Daily Mail* ran a short paragraph, telling readers who won the trophy. One year, the all-important paragraph was accidentally omitted from the edition Esmond had received at Daylesford and the fearful staff actually did a special edition, hiring a van to go in and deliver it, and taking back the edition that had left out the paragraph. All this, so that when Lord Rothermere awoke he would read about the local competition, as was customary each summer.

Thus, in the lore of the *Daily Mail* and at Associated Newspapers, Esmond's stern professional persona still had the power to strike fear into the rank-and-file journalists. But the circulation of the *Mail* was lagging behind Beaverbrook's *Express* by two million sales a day. Even more ominous was the kingdom of Cecil King, where by 1964 the *Daily Mirror* had, incredibly, topped five million circulation.

Now the strange competition between cousin and cousin, the only direct contest Esmond seemed able to conduct aggressively with something approaching the famed Harmsworthian touch, tipped in favour of King. And suddenly it was King who was being hailed as the natural successor to Northcliffe. Rothermere seemed to decline in the public eye in direct proportion to the downward spiral of the circulation of the *Daily Mail*.

For King, victory was sweet. In his own mind his ambitions and abilities had been obvious since he joined the *Mail* staff in 1923. But even though he had been made a director in 1929 and assumed executive responsibility by the time he was thirty-three, in truth a very young age, he continued to believe he had been frozen out. In his own words, 'anything I achieved was by subterfuge'. He would write later of Northcliffe and Rothermere, 'My rich uncles were insecure and unhappy men, so wealth as a source of security and happiness, the delusion of so many people, meant for me the reverse.' According to King, his uncle Harold, who employed him in the business, was 'an uncle I hardly knew.'

Yet, from the beginning, he claimed he was heir to that understanding of public motivation that so characterized his other uncle, Northcliffe. Though he had 'no idea what the man I am talking to is thinking, I have an intuitive comprehension of the thoughts of millions...'

On 15 July 1965, King appeared on a BBC television programme entitled, *The Napoleon of Fleet Street*, presented by Malcolm Muggeridge. 'Cecil King,' Muggeridge began, 'I don't suppose anybody is going to call you the "Napoleon of Holborn", but as the chairman of the biggest extant publishing empire, I suppose you could be regarded as your famous uncle's heir.'

Although this purported to flatter King, Muggeridge's compliment was quickly shown to be a two-edged sword, as he told the audience that Northcliffe's father had been a 'penurious drunken barrister', his 'meteoric success ... a by-product of Foster's Education Act of 1870' that had created 'a new, literate class – a class to which Northcliffe himself belonged'. In his time, Muggeridge explained, Northcliffe had been outwitted by Lloyd George, as his brother Rothermere was later outwitted by Stanley Baldwin. Northcliffe, moreover, had been unstable and perhaps even syphilitic. Muggeridge summed up the great press lord thus: 'Telephoneless, demented and alone, the first and probably the greatest of the twentieth century's newspaper moguls expired in a wooden hut, especially constructed for him on the roof of a house in Carlton Gardens...'

For his part, King pointed out that family lore had his grandparents meeting 'on a park bench', a distinctly lower-class beginning. As to Northcliffe's fabulous wealth, he spent it on 'houses, travel and divided it among family members.' 'My mother's share of all this wealth at any time was an allowance of £2000 a year and that was threatened with being cut off fairly frequently.'

MUGGERIDGE   When there were rows?
KING *nods assent.*
MUGGERIDGE   Between her and her brother?
KING   Mmm. Yes.

And what was it, Muggeridge asked, that Northcliffe really wanted?

'Oh, power ...' King answered dismissively.

This was the moment of his triumph over the family, and King treated it casually, although it was obvious it was important to him. But even as he ascended in the public eye, King was sliding downhill. He had become convinced that Harold Wilson's Labour Government had betrayed its trust to the country. More dangerously, he believed he was the man to right this wrong.

Only three years after his triumphant TV broadcast, on 10 May 1968, he commandeered the front page of the high-circulation *Daily Mirror* and plastered his photograph beside a gigantic headline, 'Enough is

Enough'. His message: 'Mr Wilson and his Government have lost all credibility: all authority.' But it was King who had lost all credibility, all authority, and soon afterwards he was ousted from his position as chairman of the International Publishing Corporation.

Marmaduke Hussey, at the time managing director of Harmsworth Publications, was sitting in his office when he got the flash that Cecil King had been sacked. He immediately rang Esmond saying, 'I've got the most extraordinary story but I can assure you I've double-checked and it is true. Cecil King has just been fired.'

'I'm not surprised! I'm not surprised!' Esmond exclaimed. 'He was looking more and more like de Gaulle every minute and acting more and more like de Gaulle and they've both been fired in the same week!'

More damning by far were the words of Winston Churchill's caustic son, Randolph, who appeared on *The World This Weekend* the week after King was fired. 'Well,' said Randolph, 'Mr Cecil Harmsworth King has a curious background. He had seven uncles – tons of uncles. One of them was Lord Northcliffe. He was a megalomaniac. He went mad. His other uncle, the first Viscount Rothermere – he was a megalomaniac and a coward. Mr King is just a megalomaniac.' The quote was typical of Randolph Churchill who, like King, had been helped by and appeared to despise ever afterwards the Harmsworth family.

More unsavoury charges would surface about Cecil King after his death, however. In one of them, a Member of Parliament noted in a Commons motion 'that Cecil King was controlled by a former MI5 officer identified as a leading co-conspirator in a plot to bring down Harold Wilson's government.'

The story was that on 6 February 1968, Tony Benn, then Minister of Technology in Wilson's government, had lunch with King, later recording in his diary that King was calling for a coalition government, with Denis Healey at its head. The pair discussed devaluation, King predicting there would be another. Benn's diary entry read,

> Literally as we said goodbye, he added, with an air of authority which I thought was really derived from an anticipation of his own projected powers of patronage, 'there may well be a larger part for you to play.'
>
> As I reflected on this conversation, a number of thoughts came to mind. One was that he was really slightly unbalanced . . .

Thus did Esmond's only open competitor fall from the ranks of the great and good, victim of his own ambitions. Since his father divested himself of all his interests in the Mirror Company in the 1930s, Esmond had had to stand guard against first, hot competition from the *Daily Mirror* and second, the ambitions of his hostile cousin.

Through the years, Esmond had successfully protected himself and the Daily Mail and General Trust from assault after assault from Cecil King. He had won fair and square in the single competition he felt he could engage in freely. But through the years he had had a signal ally in the fight – Cecil King himself – who, for reasons unfathomable, sought his own destruction far more actively than Esmond ever could or would have.

While Esmond battled with his competitor, Cecil King, Mike Randall was fighting to change the image of the *Daily Mail*. Randall had been one of the few journalists to be retained from the staff of the *News Chronicle* after the ill-fated merger of 1960 between that paper and the *Mail*. In almost every way Randall was a child of the *News Chronicle*: he was intellectual, liberal, thoughtful. A kind of symbol for the changing times, he wanted the *Daily Mail* to reflect higher values, above the 'gutter journalism' that was beginning to dominate Fleet Street. A kind of wunderkind, he had at the age of thirty-three briefly edited the *Sunday Graphic* during coronation year and it was generally believed that if anyone could raise the tone of the *Mail*, Randall was that man.

Randall was an associate editor on the *Mail* when, according to his own version of events, 'I heard that Hardcastle was going to be sacked.' He and his colleagues considered the situation, believing that the new editor should be selected from the inside. Mike was 'elected' to go to Bobby Redhead, vice-chairman of Associated Newspapers, and tell him this.

> The next thing I knew, I had to go and spend the weekend in the Cotswolds with Rothermere. It was there that Rothermere said, 'What would you do if you were the editor?'
>
> I told him exactly what I would do: 'I would take it upmarket, making it very unlike the *Daily Express*.'
>
> 'That is the hardest course,' Rothermere replied.
>
> That was it. No more discussion. Next thing I knew, Hardcastle had gone on his world tour and I was editor. I knew eventually I would be fired, I couldn't beat the odds, but I wanted 'to have a bash'.

Randall brought a systematic method to trying to improve the *Mail*. Many staff members noticed that he kept a small book in which he would write down all the things that were wrong with the paper. The result of this would be the rather learned monograph that Randall brought out for the edification of the staff entitled, *Why, Why, Why?* The book explained the *Mail*'s position in the market, who the readers were, what their financial situation was, their values, their interests, etc.

He outlined three key points to success: attracting young readers, getting rid of the old-fashioned image of the newspaper and becoming 'intelligent, authoritative' and full of facts.

The path to wisdom lay in abandoning old ideas that were keeping the newspaper from a loftier place in the market. Crime should not be sensational. Long stories were not anathema. Investigative reporting was important for a thoughtful readership. And divorce cases were not *prima facie* interesting.

Randall represented the new intellectualism arising from the changes wrought in the 1960s, for at the same time that London was dubbed 'swinging', to show a new freedom, intellectualism was enjoying a kind of revival in the popular mentality. One of his great achievements on the *Daily Mail*, it was thought by many of his colleagues and a great many readers as well, was to hire Bernard Levin, first as theatre critic and later as a daily columnist. Levin was the thinking man's columnist, as provocative as he was entertaining, and his presence on the paper was in fact a great intellectual coup.

Randall was furthermore an advocate of a new 'objectivism' in reporting. And he was known for inventing, along with the *Mail*'s production editor, Leslie Sellers, a graphic device he called 'the split lead', which was intended to give two leads to an important, front-page story – ostensibly to show that a topic could and often did have two sides.

But not everyone agreed with Randall's approach. His split lead, for example, was quickly labelled 'Randall's folly' by his opponents on staff, who believed that it created confusion on the page by leading the reader in two directions at once. To them, it was a visual nightmare that distorted the news and split the front page. And his disdain for scandals, particularly those dealing with divorce, seemed to many a kind of newsman's suicide.

Be that as it may, Randall initiated a policy of recruitment from the universities that attracted two young men who would eventually become famous in their own right – Nick Lloyd and Jeffrey Archer. Lloyd was editor of *Cherwell* at Oxford and Archer was a volunteer worker for Oxfam.

It was the twenty-first year of Oxfam, and the charity had wanted to raise an extra million over and above their normal income – known as 'The 21st Birthday Million'. But by October 1963 the fund-raisers had managed to find only about £150,000. It was then that Jeffrey Archer had the idea of going to *Cherwell*, where he and Nick Lloyd first met. Archer then made the proposition to Lloyd:

Jeffrey had a great idea, he said. We could raise a million pounds for Oxfam if we got every student at university to go out with a collecting box to collect for the charity. But we would need a national newspaper to back it and we would need somebody like the Beatles to endorse it. They had then become the hottest thing in the world.

I listened and thought he was crackers, but might be right. We were having an off-news week, so I gave it a go and led the student paper in the Oxfam Beatles Drive.

The two managed to talk the Beatles into the project by inviting them and their manager, Brian Epstein, to a dinner at Oxford. It was to be held at Brasenose College, and would be attended by Harold Macmillan, then Chancellor of the University. 'They agreed to that,' said Archer, 'and it was a very good evening with about twenty people there.' He went on:

My staggering memory is of Paul McCarney regretting that he had not gone to university. He was obviously very bright and he seemed genuinely sorry. He seemed to be the easiest of the four. I liked them all. Lennon was a little cynical about fame, Ringo appeared a little lost by the whole thing and George and Paul were very intelligent and interesting to be with.

Since Nick Lloyd was already part of the training scheme for the *Daily Mail*, he went to work talking the newspaper into lending its support to Archer's grand money-raising plan for Oxfam.

'Then we went up to Liverpool,' said Lloyd, 'where the Beatles were appearing in the Liverpool Empire.'

We went on the train and, because they were so big, they had to be locked into the theatre hours before the performance; and somehow we got in, carrying our boxes and posters, and Jeffrey took the pictures.

The Beatles were basically irreverent and didn't appear to give a toss. They had their pictures taken and spent two minutes, and that was it. Then they gave us two seats in the audience and they did *Juke Box Jury* live.

You couldn't hear any of it, girls just screaming, no music at all. It was very exciting.

The *Daily Mail* adopted the campaign as their Christmas project and Archer soon came up with the idea of enlisting more famous people or pop groups to endorse the scheme. He and Lloyd teamed up with staff from the *Daily Mail* and organized a carol concert in Trafalgar Square, well publicized in the *Mail*, and lo and behold, some thirty pop stars turned up to sing with the tens of thousands. In their haste to contribute, people sent their money in envelopes, in cheques, in cash, with no return address envelope to the *Mail*, and eventually much more than the original million was raised.

The following year, *Daily Mail* reporter Dickie Herd, who had helped with the project, was summoned by Mike Randall, who said, 'Go and see how Oxfam has spent the money we raised.' So Herd found himself travelling to Africa, where he spent three days and nights in a leper colony that had benefited from the money. He also went to a school in Nigeria, where Oxfam had spent the cash on seeds and fertilizers.

> The kids were able, for the first time, to make stews with vegetables in a big pot, preventing the malnutrition that had plagued them since birth.
>
> They got the seeds for vegetables from Oxfam and began growing them. And Oxfam also gave them enough money to get their parents to grow a variety of produce, and as a result there must be thousands of lives since saved in these remote little villages in Nigeria, all because of Oxfam's campaign.

These were only two of the projects funded by the '21st Birthday Million' campaign.

Back in London, Archer gained the reputation for being a phenomenal fund-raiser at a very young age, leading to his first job. And Nick Lloyd got a permanent position on the *Daily Mail* after his graduation.

The fund-raising event was popular from start to finish, but another, rather sinister event during Randall's years as editor was the jailing of two journalists in 1963 who refused to disclose their sources of information to a tribunal of enquiry into the Vassall spy case. It was a scandal that caused the resignation of Thomas Galbraith, a former Civil Lord of the Admiralty from his position as joint Scottish under-secretary.

John Vassall was the thirty-eight-year-old civil servant who had been sentenced to eighteen years' imprisonment for selling Admiralty secrets to the Soviet Union. There had been some unsavoury photographs taken by the Soviet secret police depicting Vassall in homosexual poses when he was stationed in Moscow in 1952.

Although several journalists questioned as to their sources were prepared to go to jail for contempt of court, *Daily Mail* reporter Brendan Mulholland and *Daily Sketch* reporter Reg Foster became the scapegoats for what many believed was a retaliatory tribunal set up by a government angry over the Profumo affair. Mulholland had refused to say who told him that Vassall's colleagues in the Admiralty knew he was homosexual and called him 'Aunty'; that he lived far beyond his means as a £15-a-week clerk; and that sponsorship by two officials had exempted him from the rigorous vetting that usually takes place when hiring employees for the Admiralty. Reg Foster, a veteran Fleet Street reporter who had been hired on the *Mail* by the legendary Tom Marlowe just after the death of Northcliffe, was now working for the *Sketch*. He refused to say who had told him that Vassall bought and frequently wore women's clothing.

The plight of the two men became something of a *cause célèbre* – although both did in the end serve their entire sentences, six months for Mulholland and three months for Reg Foster.

The news editor of the *Daily Mail* was Monty Court, who was the first person to go down, apart from his family, to see Brendan in prison. Court asked Mulholland's wife if he wanted anything and she answered, 'Yes, money.' Taking money to a prisoner carried extremely high penalties, but Court did not believe he could deny Brendan anything he needed, so he bought some After Eights, and put a five-pound note into one of the envelopes that held the mints. This he placed on the table between them when he went to visit him.

Since he was the first official visitor, the governor made a point of coming over and speaking to him: 'Hello, Mr Court. After Eights! May I have one?' Court was fit to be tied and, after the warden left – without picking the mint that had the fiver in it – he said to Brendan,

> 'For Christ's sake, get the money out of there! What do you want this money for?'
>
> 'I just want some money.'
>
> Well, I must have needed having my head examined, because I then said to Reg Foster, 'Reg, can I get you anything? Want any money?'
>
> He said, 'We're not allowed money!' at the top of his voice in the public visiting room! I was so scared by the experience that I vowed never to do it again and insisted that Mrs Mulholland find an alternative way of getting money to Brendan.

Monty Court was something of an old-time newshound, certainly more a Hardcastle than a Randall man, and he more or less openly opposed Randall's interdict against aggressive reporting of the grislier details of a crime, or the juicy gossip associated with celebrity divorce cases. 'For God's sake,' he asked Randall, 'what do you do with the Duchess of Argyll's divorce case?' which at the time was a newspaper sensation that challenged the Profumo affair. To which Randall is said to have replied, 'I suppose I'll have to carry some of it.' Court believed the effect on sales would be 'absolutely disastrous', especially since the *Daily Express* was playing the quite sensational story for all it was worth.

Known for his slow, laconic wit, Court was a Fleet Street character who was extremely popular among his colleagues. Joan Gabbedey was his secretary at the time and she still remembers one of Court's methods of cutting down on reporters' expenses. He would write a letter saying that, sadly, it was necessary for him 'to sober up your sources'.

Then again, it was Court who cooked up a scheme whereby the *Mail* could scoop the other papers when Winston Churchill died. They simply paid one of the nurses tending Churchill to make a phone call to a prearranged number saying, 'I'm sorry, I won't be able to get away tonight.' In this way they got a three-hour lead on the rest of the world's press.

Monty Court, who admitted readily that his style of reportage was 'by the seat of my pants', said that some of his success came from savvy, some from hard graft, but 'I did have the luck'. On one occasion when the *Express* had left the *Mail* completely behind for a story 'and we were left for dead', Monty was dreading the following day. 'But it turned out to be the luckiest night of my life. At eleven at night, Aly Khan killed himself in a car crash. This story they were going to take us to the cleaners with finished up with about five paragraphs.' The front page of the next day's *Mail* was filled with photographs of the playboy with the various women in his life, including Rita Hayworth, the film star, who was his second wife.

It was Monty Court's fate to have on his staff an older reporter by the name of Paul Bewsher – a man who caused him tremendous trouble. It was said that Bewsher had been one of Northcliffe's bright young men and that when Bewsher returned from the First World War the press baron had promised him that he would have 'a job for life'. It must have seemed so to Court who, in the early 1960s, was the one who had to deal with him.

Bewsher avowed that he hated 'the white stuff', meaning daylight, and loved 'the dark stuff', meaning night-time. And so he had managed to secure a late shift from about 7 p.m. until 2 a.m. Usually, however, Bewsher wouldn't get in until around eleven and he was usually the worse for wear, having spent his evening in his favourite place – the Press Club. Bewsher was the kind of character who put in his *Who's Who* entry that his favourite hobby was 'Walking from pub to pub'. Monty and other members of the *Mail* staff were relieved when someone omitted the last four words, simply leaving it as 'Walking'. Bewsher called his drink, which was gin and ginger ale, 'Ogie Boo' and as he had generally imbibed far too much, Monty Court came to think of him as useless.

Night after night, Bewsher was late to work and when Monty called him down, he would charm him by telling him some long-winded story or joke, taking Monty in totally. He always seemed short of money and this was a result of having drawn and drawn on the *Mail*, then failing to file any expense requests, leaving himself constantly in arrears. Thus, he was reduced to begging for money from one or other of the staff and generally making a nuisance of himself.

Like many Fleet Street characters, however, Paul Bewsher was more complicated than he looked. Early after taking over, Monty sent him to cover a story in which two tankers had collided and burst into flames in the Severn Estuary. Once he had been assigned the story, Bewsher had called the pubs round the estuary, being familiar with them all, and not only had he managed to get an eyewitness account of the collision, but he also talked to several of the survivors who had just been pulled from the water. Even though Monty learned to respect the old reporter's news acumen, however, Bewsher was still a thorn in Monty's side. Once, after chewing him out for coming in either late or under the weather, Monty found himself 'placed properly into Bewsher's timescale when he said to me, "Do you know, Old Man? I think you're the twenty-eighth news editor I've worked for on the *Mail*." '

It seemed that Bewsher lived only on rock cakes and he joked constantly about taking home the crumbs to feed to the mice in his flat. Once, Monty inadvertently hurt Bewsher deeply because he was off with the flu and Monty sent someone to his address to see if he was all right. The reporter said that he was deeply embarrassed that a colleague had been to his flat, and seen what kind of abject and squalid circumstances he lived in.

When Paul Bewsher died, as he would have wished and as Northcliffe promised, still in the saddle, an in-house sheet given out by one of his relatives on the staff was circulated. On it were written his accomplishments in life.

> Scholar at St Paul's School: Port of London Authority for short time, then Advertising Magazine. DFC First World War – Captain in the Royal Naval Air Service. Received decoration from King George V...
>
> First served in a kite balloon ship at the Dardanelles. Commissioned as Observer in the Royal Naval Air Service. Took part in the bombing of Bruges. Plane crashed into sea off Zeebrugge at night and was picked up by the glare of a British destroyer's searchlight...
>
> He never flew without his black kitten and wrote poems on night bombing flights, and a few others. Highly thought of by Lord Northcliffe, and the first Lord Rothermere took him as his sole companion on a cruise to South America because 'he was the only man who could make him laugh when he didn't feel like laughing'.

In his obituary, written by Vincent Mulchrone on 19 January 1966, it was pointed out that 'He dropped his first bombs by hand from an open cockpit' and was the 'first poet of the air'.

He was a correspondent in the Spanish Civil War and the first one in with the British Expeditionary Force in World War II, where only six British correspondents were allowed. 'It was said of him, with accuracy,' Mulchrone wrote, 'that he was always late into the office and never late on a story.'

The least-known fact about Bewsher was that he had several books of poems to his name, written when he was a pilot in the primitive aeroplanes of the First World War. 'Sometimes I fly at dawn above the sea,' he had written in his poem 'The Dawn Patrol',

> Where, underneath, the restless waters flow –
> Silver, and cold, and slow.
> Dim in the East there burns a new-born sun,
> Whose rosy gleams along the ripples run,
> Save where the mist droops low,
> Hiding the level loneliness from me...
>
> Then do I feel with God quite, quite alone,
> High in the virgin morn, so white and still,
> And free from human ill:
> My prayers transcend my feeble earth-bound plaints –
> As though I sang among the happy Saints
> With many a holy thrill –
> As though the glowing sun were God's bright throne.
>
> My flight is done. I cross the line of foam
> That breaks around a town of grey and red,
> Whose streets and squares lie dead
> Beneath the silent dawn – then am I proud
> That England's peace to guard I am allowed; –
> Then bow my humble head,
> In thanks to Him Who brings me safely home.

The nature of working on the *Daily Mail* was that none of the journalists who came and went – no more no less than a stint in their careers – had an overview of the life of the paper and the other practitioners of the trade who worked alongside them at the *Mail*.

It was only in the course of doing their job, writing an obituary or looking up an entry in *Who's Who*, that they were apprised of the life's blood of the *Daily Mail*. Then, at last, a man like Paul Bewsher could be viewed in the context of his remarkable life and career.

Now it was Monty Court's turn to put his imprint on the newspaper of which he was the news editor.

No mean accomplishment for a desk man, Court initiated three major campaigns that resulted in legislation to halt practices that were putting the public at risk.

In one of them, the photograph of a five-year-old child, Jacqueline Jones, was published in the *Daily Mail* after her nightie caught fire as she was playing with her favourite doll in front of the living-room fire. 'How many more, Mr Brooke?' the headline asked the Home Secretary. Another story entitled 'A life for 5d' stressed the low cost of flame-proofing children's nightware. 'In just 85 seconds a child can be killed or disfigured,' the article went on to explain, showing photographs of an experiment that demonstrated the difference between non-flame-proofed and flammable nightgowns.

Court had two children of his own and one of the first stories he did when he joined the *Daily Mail* was on a small boy whose house was hit by a plane that crashed only a few seconds after take-off. Court remembered the influence the young boy had on him:

> Brian Gibson was then nine, and he went back into this inferno to rescue his cousins and was awarded the George Medal. He got terribly badly burnt and I did a series of stories on him from the time of the crash. I visited him several times in hospital and saw the agonies and saw lots of kids in burn units so that was why I was particularly sensitive about fires.
>
> You could buy some solution which you dipped normal untreated cotton in and it did render it to a certain extent flame-proof but not properly. In the days of open fires when there was no central heating, it was common for children to stand in their nightclothes in front of the fire. It took years and years to get adequate safeguards.
>
> I didn't necessarily think about it as consumer reporting but just, 'This is the bloody newspaper's responsibility, its duty.'

Court was responsible for another campaign after he went for a meal at Smithfield and decided to order steak. He happened to mention to the waiter that the meat 'looked nice and fresh', and the waiter responded that they now had powders that 'you could put on the soles of your shoes and bring it up looking red and succulent'.

The *Mail* led the way against this practice by documenting the illness that could result when families ate meat treated with the dyes that were frequently put on them. In a leader entitled 'The Red Meat Racket' the *Mail* took the authorities to task for waiting for a newspaper to lead the way. 'As a result of our disclosures, the Meat Traders' Federation has advised its members to drop the colouring agents pending the result of a Government inquiry, now proceeding.'

And on 20 December, in a front-page story, the *Daily Mail* wrote 'Meat Victory: Minister will stop powders'.

The use of dusting powders that make stale meat look fresh is to be stopped, the Government announced yesterday.

The end of the artificial 'freshening' racket follows a Food Standards Committee investigation...

The ban was announced in the Commons and the Lords after eight days of campaigning by the *Daily Mail*.

It was also under Court's direction that the practice of recutting worn-out tyres was put under investigation, leading to another fully fledged campaign against what the *Mail* called 'Killer Tyres'. The news team assigned to the topic found that there were twenty-six dealers in the London area alone selling the recut, regrooved tyres. Some of the tyres they investigated in 1964 had been found to be manufactured as long before as 1938. The *Mail* wrote,

Reporter Chris Underwood and a colleague went to one of the advertisers, the Pentonville Tyre Service, in Penton-street, Pentonville, London.

Without revealing who they were, they asked for four 16 in. recuts for an old Vauxhall. The dealer, nodding at a huge pile of tyres on the pavement, said: 'Help yourself. They are all recuts.'

By April 1965 the Transport Minister announced the ban on the sale and use of re-cut tyres on cars and vans.

Despite the success of this campaign and the others, however, Monty Court's days at the *Daily Mail* were numbered. A great fan of horse-racing, Court made a point of going to the Cheltenham Races every March and in 1965 he had just come back into the office when Joan Gabbedey said that the editor wanted to see him.

As Monty Court remembered it, Mike Randall stood in his office, eating an apple. He walked across to the fireplace and leaned against it, still chewing, and said, 'Things aren't working out.' Many years later, Court said he could still remember Randall's loud smacking as he ate the apple during the sacking.

Then again, Randall sacked another well-known figure on the newspaper – the fashion editor Iris Ashley. When Randall made the decision he must have been aware of the chance he was taking of antagonizing Rothermere. He said, several years later,

Iris Ashley had been the former girlfriend of Lord Rothermere so it was extremely difficult. The main thing was that the stuff she wrote was far too upmarket all the time. She wrote about all kinds of things that our readers couldn't buy, and in the end I went to Rothermere and said, 'I really think she has had her time with the *Mail*, she's not in the right market', and he agreed and I'm sure he gave her an enormous pay-off.

It was the end of an era; for better or worse, a new set of values was overtaking the public and the Sixties were swinging in. Perhaps it was true that Iris's extravagant style was no longer in step with the times. But her friends believed Randall would in the long run pay a high price for his ruthless culling of the staff. One of Iris's friends, columnist Godfrey Winn, wrote her a note of sympathy when he heard that she was out:

> It seems to be a suicide policy the present editor is pursuing. First he axes Quentin Crewe, who has great brilliance and really is in the know and he has sources ... which the ordinary run of journalists haven't and ... then he forces you to resign who has such authority and prestige and so many powerful friends in the fashion world ...
>
> I think [Rothermere] is in a terrible state himself over what has happened to the *Mail*, and if I was a proprietor, I would interfere before ... disaster. His argument is that the present madman must be given enough rope to hang himself.

Randall was no madman, but he did cherish some peculiar notions. One of them was that Lord Rothermere was a Liberal. He concluded this from a set of events that occurred more than once. Randall had to go to dinner with Rothermere at Warwick House from time to time and he would be able to bring him around to the newspaper, usually over the brandy. And Rothermere would say, 'Yes, yes, yes, okay, if that's what you think, you do that.'

> Then on the 5.30 telephone call, I'd suddenly get a blat on the telephone. I could detect that there was somebody else in the room. 'What the hell do you think you're doing?' Rothermere would ask him.
>
> Mike would say, 'We agreed that.'
>
> And Rothermere would reply, 'No, I don't remember it. I don't agree at all.'

Randall believed Rothermere did agree, but he had been attacked by his friends. Randall was convinced others were listening in the background. Rothermere might not be strong in his beliefs, but beneath it all, he was a liberal man. True, Randall would admit, Rothermere was outwardly clothed as a Tory. But at heart, Mike believed, he was a Liberal.

To some extent, Randall was probably projecting his own values on to his proprietor. Then came Randall's personal catastrophy: he developed serious back trouble and was forced to lie still for about six months. In the interval of time, it seemed to the writers on the staff who were loyal to Randall that his power was being eroded. Said Peter Lewis,

> So Bernard Levin and I rang him up and said, 'We're coming to see you.' Once

we were there, we said, 'We don't know if you know this, but we think they're trying to get you out.'

He said, 'No, it's the first I've heard of it.'

'How is your standing with Lord Rothermere?' we asked him.

'Well, I don't have any contact with Lord Rothermere, or hardly any, since I became editor because when I became editor I submitted my plans, my programme for the *Daily Mail*, and it was accepted and so I took it that I was to carry that out.'

So we said, 'Have you been in constant touch with him since then?'

He said, 'Well, no.'

This didn't sound very hopeful, and secondly when we said, 'Who among the senior executives' – we went through a list – 'shall we ask to sign a letter?'

All too often he said, 'No, I don't think I should ask him.'

So we went away from his house pretty gloomy because we said to each other, 'I don't know what we can do to save him,' and indeed he went, quite soon after.

If, in fact, the first Randall had heard of the possibility of his sacking was from Lewis and Levin, he did believe his days were numbered from the moment Arthur Brittenden was brought on to the newspaper. Circulation had fallen – in large part because the *Mail* had failed to raise its prices when its competitors did. When at last it did raise prices, as it inevitably had to, it suffered a big drop. Nevertheless, Randall had built a constituency, both among the writers on the staff and the readers who bought the newspaper. Perhaps it was the writing; possibly it was Monty Court's intelligent campaigns; maybe it was both.

Nevertheless, practically on the eve of the *Daily Mail*'s editor winning the coveted 'Journalist of the Year Award', Mike Randall was sacked. And whether or not Randall's days had been numbered since the hiring of Arthur Brittenden, the latter did become the next editor. There was a story that made the rounds, unsubstantiated but widely told, that at the time of Randall's firings Vere Harmsworth, innocent bystander and interested observer, said to Brittenden, 'Let this be a lesson to you, Arthur, not to win any awards.'

It was surely a joke. Vere Harmsworth had no serious objections to the winning of awards. But if the truth were told, Esmond's son believed that the real measure of a newspaper's success could be found at 'the box-office'.

10

'Walk Tall'

The men who reported from the north of England believed they were the salt of the earth, the best reporters in the land. Those who went south were softies looking for an easy life. And during bouts at the pub in Manchester it was not uncommon for the youngsters to swear they would never go to London, but stay where the journalism was pure.

Especially in Manchester, there was a strong tradition to live up to. Jimmy Lewthwaite was the all-knowing night news editor, and when Jack Crossley joined the office, he was put on the late shift, where he became one of Lewthwaite's boys. 'Lewthwaite', said Crossley, 'believed in accuracy and integrity. If you got a fact wrong, it was an unforgivable sin. He bred into me the need to ask ten questions to get one fact.'

Lewthwaite once sent Jack Crossley to cover a murder story in Blackpool by bus. 'By bus?' Jack complained. 'And bring back the receipt.' He then said, as he always said to any reporter going out on a story, 'Keep in touch, Old Man.'

When he was breaking them in, Lewthwaite called his reporters by their last names. When he began calling them by their first, it meant they were learning their craft. At last came the day when the newcomer was asked for a drink at the pub. That meant the reporter had finally arrived and Lewthwaite thought he could carry his weight. The men drank halves of bitter. The first drink was inevitably 'one for the road'. Then there would be a 'final'; then a 'final binder'; then a 'final flying binder'. And, as often as not, they all ended up having a plate of Lancashire hot-pot cooked by Lewthwaite's wife.

Louis Kirby, who was broken in at the Manchester office some years before Crossley, remembered Lewthwaite as a taciturn man with bright-blue eyes. 'He would come in to take over for the night,' said Kirby,

and he would be wearing a jacket that had holes in each elbow. And he used to walk around whistling tunelessly and speaking as little as possible to anyone. And I went in on Good Friday, and Lewthwaite started whistling tunelessly, and took off his jacket, and nodded his head to indicate I should go with him. And he went out, down the steps of the bureau, and I found myself in church. So we knelt down for a service and stayed there for half an hour. Then, still whistling tunelessly, Lewthwaite took me into a pub and we had some soft drinks and there he spoke for the first time.

So many first-class reporters came through the Manchester office that it took on a kind of cult status in the business: the great Parliamentary reporter Walter Terry served his apprenticeship there, as did Rodney Hallworth, one of the *Daily Mail*'s greatest crime reporters. Harold Pendlebury also started in Manchester, honing the style he would use to charm his sources and learning how to get a worthwhile interview.

Brian MacArthur had gone from Leeds University directly into reporting for the *Yorkshire Post*, where he was told by a friend that there was a job on the *Daily Mail* in Manchester. By now the news editor was Ken Donlan, another news legend. Said MacArthur, 'Ken had this team of young guys whose lives he terrorized. You had to wear a neat dark suit and white shirt. I had an interview. We went through "What have you done?" all that, he then said, "You're highly strung, aren't you?" I jumped and said, "Am I?" Well, I got the job.'

The life of a beginning reporter could be difficult. He might get a call at 8 a.m. saying, 'Get over to Sheffield and follow that story on page four of the *Daily Express*.' If he was dumb enough to say 'What story?' he was finished. As soon as he got the story, he would be put straight on to 'copy' and he then dictated the story over the telephone.

MacArthur ran into trouble pretty quickly because he had had a tiff with the woman he wanted to marry – a TWA air hostess. So when he should have been at work, he went down to Heathrow to give her an engagement ring on her stop-over on the Frankfurt–Washington flight. He presented the ring, she accepted and he hurried back to Manchester. 'Two Saturdays later she got married to an accounts executive at J. Walter Thompson,' said MacArthur.

Anyway Ken Donlan, the next day, totally froze me out. Everybody was invited out to lunch but me. I was left on the news desk on my own. That was the signal of his displeasure.

So after this unfortunate love affair and to console myself, I bought this really swish corduroy coat, three-quarter length, dark-green muddy corduroy, and I was going out on a job where you had to be photographed. And Ken said, 'If you work for the *Daily Mail* you can't wear a coat like that.' And he fetched out his wallet and said, 'Here's £10. Go get yourself a decent coat.'

A piece of advice Donlan gave MacArthur when he was just starting out was. 'Just tell the story.' MacArthur believes to this day that it is the most profound piece of journalistic advice he has ever had. And if your copy was bad, he would walk right up to you and rip it up in front of your face. 'He was a brilliant news editor,' said MacArthur. 'When there was a tremendous train crash, he moved the news desk out to the crash and filed from there.'

It was Donlan, too, who originated one of the most frequently quoted aphorisms in the *Daily Mail* lexicon. The targeted opposition was the *Daily Express* and the whole thrust of every reporter in the *Mail* office was to smash the opposition. All too often, however, there were five *Express* reporters assigned to every one on the *Daily Mail*. At least, that was how it felt. Ken became famous because one of his reporters rang up one day and said, 'There are five guys from the *Express* and only me from the *Mail* on this story. What should I do?'

'Walk tall,' came the answer.

Perhaps the most famous of the reporters ever to come out of Manchester was Vincent Mulchrone – raconteur and writer. Both his chat and his introductions were legend in Fleet Street. He began on the *Daily Mail* when he met a reporter from the office. He had just been laid off by the *Mirror* and the reporter said, 'Come and see me later.' Later that day, he came on staff.

Shortly after Vincent joined, there was a very rare visit to the Manchester office by Lord Rothermere. The reporters were lined up for presentation and appraisal, Mulchrone among them. 'Where did you work before you came to the *Mail*?' Esmond asked Mulchrone.

'At the *Mirror*, Sir,' was the reply.

'Why did you leave?' queried his lordship.

'I was sacked, Sir.' Other reporters snorted with embarrassment, but Lord Rothermere simply nodded without comment and moved on.

When Louis Kirby first met Vincent Mulchrone he was the star of the Manchester office. But it wasn't long before London began to notice 'the general grace of his writing' and he was invited down. For a time he resisted, because he didn't want to uproot his wife and three children. Eventually, however, he ended up on the London staff of the *Daily Mail*. By now Louis Kirby was based in Dublin and Vincent recommended him to the editor in London, an action that endeared him to the young reporter.

When I got there, the first thing Vincent did was to take me across to a little pub, the Harrow, in a backstreet very close to the *Daily Mail* offices just off Fleet Street where he had champagne every morning, as soon as the pub opened about eleven o'clock. Then it was back to work. It was the start of his day; then he would perform absolute miracles on his typewriter.

The life Mulchrone lived was one of crossing and recrossing the globe, following the royals or covering the Olympics or keeping up with breaking news in Moscow or other capitals of the world. His wife took care of all the household responsibilities, including the raising of their three sons. His son, Patrick, remembered what it was like to try to get a glimpse of his father:

> I think we knew the way to Heathrow Airport before we knew the way to the local church, and Heathrow Airport was a good thirty miles away but my mother could do it blindfolded. She wouldn't drive to town, she wouldn't drive further than the local shop, she didn't like it, but she could get in and out of Heathrow like threading a needle.
>
> We would get calls at all hours of the day and night; even in our pyjamas, we would go to the International Building or the Queen's Building and stand outside the arrivals doors. There was a strange thing at that time – Heathrow used to have conveyor belts that would take the baggage into the arrivals halls but they'd come out through a sort of valley so you could see the baggage going in. You'd literally know exactly when he was going to come out through that opaque door.
>
> One time when he was coming in from somewhere exotic and going out to somewhere cold, and there was no time to get home, my mother was rung from some far-flung place and told, 'Pack all my cold gear, my heavy gear.' And he unloaded his suitcase on the floor of the arrivals building while she shovelled the lightweight stuff in. We three boys stood in our dressing-gowns watching my mother transfer hot-weather kit from a suitcase into a bag.

There was a great sadness about Vincent Mulchrone that many of his colleagues and even his sons recognized. He had wanted to be a poet, a writer of lyrical prose, and he had never made it. 'And the sadness with Vincent was he couldn't just settle for being the greatest at what he was. That was always about him. When you knew him well, there was a regret in him that he hadn't further achieved, but he was the icon of newspaper reporters in Britain.'

Another theory was that Mulchrone wished he could be writing for a Labour newspaper and, said Vere Harmsworth, 'he always was tortured by the fact that he was writing for a Tory newspaper. His heart was really on the left.' Harmsworth, now Lord Rothermere, continued:

> He was a great companion; we used to play golf. The caddy used to come out with the iced champagne at strategic positions, and be waiting for us . . . Vincent loved that sort of thing.
>
> There was definitely a sad streak that was in him. He was a man full of heart. I went to his funeral. It was remarkable in the sense that there were people

virtually hanging from the rafters, he was so well loved. When he was buried, there were crowds of people standing around. It was very moving.

Before his premature death at fifty-four from leukaemia, Vincent Mulchrone made his imprint upon the minds of his colleagues with his brilliant introductions, which he wrote with his gold pen, padding over to the 'arrer' for a half a bottle of champagne whenever he needed inspiration.

One of his wilder introductions read:

I was shaving waist deep in the Areguma, a pastry slice for a mirror, when this cannibal swam down the river bed and grabbed my ankles.

Well, I mean, I'd searched London without success for a chrome mirror. The pastry slice, my wife's idea, was the ideal substitute. A girl in the chemist's had suggested a compact. I'm glad I said no. The cannibals, apart from the taste for homo sapiens, have another for homosexuality. Happily, the one who dug his nails into my ankles wanted only to play crocodiles.

Or more prosaically, Mulchrone writes about a slightly atypical lunchtime:

I lunched backwards yesterday. 'Good morning sir,' said the waiter.

'Goodbye,' I replied, and for an aperitif ordered coffee and brandy.

He reacted with an aplomb which, if you could bottle the stuff, would be worth a guinea a sniff. 'Certainly, Sir,' he said and passed on the order...

'Then,' I said with increasing firmness, 'I'll have La Tranche d'Ananas au Kirsch, *followed* by roast beef and Yorkshire pudding. And to follow – soup. A little chilled Vichyssoise.'

He didn't bat an eyelid. He reacted to my choice with such pleasure that I thought he was going to smack his lips. Taking firm control of a mounting hysteria I went on: 'And last of all I'll have a glass of dry sherry.'

The iron-nerved servant inscribed a last hieroglyphic on his pad and, without a trace of irony, asked: 'Would you like some olives and nuts with the sherry, sir?'

In a vain effort to regain control of the situation I told him that my purpose was to lunch backwards. 'Of course, sir,' he said. 'Would you prefer the bill *now*?'

Of his many introductions, perhaps the most famous was written on 30 July 1966. It appeared under the headline, 'World Cup or World War': 'If the Germans beat us at our national game today, we can always console ourselves with the fact that we have twice beat them at theirs.'

And, finally, the classic beginning of Vincent Mulchrone's obituary on Winston Churchill: 'Two rivers run silently through London tonight, and one is made of people. Dark and quiet as the night-time Thames itself, it flows through Westminster Hall, eddying about the foot of the rock called Churchill.'

A genuine Fleet Street character, Vincent Mulchrone ran into heavy trouble at the *Daily Mail* because he failed to file his expenses – for quite a long time. Eventually he had run up a bill of some £7000 and the managing editor told him he needed to file his expenses by Friday. So unappealing was this prospect to Vincent that instead of agreeing to file as requested, he resigned on the spot. The *Daily Express* was constantly after him and, rather than fill out the necessary forms, Vincent was willing to go.

One of the senior editing staff, Gordon MacKenzie, sought to keep him:

So I took him out to the Ivy and ordered a bottle of champagne and I remember saying, 'As this is the last bottle I'm going to be buying you, we'd better make it Dom Perignon.'

So we had a bottle and we drank it and he said, 'If that's the last you're going to buy me, then I'll buy you one.' We had another bottle of Dom Perignon and drank it, and then he said, 'I think we could do with a third.' So we ordered a third bottle.

The manager of the Ivy now whispered in my ear, 'If you intend to drink any more champagne, I delicately suggest you should have something to eat.' So he came along with a little basket with gull's eggs, put them down and by this time I think we were well into our fourth bottle. It was really quite dreadful and I couldn't see or eat or talk.

By this time Vincent had agreed to have a go at staying on.

My wife got me to bed somehow and I woke up the next morning and to my astonishment I felt, well, I didn't have a hangover and I thought, 'This is just proof of how important it is to drink Vincent's champagne.' And then I ran my tongue over my teeth, all I could feel was sharp things, pointed edges, all the way along like a saw and I thought, 'Somebody's hit me and I've lost all my teeth.'

So I struggled to the bathroom and there in my teeth were gull's egg shells. We were so drunk that we'd been putting the unpeeled gull's eggs in our mouths and eating them whole!

During these years when characters like Donlan and Mulchrone were making their mark on the *Daily Mail*, the man who would one day come to be known as 'Mr *Daily Mail*' was abroad in America, honing his skills.

His first stint was as foreign correspondent for the *Sunday Dispatch* and it was here that David English made the acquaintance, in 1959, of Alan Watkins, who was at the time reporting for the *Sunday Express* in New York City. Watkins said that there were several attempts to turn his mind against David English by his colleagues on the sister publication, the *Daily Express*. 'You've got to watch David English, you know,' they would say to Watkins. 'He's a very sly character and a good operator, and he'll pull a fast one over you.'

So Watkins was appropriately armed when he first met 'this rather charming, sort of boyish chap, in a blue-striped shirt, very neatly dressed, and we got on really very well. He never told me anything and I never told him anything.'

The pair of them used to meet one another in one of the bars along Third Avenue. Watkins remembered that one Saturday morning, when they got in, they were both being requested to go and investigate a story about 'a chap on the Eastside who had in his apartment a giant Peruvian earthworm, some two feet long'.

> Of all the things going on in the world! We were charged to go to this place, this man's apartment. We were to spare no expense and even hire a photographer to photograph it.
>
> And I said to David, 'These things, I don't like these earthworms. I don't like the sound of this at all, I don't want to go. It will upset me.'
>
> And English said, 'Come along. Be a man. Pull yourself together. Why don't you let me buy you lunch?'

But Watkins could not be persuaded under any circumstances. And he let it be known he would rather English got the scoop than go along with him, even to the extent of losing his job.

> 'Well, all right, then,' David said finally. 'We'll tell them that the man won't let us in, that he's guarding this earthworm. We'll both send identical cables.'
>
> We both behaved, journalistically, in a scandalous way owing to my cowardice, and David showed himself far from being the chap who would pull a fast one, instead to be a great friend who didn't mind looking out for his comrade's susceptibilities.

It was true among the press corps in the United States, English was becoming quite a popular figure, as well liked by the Americans as by the British. It was completely in character, then, when the New York newspapers went on strike, for David to organize a strike-breaking newspaper.

English was fascinated by what might happen if one combined British and American journalism. 'Really you could get the worst of both worlds or the best of both worlds,' he said.

> So when the papers shut down, I had this great idea to start a paper. We hired offices, and then I found a printer in White Plains – the *White Plains Reporter*

Dispatch, which is now a gazette paper, but was independently owned in those days, and they were ready to print the paper.

So I got a whole bunch of American guys, all out of work and three or four Brits and we all put in whatever we could put in, took shares in it. And we got advertising guys who were also out of work. I was the editor. We got the drivers' union to distribute it for us.

So I went to see the Mafioso in charge of the drivers' union and we did a deal with them. They were only too happy to do it because it got some money for their men and it maybe was putting pressure on the papers, but to me it was a laboratory combining the two forms of journalism.

Where the newspaper fell down was on advertising – not in selling, all the major department stores wanted adverts – but in collecting, because the *New York Chronicle*, later called the *New York Standard*, wasn't going to be paid for at best thirty and at worst ninety days.

English had thought the banks would lend them operating costs, but the banks thought the new newspaper would fold the minute the dailies came back.

After about ten days, the newspaper was running out of money and no one knew where it would come from. Said English:

I went to see a man called Waxy Gordon. He had some office on Broadway. Anyway, we did a deal which of course virtually took away all the profits, but allowed us to go on producing the paper.

The Mafia were able to collect all this advertising money which had amounted to probably millions, at least a million and a half. We all got our money back, we got about three times our investment but as we'd worked night and day for weeks, we all took a salary as well . . .

But, of course, had we been able to structure it properly, they would have had about twenty times our money because we really did get quite fat in the end.

The fat was taken up by the Mafia and, far from being repelled by these denizens of the deep, English was actually transfixed. He loved their names, their *Guys and Dolls* glamour, their overstated mannerisms – he loved America. It was all part of his great exuberance for living, his enthusiasm for all that he encountered.

The strike newspaper was a learning experience, however. Confident as always that he could organize others into a coherent working unit, his actual capacity for sustained leadership was established by the New York experiment.

English advanced from being the foreign correspondent on the *Daily Express* to the Washington correspondent and finally to the chief foreign correspondent. When, in 1965, he returned to the *Express* in London, it must have seemed something of a let-down. America had a popular mentality, and one that someone as sparky as English was bound to benefit from. England was still austere, the entrepreneurial spirit was minimal and the country seemed grey in comparison with the flash of the United States.

Once home and back working at the *Express*, however, English was able to move from foreign editor to associate editor swiftly and with relative ease. He seemed to know instinctively how to cut through the political morass and get what he wanted. None of his subordinates would ever discover exactly how he did it, but one of his earliest achievements on the newspaper was to set up a special investigative team that became known as the 'SMERSH Unit'.

English's idea was that he would have a core team who were experienced in hard news reporting and who could descend on big stories instantaneously. They would then blitz them with in-depth reporting, analysis and background, in the process annihilating the competition. English recruited a team which consisted of Andrew Fyall, Jim Davies, Struan Coupar and Colin Smith. Others like Gareth Parry and Ivor Key were also enlisted later.

The team was completely separate from the rest of the *Express* newsgathering operation. They had their own room in the building; it was rather posh. By some reckonings, it was of a higher standard than the office of the editor, Derek Marks.

The room was well-equipped with reference books that weren't available at the *Express* library. And there were special deliveries of magazines that were too expensive for other departments to order. The unit had its own tea, coffee and soup machines, and these were negotiated directly. None of the reporters inside the unit knew where the budget came from, but it didn't take them long to realize that they were much better equipped than the news reporters. They had their own secretary as well; they *even* had their own copytakers.

Most critically for the success of the unit, none of David's men was able to work on the shift rotas of the news desk and, for all their sense of prestige, it wasn't long before the group began to feel isolated and ostracized.

David actively encouraged the team to drink in separate pubs, and an *esprit de corps* informed the group to the extent that they knew they were the élite, and they began to like it. English's methods were so stylish and professional that gaining plaudits from him was the shared goal of the united group. On the other hand, he expected to be able to put his finger on the entire group at a moment's notice. The wife, the family, the girlfriend – everything had to take a back-seat to the unit.

The young David English gave an impression of success. Said Jim Davies,

> He dressed very smartly, very well, very trendily and he liked us to dress quite well. He used to make the occasional remark to me and he used to say, 'You must wear a tie if you interview anybody.'
>
> His clothes were pretty expensive. He had a rather classic handsome face, his hair was always rather stylishly cut and he had great charm. If any of us ever brought wives or girlfriends to the bar and introduced him, he'd charm them off their feet.
>
> David always had an aura of power around him, he was very easy with people, he was an easy conversationalist, he had quite a depth of conversation, with pretty catholic tastes and he was so easy to talk to that people naturally felt at ease in his company.
>
> I think some women saw him as a romantic figure, others were simply charmed by the conversational ease. As my then wife once said to me, women have a sense of knowing when a man genuinely liked women and he liked women. She said she felt all the time that he didn't have to make an effort, he genuinely did like women, not in a sexual sense of trying to make a contact.

So far as English's own home life went, his reporters had the impression it was rock solid. He and his wife Irene were very close, and she was reputed to have made a great deal of money in the launderette business. Jim Davies again:

> I used to get the impression that she was a tower of strength for him and that when he went home there was a cocoon of support and warmth and love and friendship and I think genuine admiration. I barely knew her but I got the impression that she absolutely not only loved him but admired him tremendously as well. Certainly he was incredibly loyal to her.

Some who knew him well speculated that it was this very strong marriage that was 'the real strength behind David'. But as far as the team was concerned, if they wanted to leave work a little early there was always the feeling they should perhaps have stayed.

One of the first successes of the team was a major hospital scandal in South Wales at the Ely Mental Hospital of which reports of brutality and deprivation were beginning to hit the headlines. English went into conference at about 10.30 one morning, proposing to the editor that an in-depth investigation was appropriate. The editor said there was only one reporter there, John Christopher, and he couldn't possibly do all that English was proposing in a day.

What those in the unit heard later was that English had agreed with Marks that no single person could handle it, but 'my boys can'.

Jim Davies remembered later what it had been like: 'He sent four of us down by private jet from Denham Airstrip. This was like a Stuyvesant ad, the office car took four of us up there, we all had a quick briefing from David as to what he was looking for and we were told, on the plane, to apportion the job between ourselves.' John Christopher was notified and met the men a short time later in a big car, and they blitzed the town, collecting all the information, and had the copy over by 7 p.m.

The team always filed their copy separately and David himself took it over. He then did 'an American rewrite job', wherein, in about twenty minutes, he was able to bring thousands of words together, rewrite the story and make it seamless. This, in the days before the computer.

This was the team's first big triumph. David was euphoric and he told them over the telephone that the plane wasn't coming back for them. They were to ask which hotel was the best in Cardiff, book themselves in, take in a night-club if they liked, charging whatever they liked in food and come back the next day. Although David himself rewarded them fulsomely, the news desk and even the editor seemed remarkably silent. There were no congratulatory cables or pats on the back. It was difficult to avoid drawing the conclusion that jealousy was running rampant throughout the building.

Another notable success for the team occurred when Rolls-Royce landed the biggest ever aircraft engine order – the RB211 engine that was destined to drive the 747 aeroplane around the world. It was a major success story for the British aero-engine industry and David said, 'Right, we're not just going to carry a story saying that Rolls-Royce have landed this contract, we want to go and take this factory apart.' He instructed the team to talk to the chairman, to the workforce, to the unions. He said, 'I want everything and I want the townspeople of Derby. Let's go for it.'

Then he called the head of Rolls-Royce, who resisted the idea, saying that it was impossible to get together the kind of people English needed in such a short time. Instead, he offered to do it the following week, declining the instant publicity.

English then, so goes the story, called the *Express*'s air correspondent and asked him, 'How well do you know Tony Benn?' who was then Aviation Minister in Harold Wilson's government. 'Well enough,' was the answer. So he said, 'Get him to call me.' In fact, Benn did call English, whose enthusiasm for the story was so infectious that Benn rang David back ten minutes later, saying, 'I think he'll speak to you now.' The team then shot up to Derby, did the blitz and the *Express* again outclassed every other newspaper in the field.

This was the upside of working for David English. But if one of his men didn't do the job too well, he came down publicly on the offender, making him feel inadequate and small. Still, the rewards were great if the reporter made the grade. It was generally believed among the group that Gareth Parry, one of the earlier members of the squad, gained his year's tour of duty in Vietnam, where most reporters of the day were frantic to go, as a result of his good work. Ivor Key was sent to New York. The team were getting jobs abroad, they were getting the cream of the assignments and they were getting salary rises.

And they were loyal to David.

It all lasted a glorious eighteen months, until David went to Spain on holiday. While he was away, the team was disbanded, the members dispersed into different areas. Upset, they called him on holiday and he said, 'What did you expect?'

It was then clear to the team, if they weren't aware of it already, that English had been using the unit as a launch pad to his own success. In fact, when one of his competitors within the ranks of the *Daily Express*, Tim Hewitt, asked several of them to his flat for drinks and they reported the fact to David, he told them to go, but to remember what was said and to tell him later. While they were there, he said, they were to look over the flat carefully, seeing how it was decorated and remembering the books in the case. That was the more complicated side of his nature. That was David English.

But then, after he had left the *Express* to edit the *Daily Sketch* for Associated Newspapers, within weeks of becoming editor, David English had called each and every man on the SMERSH Unit and offered them a job on his paper. The same offer came again after he began to edit the *Daily Mail*.

That was David English as well.

Howard French, editor of Associated Newspapers' *Sketch*, was not surprised to receive an invitation from Esmond Rothermere to dinner at Warwick House. Both men knew they were going to discuss 'the crisis at the *Sketch*', which Howard edited. There was no question in Howard's mind that the newspaper was failing and since he was editor he was to some extent responsible. But he was a reasonable man: he knew a paper with the limited resources of the *Sketch* was in no position to compete with the well-funded *Mirror*, its tabloid competitor. By the same token, the times were changing and the *Sketch* reflected the past more than the present.

The Swinging Sixties had brought about attitudinal changes on the part of the public and many readers were expecting more salacious material in their newspapers. There were also rumours that a brash young entrepreneur, Rupert Murdoch, was about to bring out a newspaper. Many were predicting disaster. What did an Australian know about the British newspaper market? And what of the man he had chosen to be his editor, Larry Lamb, though acknowledged as quite a competent newspaper man; could he succeed in changing the old *Daily Herald*, a stodgy, failing trade union newspaper, into a lively daily with a youthful readership, when others had failed? It seemed dubious.

Howard French was an old-fashioned man. And Esmond even more so. The two had no illusions about which way the rambunctious tabloid market was going – in the direction of 'soft porn'. Rothermere said to French, 'Look, I'm a very rich man and I do not need the *Daily Sketch*, and I'm certainly not going into that market.' Even though his own position was at stake, French agreed with the decision. The two also agreed in theory that the *Sketch* was finished. It would not be able to make the stretch against the hot competition of the late Sixties.

Howard French was crusty and colourful, and dozens of tales circulated about him, a few of them true. True, for example, was the one that he spiked the Sputnik story. In one version he said he would be damned if he would give credit to the corrupt Soviet regime. That wasn't true. The reason French spiked the story was because the paper had gone and only a few thousand copies would have made the streets. That *was* true. Still, the more colourful version became part of the legends attached to the Fleet Street editor.

Louis Kirby was a leader writer under Howard French, and he never tired of repeating some of French's more famous malapropisms. Kirby's favourite: 'I'll tell you one thing. The Russian bear will never change his spots.' Another: 'You do realize we're falling between three stools.' Howard French wore a dramatic moustache, and Louis was fond of telling one story in which Howard marched up and down, flopping his moustache – and going 'MMMRRRRrrrr' – while looking out of the window. At last, he turned to Kirby majestically, saying, 'I want to make a declaration of policy about Rhodesia.'

Kirby said, 'Yes?'

Said French, 'The main trouble is that I can't think what to say.' When the Deputy Editor asked French, so goes the tale, which story he thought they should splash on, Howard replied, 'It's simple. Splash on the best story.' These were the kinds of anecdotes one heard about Howard French.

French, like any editor on Fleet Street, had his detractors. But in the main he stood out among them as one of the very few – in fact, probably the only one – who was actually *likeable*.

French was acquainted with Esmond in his professional capacity, but despite his seniority in years the person he had really hit it off with was Esmond's son, Vere. Pretty well unnoticed by the rest of the staff, a genuine friendship had developed between the two men, with the result that French and Harmsworth sometimes went sailing together. What French liked about Vere was his outstanding character and quiet calm. Beyond the fact that he liked him, French believed strongly, and against the conventional wisdom of the time, that Vere was rather clever, very capable and extremely shrewd.

He remembered one time when he went on holiday with Vere. The plan was to sail from Flumenica around the heel and toe of Italy, eventually going across to the harbour at Dubrovnik, before returning home. But when they went into the straits of Messina, and a little past, the wind seemed to be blowing up a bit, and they watched two trawlers turn round and run back towards the Cape. According to French,

> The question was should we go on, or should we run for shelter? It was really six of one and half a dozen of the other. But Vere decided, and correctly, to turn back.
>
> Well, we had a terrible time, big sea running under us and a terrific wind, and we were broaching all the time, and Vere was steering and having to use the engine to keep the bow up. So there was suddenly a great whoomph! and a porthole in the bow had stoved in. The water was rushing in. So I rushed down to stuff a pillow in, and the one hired hand aboard was helping me. We sawed up some oars, put in more pillows, eventually closing the porthole.
>
> When we came up on to the deck, we found Vere alone, totally calm, without a hair out of place, guiding us through the storm. The gales were blowing ferociously, but he managed to get us into a little harbour and we were up all night, tending the lines and the ropes and one thing and another. This took place some time around 1960, but I became convinced that Vere had unusual physical and moral courage and that he would do well when he came to take over the company.

What happened next would signal an important idea in the history of the company and it was French who suggested it at a staff meeting. There was this notion floating around Associated Newspapers that the *Daily Mail* might do well to go tabloid at some point in the future. And somehow French came up with the suggestion that although the *Sketch* was certainly on its way out, it might still provide a good training ground for a young man of promise to have a go at putting out a tabloid. And the young man he suggested was David English.

There was a saying at Associated that permeated every level of management and it was, 'Success has many fathers and failure is an orphan.'

Later on, the idea of hiring David English would be claimed by many as being their own. In one version John Gold, who was editing the *Evening News* and who had worked with English in America, had made the suggestion. In another Vere's mother claimed that Northcliffe visited her in a dream and told her to tell Esmond to hire David English. Still another credited Bobby Redhead, cousin to Vere Harmsworth and managing director of Associated Newspapers. Certainly, a man as august as Marmaduke Hussey would not be ashamed of taking the credit for being the one actually to make the contact with English and to woo him to the ranks of Associated Newspapers – and even to boast of it many years later.

Success did appear to have many fathers, at least in the case of David English.

A short time before English actually took over the *Daily Sketch* in 1969, a young woman managed to talk her way on to the staff as a diary reporter. She was extremely pretty and very capable, but she had already been rebuffed at every Fleet Street door *twice*, before succeeding in getting on to the staff of the *Sketch*.

From the age of twelve, Anthea Disney had wanted, for a variety of reasons, to be in newspapers. The one she chose to emphasize was her curiosity: she understood a reporter was paid to point and ask anybody anything and not be considered rude, something her mother had told her not to do. This forbidden desire would carry her through her first rebuff by Fleet Street and into training at IPC's *Woman's Own*, where she learned to be a sub-editor and a feature writer. Although she ended up as a feature writer at the magazine, she knew the world of women's magazines wasn't for her. Thus, she went for a second round of rebuffs on Fleet Street, the only place she really wanted to be. She said:

This time, I was told to go away again!

But there was this managing director at the Associated Newspapers, Jack Hammond, a lovely man in his mid-fifties. He said, 'We may have work as summer relief because we can't give you a job since you don't have experience.'

Two weeks later I got a call from Jack, who offered me £30 to come and work on the diary as the relief. At the end of my time, they hired me as a diary editor. I used to hang around before and after work, and everyone went home or to the pub by six o'clock, and I figured this was my opportunity. I could get extra assignments.

Then David English came. The newspaper went from this death-struggle tabloid to, well, we knew it wasn't going to survive, but it was suddenly fun. Whatever the new journalism was, David looked around and basically said, 'Anybody alive, hold up your hand.'

So I held up my hand and he sort of waved across the newsroom and said, 'We'll be talking,' and he had me write a series and other things for him. He sent me on a long haul to get Brigitte Bardot, who had never given an interview at that time, to write a series about her and her life and I spent a week with her and got her to do that.

Then, one day, English called Disney into his office and gave her a book called *Black Like Me*. After she had read it he said, 'What do you think of it?' She asked him what he had in mind and he said it would be very exciting if 'we could pull it off here'. And he offered Anthea Disney the chance to go to Birmingham as an Indian and experience prejudice as an Indian might, writing a series about the experience.

Anthea was thrilled to be noticed, excited to be doing something 'hot and important and potentially socially relevant'. And she didn't think it could in any way hurt her career.

What I didn't think about was what living in a cold-water flat in the middle of winter would be like, with local boys outside trying to kick you as you went past because you were one of 'those coloureds'.

I never thought about what the reality would be. The reality was dismal. And getting to be that colour was hard...

I found this doctor in Puerto Rico who used these drugs. I said, 'Is this dangerous?' and he said, 'I don't think so,' and that was the long and the short of it! His only fear was that there could possibly be liver damage. He tested my liver every three or four days.

I would lie on the roof of a medical centre in Puerto Rico. I had to lie on the roof because I had to be stark naked because you couldn't have marks from a bikini.

I had to have my hair parted in different places so my scalp got darker. I had to have my hands held open so it got in there and I had to have my toes open. It was incredibly hot. The doctor used to have someone come up and throw a bucket of water over me because I passed out once.

Of course, now looking back I hope I haven't damaged my skin with skin cancer. I have blotches which never go away which are just darkened pigment. After I was that colour, it kind of lingered in patches. It's not disfiguring. I'm not about to sue poor David English over it!

On the first day of the story, the entire front page of the *Sketch* was Anthea Disney's face. There was nothing else except a box that said, 'To find out what this woman has done, buy the *Sketch* on Monday.'

After her story of prejudice and humiliation started as promised, it vaulted Anthea on to every talk show in London. She was on the front page of every newspaper and magazine, and became an instant celebrity. And she was not yet twenty-five years old.

If Disney entered an Indian restaurant, she was frequently met by applause and 'I can tell you, I didn't pay for an Indian meal after that for months.' But the difficult part was that people who didn't recognize her went on exposing her to prejudice, so while she was relatively famous, the experience still stung her. 'It was like a slap in the face,' she said. 'I wanted to say, "No, no, it's all over, it's me again."'

Her skin remained dark for over a year and it went through all the colour changes as she went back, a strangely dispiriting experience. For about six weeks she was a 'disgusting jaundiced colour'. But the episode established her firmly in Fleet Street as a true professional, the first step in a career that would eventually lead her to become the editor of America's biggest circulation magazine, *TV Guide*, and eventually the head of HarperCollins in New York.

Another young talent, Mac the cartoonist, had been on the *Sketch* for a year, in his own view languishing from lack of proper exposure, when David English took over the newspaper. He immediately gave Mac a double-page spread in the middle with a photograph of his wife and family and himself, along with a sampling of cartoons. 'Mac is one year old today,' read the headline.

> Then David sent me off to a nudist camp. There had been a story in the paper about a vicar who had to give a service at a nudist camp. I'd done a cartoon about this that had created a lot of interest.
>
> Every morning, we had this morning news schedule, it told you all the things that the reporters were covering during the day. The next morning I picked up my schedule and it said: 'Mac the cartoonist goes to nudist camp.'
>
> I went down to one and they had a nudist convention going on and they had very young and middle-aged and some very very ancient people, all shapes and sizes. And I had to take my clothes off.
>
> I drew a cartoon with me holding a cartoon in front of me and two or three nude girls were pulling the cartoon away from me. This was a big spread, 'Full-frontal Mac', they called it.
>
> That was the way David would promote you and help you. He's just been wonderful for my career.

Stunt journalism? Maybe. Yet English created an excitement among his readers, a need to read the *Sketch* in order to keep up with what was happening. As Vere Harmsworth had implied, a keen interest in the box-office was certainly a central focus of David English's developing style of journalism. But there was a serious side to him as well.

John Edwards, a hard-news reporter who met David earlier when he was on the *Express* covering the Chicago riots at the Democratic Convention in 1968, was also working on the *Sketch* when English came in. He believed the real beginning 'of David's very dramatic entry into the so-called Hall of Fame of British newspaper journalism' was over the My Lai Massacre:

> On the *Daily Sketch* we produced a four-page pull-out headlined: 'If this is true, America is finished'. We bought the pictures from a very strange newspaper in Ohio. That was the beginning of him. Yes, he had been big, but that was the real start.
>
> I know that many letters that flooded in to him from publishers, congratulated him on this marvellous pull-out. So, things just started to explode then.
>
> And for me as well personally. The majority of my work was here and he put me to work, with three major pieces a week.

Thus the cult of David English began.

11

The End of the
Lunch Club

Unexpected things can and do happen in life, although these events are usually assimilated so quickly that living gives a sense of stability it rarely possesses. Now, in the life of Esmond Rothermere, one of those unexpected events occurred, with far-reaching effect.

Esmond lay on the beach sunning himself while on holiday in Jamaica and noticed a young matron approach the water. With no-nonsense discipline she stood by the sea, blew a whistle, and her six sons emerged from the water and marched back to the hotel behind her. This caught the press baron's attention. Among the many worries pressing in on Esmond at the time was the possibility of the extinction of the Rothermere title. His son Vere had been married for nearly ten years, but he and his wife Patricia had had only two girls.

It was rather a strange thing that during the Sexual Revolution, when flower children, hippies, feminists and rock stars dominated the centre stage in both Britain and America, when hashish, pot and LSD were the buzz words of communal living, Esmond sat on a beach in the Caribbean and pondered the exigencies of primogeniture.

Esmond, at sixty-eight, was as handsome and as charming as ever. Women found him no less irresistible than they had in the past – although in fact he was not ageing as well as appeared. He had had two major strokes in the late Fifties that had been given out as heart attacks. And as early as 1961 he had been diagnosed with the beginnings of Alzheimer's Disease. It is possible, though not documented, that his health problems, kept secret from all but the closest members of his family, were affecting his business decisions. Despite this, he and Mary Ohrstrom were tremendously attracted to one another and when she came to London he took her out to lunch.

The pair began sending messages across the Atlantic, via a courier whom Esmond hand-picked for the job. The secret courtship caught everyone off guard. Perhaps it had been planned that way.

Mary was the eldest daughter of Kenneth Murchison of Dallas, a well-known Texan, with good contacts in the oil industry; she was married to Richard Ohrstrom, a businessman in Virginia. Much was written or said about Mary's determination in securing the affections of the Viscount. In fact, the attention of an older man, sophisticated in the ways of the world, attentive, titled, charming and handsome, must have seemed to the Texas matron the most overwhelming event of her life. If the man did not take her by storm, the situation did. She divorced her husband and married Esmond, becoming the third wife of the second Viscount Rothermere.

Esmond had promised one of his close women friends that if he decided to marry again he would consult her first. He did not. He had told both his daughters the same. But Lorna found out by letter, a day too late to attend the wedding, and Esme received a call three days before the event. On the telephone, Esme said to her father, 'I'm sure she's small and dark. They always are.' Yes, Esmond conceded, Mary did fit the pattern.

Esmond's son Vere found out about the marriage when he received a transatlantic telephone call from his wife Patricia, who was out on the west coast of America launching a ship. And Patricia found out from a *Daily Mail* reporter who was there with her to cover the event. She asked him, 'Does Vere know?' The reporter wasn't sure, so they found a phone box and rang through to Vere, telling him the news.

Esmond's marriage hit the office the same way it hit the family – no one had known about it. Esmond's managing director at the time was Marmaduke Hussey, who found out about it when he received an unexpected telephone call from the editor of the *Evening News*:

'Here Dukey, I've got a problem. I've just got a photograph of the Chairman's wedding, but I don't know anything about it and what do you think I should do?'

'Well,' I replied, 'I won't tell you what you ought to do, but I will tell you what you're bloody well not doing. You don't print that picture until I find out more about it.'

Esmond, it became popular to observe, was not a good picker of wives. But this aphorism was not wholly true. His first wife, Peggy, the mother of his three grown children, had been lively, beautiful and intelligent. The couple had been very much in love when they married, but they had been too young to make the long-term commitment that marriage requires. Like many men in his position, Esmond continued to carry on affairs after his marriage. Peggy was too spirited to take this lying down and retaliated in kind. Thus a marriage that would no doubt have unravelled over time – simply by attrition – halted abruptly instead.

Esmond's second wife, Ann O'Neill, was a curious mixture of caprice and cruelty such as only the most privileged among the English aristocracy can produce. Ann enjoyed Esmond's position and money, and certainly she liked the sex, but she had no capacity for love, and loyalty was a trait unknown to her. Like so many women of her class at the time, she was successful socially, but failed as a human being. Since her own father had been distant and self-indulgent, Ann was especially cruel where men were concerned. This subconscious antagonism to men would eventually come back to haunt Ann when her son by Fleming, Caspar, who was the living embodiment of the troubled psycho-sexual relationship between his parents, committed suicide in 1975.

There was an ironic sideline to this terrible event. Ann Fleming had called New York socialite Jane Gunther to ask for help in trying to deal with Caspar before he died. Jane was the widow of the famous writer John Gunther, who was known for his 'Inside' books and also for a moving account of the death by cancer of his first son, Johnny: *Death Be Not Proud*. The two women knew one another socially and had many friends in common. Like Ann, Jane was recently widowed, both were prominent in high circles and both were trying to raise sons alone. Ann knew very well that Jane had a gifted son who was troubled and that Jane seemed to have dealt with the difficult passage through his teenage years particularly well. She called to find out what Jane had done, clearly in the hope that it might help her with Caspar. Jane Gunther talked with Ann Fleming for a long time, saying what she thought might help, before the tragedy occurred.

But there were such signal differences between the two women that Ann's cry for help could not help but fail. Although Jane Gunther was beautiful and rich, the darling of the New York social set, she had a streak of Puritanism and self-discipline Ann could never hope to emulate. She was formally educated at Vassar and her mother had been a schoolteacher. Like Caspar, Jane's son was bright and gifted, but John Gunther had heart and had loved him very much, unlike Ian Fleming who frequently confused his son by rejecting him as cruelly as he did Caspar's mother. After Caspar's death the Charterises bonded together, referring to the event as Caspar's 'choice', when in fact everyone knew, but was too kind to say, that Ann and Ian had failed the boy.

One of Esmond's most endearing characteristics was his understanding of human frailty, and with good-natured affection and a great deal of panache, he retrieved the friendship of both his first wife, Peggy, and the more difficult Ann, inviting them both to social events at Warwick House, where they appeared to enjoy themselves very much.

Esmond's son Vere also possessed this rare tolerance of human frailty, accepting it as one of the terms of endearment. He had married Patricia ten years before, and he was glad to see her finding her feet socially as she became a stylish hostess whose parties included such diverse types as Princess Margaret, Barbra Streisand, Patrick Lichfield and Andy Warhol. Patricia was great fun. She had a way of bringing together the well-born and the self-made, the gifted and the glamorous.

Favoured from her youth by looks and intelligence, in her present position at the centre of things she excited envy as well as admiration. But, for all her success, she had been born middle-class and in the British society of the time, it was viewed as a serious impediment to her easy acceptance by the aristocracy. For Patricia, whose gifts were great but whose confidence was less assured than it looked, confirmation of her acceptance by the world was important. And many who sensed her need withheld their approval. So a strange paradox arose. No matter what Pat achieved, in her own eyes it was always too little, and no matter what she had, it wasn't enough for her. Vere was a kind of curious bystander in Patricia's spectacular social life, because he was able to take for granted everything she pursued, and his main pleasure in their social life consisted of his pride in his wife.

For Patricia there were also health difficulties. In particular, she had had a hard time in giving birth to Geraldine, her second daughter, who weighed nine pounds. Then again, when Camilla was born seven years later in 1964, both mother and child nearly died on the delivery table. The reason Patricia and Vere had not had a son was that the doctors had told her if she had another child she would be endangering her life.

Against this background Mary Rothermere, Esmond's new wife, became pregnant. Legend has it that she wrote to Patricia giving her the news on New Year's Day 1967.

The story of how Patricia met the challenge, endangering her life by becoming pregnant herself, has been recounted many times. For once, she took care of herself and read a popular book of the time about determining the sex of her child. A religious woman, she also prayed her unborn child would be a boy.

In the end Mary had a son in June 1967, Esmond, or 'Little Essie', as he was called then, and Patricia had Jonathan in December of the same year. The title was thus assured and would pass eventually to Jonathan, but Patricia's health suffered seriously as a result of the birth. Although Jonathan was a source of growing pride to the Harmsworth couple, Pat paid heavily. It was not only for this but also for her loyalty and vitality that Vere loved his wife.

As for Mary, she was not physically vain, as Ann Fleming had been, caring not very much for the latest fashions and expensive jewellery that went with being a viscountess. Some saw this as a virtue; others implied she was a frump. Certainly, Ann Fleming was delighted to outdress her when they happened to attend the same social events.

Arthur Brittenden was editor when Esmond married Mary, and for him the dramatic story of his proprietor's marriage to an attractive young bride, some thirty years younger, became completely natural after he grew to know the couple socially. One important change was Rothermere's presence in the building. There was an anecdote that made the rounds at the time that on the first Monday morning the couple spent in London, Mary asked Esmond, 'What time are you going to work?' and the proprietor, who had felt no compunction in absenting himself from the building for long periods of time, came to his office, staying the full day, and he continued to do so whenever he was in town.

It was Brittenden's impression that Mary gave Esmond a confidence that he had lacked, because she built a new social life for him, inviting public figures of the day. But Arthur knew Rothermere only within the confines of the years he worked for him and was therefore unaware of the glittering social life Esmond had enjoyed in the 1920s as a Member of Parliament; or indeed as a close friend of the Prince of Wales and Mrs Simpson in the 1930s; or during the days of Ann Rothermere's social supremacy in London. Indeed, Rothermere's term of office was long enough for no one except his children, now adults, to remember the milestones in Esmond's life.

Nor did Brittenden know the history of Ann's interference in the running of the *Daily Mail* and the sometimes disastrous effects it had. One day Arthur said to Mary, 'Everybody is saying the paper looks very good now. But you know, it should be publicized. Esmond takes the view that people will just find out and that's that.'

To which Mary replied, 'Leave everything to me.'

In a day or so, Esmond rang to invite Arthur and his then wife Ann to Monte Carlo, saying that he and Arthur would discuss the newspaper while Mary and Ann shopped. Arthur was now hopeful that he would get a budget to promote the *Daily Mail*. Three days into the trip Mary asked, 'Has he discussed promotion?' Esmond had not. A week into the trip she repeated the question. Esmond had still not raised the issue.

Early on the last day she said to her husband, 'Now look, Esmond, you have come here to talk to Brit about the newspaper,' and he replied, 'We'll go down to the plage and have a talk.' Once there, Arthur renewed a request for promotion of the *Daily Mail*. Esmond replied that the idea was 'absolute rot' and he didn't want to hear about such a thing again. So Arthur and his wife, and Mary and Esmond returned to London without accomplishing what Arthur had intended.

Although to Arthur's mind the holiday ended in failure, Esmond had obviously decided the days of any wife of his interfering in the conduct of the newspaper were in the past. And although Mary's method of interference was vastly different from Ann's, who actually placed friends on staff and planted stories in the paper, still Esmond had no intention of a repeat run.

Arthur nevertheless thought the couple were happy together and, in particular, he believed that Esmond was delighted with his baby son.

One afternoon Brittenden was summoned to Daylesford on business and usually on such occasions Esmond met him at the door. But this afternoon the butler answered. Mary said, 'Oh, Lord Rothermere is in the living-room.' And, as he made his way there, Arthur was 'astonished to hear, as I approached, Tom Jones on the record player and there was Esmond sitting on the floor with his son, singing to Little Essie who was thoroughly enjoying it'.

When Esmond and Mary came to Arthur's and his wife's London flat for lunch, they were delightful guests who seemed to enjoy everything. Their unpretentiousness impressed Arthur, because when he visited Warwick House there was a sense of butlers and chauffeurs and gracious living.

At Daylesford weekends Arthur was often hidden away by Mary so he could read all the Saturday newspapers and at the same time avoid playing tennis, a game he was not good at. Esmond would try to seek him out, but soon enough he would find another guest to play with.

Esmond didn't drink spirits at lunch-time, but he always prepared dry martinis before dinner, which was always served 'absolutely at 8.15 every night'. Arthur was once present when one of his granddaughters said to him, 'You know, Grandpa, wherever I am in the world, I look at my watch and I work out when it will be 8.15 in England and I know that you will be sitting down for dinner.'

Many of us who were executives were working class or middle class, and Rother-mere transported us into a somewhat different world. As soon as you got there your luggage would disappear. By the time you got up to your bedroom everything would have been unpacked. Your clothes were hanging, your wife's as well. Your underclothes were in one chest of drawers and your wife's were in another.

From time to time during the course of the day you would find that a set of clothes had been laid out on the bed and presumably the butler decided what each guest should wear from his collection of clothes, either for tea or for dinner.

It wasn't always black tie and in the morning you would go into the bathroom for twenty minutes, and when you came back in, in some way the staff were aware that you had been missing from your bedroom and again, there would be a pair of slacks or a country suit or whatever.

It was forbidding in that sense and it was a way of life to which Esmond was totally accustomed. But a lot of his guests had never known anything like it.

The managing director at the time, Marmaduke Hussey, who certainly was not unacquainted with weekends in the country, could nevertheless feel daunted by the rigours of Daylesford. When he and his wife Susan were invited they were each given a bedroom. That evening, Hussey sneaked down the hallway and spent the night in his wife's room. 'The next morning, I went along feeling no end of a dog with a pillow under my arm and then rushed back to my bedroom afterwards, felt like a bachelor again and ruffled all the sheets!'

The most spectacular event sponsored by the newspaper after Esmond's marriage to Mary was the *Daily Mail*'s Transatlantic Air Race of 1969, and the couple hosted a dinner in honour of the occasion. It marked sixty years of the newspaper's support for the air industry, beginning with Blériot's crossing of the Channel in 1909. Organized by Brian Harpur and his then deputy in charge of promotions, Norman Heath, the Great Air Race marked the first time the British Harrier Jet was seen by the public.

Norman Heath was famous inside Associated Newspapers for being a bright, energetic, enthusiastic man who had been left behind at Dunkirk. He was part of the Queen's Royal Regiment, and he and the other men had been sent up near the Belgian border to fight, getting back to Dunkirk too late to be picked up. Their swift and dangerous passage southwards to Cherbourg and at last home had become legend at Associated among journalists and managers alike. Heath and the other men commandeered a laundry truck, were forced to abandon it, slept in ploughed furrows in the rain, fought off rats during the nights (more frightening than anything else Heath experienced in the war) and finally arrived back in England ten days after Dunkirk.

But it was in Yorkshire, when training troops for battle, that Heath had had the ultimate nightmare experience. As he travelled down a hedged road on a motor bike, a tank came barrelling through the hedges, driving his body into the mud. His face was lifted off and his leg ripped nearly from his body. Heath remembered ruefully that his wife was eight months pregnant when she first saw him – at a time when they wouldn't even let him see himself! The next fifteen months were spent in hospital, as plastic surgeons rebuilt his face, an experimental process since the skill was a relatively new one. Ironically, his regiment was later sent to Arnhem and killed, almost to a man. Lying inert in the hospital, his face and leg held in place by a series of weights, he had until that moment considered himself unlucky.

'I've had my life, too right,' said Heath, whose surgery was successful and who dedicated much of his spare time afterwards to caring for the infirm and the elderly. His good works and high spirits earned him the respect of his colleagues. Especially as regards the Great Air Race, he worked tirelessly to make it a success. At the time it was held, Heath moved into a caravan outside the Post Office Tower where the race started, and he didn't return home until it was all over.

The basic rules were that anybody could take part – service people, small aircraft, service aircraft, Navy aircraft, etc. – so long as they followed the laws of the land. The entrants raced from the top of the GPO Tower to the top of the Empire State Building, where they had to clock in to see who won. The last lap of the race could be in taxicabs, buses, by car or whatever the entrant could think of. The event enjoyed tremendous publicity, with the BBC devoting an hour to a programme called *Race You to the Top*.

At the time, the Harrier Jump Jet had not been seen in public, and the idea was to use this great event to sell it to America. Heath said,

We built a helicopter pad outside the Tower. The Air Force had the Harrier and it actually came up from a disused coal-yard at St Pancras. And they went down in the middle of Manhattan. For this, coal-yards were cleared, but we hadn't appreciated the underdraft of the Harrier and it blew a hole when it went up.

There was dust all over the place, and you could get a couple of cars in there. For some five years, I was getting claims saying, 'Our stock has been spoiled by the dust put up by the Harrier.'

The dinner held afterwards was attended by a number of glittering celebrities. Prince Philip was the guest of honour and Freddie Laker was there. The menu then was an exact reproduction of the dinner served by the *Daily Mail* at a celebration of the transatlantic crossing of Captain John Alcock and Lieutenant Arthur Whitten-Brown from Newfoundland to Ireland on 14 June 1919. It included 'Melon Frappé au Maraschino, Oeufs Poches Alcock, Suprème de Sole à la Brown, Poulet de Printemps à la Vickers Vimy, Salade Clifden, Surprise Britannia, Gâteau Grand Succès and Café'.

The celebration was destined to be the last great occasion attended by Esmond as chairman of the company. For though it was a tremendous public relations success, inside the firm the event was covertly criticized.

The company's fortunes were waning, as were those of others whose profits were newspaper based. A growing number of executives believed that Associated Newspapers was no longer in a position to sponsor events that were mainly promotional. It had reached a point, though no one liked to admit it, where the continuance of the *Daily Mail*, as well as of Associated's other national newspapers, was actually at issue.

As early as 1966, when Arthur Brittenden took over from Mike Randall as editor of the *Daily Mail*, there had been those who had begun to wonder about the survival of the newspaper. Its circulation continued to slide against the competition and the public no longer considered it a leader in the middle market. But even at the most prosperous news-papers on Fleet Street, production costs were escalating to such an extent that a general sense of malaise had settled in. It was difficult to deny that the newspaper industry itself was in a general decline.

On the *Mail*, it was thought that Arthur Brittenden was the logical man to follow Randall as editor because he had been a powerful force at the *Daily Express*, the *Mail's* main competitor. Whatever the *Express* was doing, so went the logic, the *Mail* should emulate, because that newspaper's circulation continued to be high, while the *Mail's* lan-guished. Although Randall's thrust had been intellectual, and that in itself was laudable, the paper needed a more popular approach if it were to continue. It was for this reason that Brittenden was welcomed by many factions.

Unusually for a paper with popular inclinations, the *Daily Mail* did have an enclave of highly intellectual writers, the sort who might have been thought to be more appropriate for a broadsheet. They included education correspondent Roy Nash, theatre critic Cecil Wilson, senior feature writer Julian Holland and daily columnist Bernard Levin. In the same office was a rising young star named Barry Norman.

Norman had begun life on the *Mail* as a gossip columnist, but by his own admission he was terrible at the job. What saved him was a rather amusing writing style, and when he later managed to dissociate himself from gossip and go into celebrity and show-business reporting, that new subject matter, wedded to his light touch, ensured his success.

Norman rather hero-worshipped the older men in his office. He said:

It was really listening to the conversations that they had, particularly Julian and Bernard. They educated me to all kinds of things – politics, drama, literature. Then eventually I timidly joined in the conversation and, because they treated my contribution seriously, I joined in more and more. I learned a hell of a lot from both of them. They were better educated, self-educated I guess, than I was. They had done the kind of reading I should have done by that time.

They talked about things with such enthusiasm and knowledge ... So they sort of woke me up, in a sense. I don't think I was a fool in any sense, but I'd probably been intellectually lazy and I'd needed that sort of stimulus – that two very lively minds arguing in your presence can provide.

Brittenden organized a kind of Friday Lunch Club that Barry Norman and Julian Holland were frequently invited to attend. Feature writers and executives went together to an Indian restaurant near Leicester Square, where they discussed issues of the day. The men paid for themselves; it was a casual affair that nevertheless conferred honour on those who were invited.

Julian Holland could be difficult in the way talented men sometimes are. He had won the award as Hannen Swaffer Descriptive Writer of the Year in the same year that Mike Randall won the Journalist of the Year Award. That accolade had turned out to be Randall's swan-song, but Julian continued to prosper on the *Daily Mail*.

The feature that won the award for Holland was a one-page, in-depth analysis of cancer. Richard Dimbleby had just died of the disease and he had been one of the first celebrities to admit it. Said Holland,

> This was about 1966. In the popular press the word 'Cancer' had been mentioned, but not talked about. It was occasionally referred to as 'the big C' but not to the actual word.
>
> When Richard Dimbleby died, Mike said he wanted me to explain all about it and what cancer was and what happened to Dimbleby, what was being done about relief, cures, etc.
>
> I was given a long time in newspaper terms – a month to five weeks to spend on it. The Dimbleby family helped.

Holland was considered to be a great asset on a newspaper edited by Mike Randall. But by his own admission, he could be temperamental. The features editor at the time was Gordon MacKenzie, who didn't always agree with Holland's approach.

> One of my major articles was butchered. It was about 800 words and I was told there was no room for it, I was told to cut it back. And I said I couldn't. In the end it appeared at 400 words and I wasn't very proud of it. I raised hell about it. That was accepted ... Gordon could send everybody away feeling okay. He was a very skilled operator.

Was this the sort of thing that got Julian Holland into hot water with Arthur Brittenden? He was never to know. But Barry Norman believed that he was in the same tub because of his friendship with Holland. The result was that neither of them was invited any more to Brittenden's lunch club. Norman said:

> I couldn't quite understand it. I never did. And it was bad news. I mean Julian

obviously knew that he'd fallen out with Arthur, but after it became widely known, we would go into the pub in the evening, the Mucky Duck downstairs in the *Daily Mail*, to have a drink before going home, and executives who used to come and join us for a drink would actually skirt round us and go down to the other end of the bar. Whatever we'd done was terrible!

Another writer who fell foul during Brittenden's tenure as editor was Bernard Levin. But it turned out to be something of a repeat performance of a similar event that took place under Mike Randall.

Levin had been theatre critic under Randall when he volunteered to do a weekly column. 'Then, in a fit of lunacy,' said Levin later, 'I said, I'll do a column *a day.* "That's a very good idea," says Mike.' Bernard continued, quite successfully, with his daily column that was on free-range topics. He had no restrictions. He could write on 'topics covered by the specialists' or on 'anything at all'. In fact, Bernard had written his contract himself in order to ensure he wouldn't be shot down – by the editor or even the proprietor.

But just before the 1964 election Levin wrote a series of columns that did not augur well. Essentially, he wrote a column for three days running about each of the political parties vying for power, giving his arguments for or against specific policies. Then, on Day Four, he explained whom he himself would vote for. The first paragraph of the column began like this:

> I speak for myself; and I now find myself hoping, as well as believing, that it will be Mr Wilson who goes to the Palace tomorrow...
>
> I love Mr Wilson even less than I love the necessity for him; but who will now deny that it was Lloyd George, not Asquith, whom Britain needed in 1916?

The comparison between Harold Wilson and David Lloyd George was something of a stretcher. But all right, besides that, the column created its own row. Although the *Mail* ran a long leader in favour of the Conservatives, Wilson, said Randall, 'got in by the skin of his teeth'. The upshot was that Rothermere threatened Levin with dismissal, instructing the managing director, Bob Hammond, to dismiss those responsible. Hammond, Randall said, asked the proprietor if he could take care of the problem in his own way and Esmond agreed. The result was that the matter was allowed to drop. It seemed to be the end of it.

But not quite. Six years later, Levin used the same device for the 1970 election – again, three columns describing the position of each party; again his own vote on Day Four:

> So, for me, the scale turns to Labour. I think that the Labour policies and achievements are slightly preferable, and the Labour team is decidedly preferable,

and will remain so until the Tories, with another five years of Opposition, can get rid of the dead wood and create a genuine alternative.

That Levin had done it before and knew from experience the ripples the columns might make gave the impression, subconsciously at least, that he might be ready for a change. At any rate, Levin did resign over the matter. It fell to Barry Norman to see him through the night.

I'd been working late and my office was along the corridor from Bernard's and I went in and there was Bernard looking very unhappy at his desk. So I popped in and said, 'What are you doing?' because he'd usually got his column finished and had gone by about six. He said that they were putting tremendous pressure on him to tone this down or even to change it.

So Barry Norman went to the pub, brought back some beers and every time Levin came back from the editor's office the pair discussed what was happening. Norman had the impression Arthur Brittenden was criticizing the column and he thought Vere Harmsworth was also involved.

The upshot was that Bernard resigned the next day, having slept on it first as Norman advised. 'So that was my contribution. I sat with Bernard Levin the night before he resigned from the *Daily Mail*.'

Like Levin, not everyone was content at the *Mail*. In what was to become a classic example of the style of Jack Crossley, who had come down from Manchester and was now news editor, Brian MacArthur was given to understand how the system worked when he first began reporting in London:

MEMO
from Jack Crossley to Brian MacArthur, Oct. 12 1965

On a matter as unurgent as the British Council Courses for overseas tax inspectors, I do not think it justified 17 shillings on taxis.

If you are going on a job that is going to run up a taxi bill as high as £1 14 shillings (taxi vandalism), it is far better to contact the firm with which we have a hire account. Even so, 1 pound 14 shillings seems a lot for Jamaica Road.

I have had to reduce the amount of money you spend on taxis and also cancel an item for newspapers and journals etc. I am afraid the management will not allow that.

By the way, it is a firm rule that expenses must be typed.

Finally the contributions department do not like lumping telephone bills all together at the end of the week. They should be done story by story.

Sorry to be so vicious but we might as well get it straight right away.

Welcome to London.

Signed, Jack

The Memo, symptomatic as it might be, hadn't really upset MacArthur, but the whole ethos of the *Daily Mail* did. He had originally wanted to become a *Guardian* reporter, when he went to work for the *Mail* in Manchester, and this was still his great desire. MacArthur described his attitude in no uncertain terms. 'I hated the *Mail* in London. I really passionately hated it, and on my fifth day – I've still got the letter – I sat down and wrote my letter to the *Guardian* saying, "You've got to rescue me. It's a nightmarish place." '

He didn't mind the limitation on taxis he could take, but he disliked being himself like 'a taxi in a rank'. The stories simply weren't fulfilling to him and Brian wanted to write. An example of a story he didn't write was one about Billy Wallace. MacArthur said, 'Billy Wallace, a well-known figure in the gossip columns of the time, got married and I did this piece on the last of the playboys. I had the biggest byline imaginable – about 36 point – and not a single word underneath it had been written by me. I thought this was bloody daft.'

That was one thing. But even when MacArthur got involved on the newspaper's investigative team, again whatever he wrote was rewritten. It was a sub-editor's newspaper, Brian decided, and he simply didn't want to work on that kind of publication. Within a year of coming to the *Mail*, he got a job at the *Guardian* and never looked back.*

Marmaduke Hussey had joined Associated Newspapers in December 1949, taking part in a management trainee programme sponsored by the company. Hussey was a war hero who had been wounded in the hands, hip and spine in the Battle of Anzio during World War II. He had nearly died then, and he nearly died again five years later when he developed osteomyelitis from the bullet that had lodged in his spine. He wasn't embittered by the difficult days of convalescence he had endured, but he had become somewhat philosophical about earning a living. Nothing about the newspaper business could ever be as difficult as the five years preceding it, he decided, and although he was ambitious, he was keen on enjoying life as well.

One of his first jobs had been doing publicity at the Manchester *Daily Mail*, which required *inter alia* organizing a bathing beauty competition. He thought this rather fun and it certainly beat lying in a hospital bed for whole months at a time. He believed most of his generation felt the same way as he did: they wanted to forget the past and get on with living. And in fact, from the time it became clear he would live, Hussey

---

* MacArthur went on to become executive editor of *The Sunday Times*, associate editor of *The Times* and the author of several books.

gave as little thought as possible to what had happened to him.

He joined Associated Newspapers a little before Mick Shields, a clever, colourful and good-looking man who had a flair for numbers. Later in life, Mick would tell a close friend that when he found himself preparing for life, fit only to teach, he decided to go to the London School of Economics and study statistics and economics. This led naturally into the area of advertising at Associated Newspapers and Mick moved into the forefront of the statistical fields that would one day develop into fully fledged market research. Familiar with the Gallup Poll, Mick pretty much invented single-handedly the National Opinion Poll and helped develop it into the MORI poll used by the media today.

The opinion poll was used by Associated Newspapers as an auxiliary research tool in the advertising department. But Mick was quick to extend it to other areas. Legend had it that he wooed Esmond with his prediction that Harold Wilson would win the 1964 election. On the say-so of Mick, so goes the story, Esmond decided not to hold the election party he usually hosted because Mick was predicting the Tories would lose.

By 1967, Marmaduke Hussey and Mick Shields were both tipped to succeed R. F. Hammond as managing director of Associated Newspapers. The decision was crucial as the company was foundering, as were most of the newspaper businesses in Fleet Street. Production costs were escalating from overmanning and union demands. The lack of a coherent overall plan for the company also contributed to the general malaise at Associated. For at least a decade, and probably longer, Esmond had tried one thing, then another, in much the same way he had chosen his editors for the *Daily Mail*, first one man, then another.

The only side of the business that truly prospered was the provincial press. When Esmond's father Harold had begun his conquest of the provinces in 1928, buying up local newspapers and forming a chain called Northcliffe Newspapers, it was largely regarded as 'Rothermere's Folly'. Indeed, it had resulted in a ruinous war with the Berry Brothers who preceded Harold into the provinces and had theretofore enjoyed the primary position in the market. The circulation war that then occurred led them and Rothermere to the very brink. It nevertheless resulted in a foothold for Associated in the provinces and the newspapers that were retained were destined to become extremely profitable. It was one more case of Esmond's father being right.

Esmond's major contribution to Associated, and one that for many years remained unsung, was his strengthening of the base of Northcliffe Newspapers, now owned by the Daily Mail & General Trust. Adding to Harold's base, Esmond acquired papers in Hull, Grimsby, Derby, Stoke,

Gloucester, Cheltenham and Swansea. The provincials, uncontaminated by the unions that plagued the national press, made good profits; labour relations were generally smooth and co-operative, in marked opposition to the events now developing in Fleet Street. There, the unions were dictating the terms.

Ironically, Northcliffe had in the second decade of the century been a strong supporter of the rights of the work-force, indeed he was one of the first in his business to recognize that workers had any rights at all. Paternal in his outlook, he had initiated some of the first industrial agreements, with the underlying purpose of protecting his printers and other workers. When the veterans returned from World War I, he was among the small group of industrialists who did not lower their pay.

A situation not unlike the one that occurred after the First World War evolved after the Second. Temporary staff had been manning the presses, but returning veterans wanted their old jobs back and, more important, felt it was their right. But the newspapers just after the war were limited in size by rationing. The result was that the temporary workers stayed, the veterans were re-employed and they worked together to produce fewer pages. Under the usual conditions of business such a situation could not long be permitted to exist. But circulations were burgeoning in post-war Britain. Most people were buying two or three newspapers a day and the companies did not feel the pinch.

In the 1950s union members began to negotiate in earnest the personnel required to man the production of longer newspapers, with the net result that the number deemed necessary to produce a twenty-page newspaper now took more staff than had a twenty-four page paper produced before the war.

It was at about this time, moreover, that what was commonly known as 'Old Spanish Customs' began to predominate in Fleet Street. These essentially meant that every time the national rates were renegotiated and the hourly rates increased, so did the overtime rates, as well as excess charges now being attached to the hourly rate. It was a system of index linking that put a particularly heavy burden on the newspaper.

The Newspaper Proprietors Association was ineffectual in dealing with the problem. An agreement might be reached in theory among the proprietors not to honour a demand, but in practice they were in hot competition with one another. Agreements made in the morning were often broken in the evening when the papers went to press. In terms of costs, the situation continued to deteriorate and it took massive circulations to support the rapidly increasing costs of labour. For a considerable time the circulation of the *Daily Mail* and its sister publications, the *Daily Sketch* and the *Evening News*, had been decreasing, although at differing rates. This boded ill for the business as a whole. Nor was it helped by a growing attitude on the part of Associated's national newspaper staff that they were so prestigious that the other more profitable sections of the business should help foot the bill for them.

The provincials certainly did their part; and up to a point relations between unions and managers at Associated had always been more cordial than at other newspapers, with a comparatively high degree of co-operation.

The choice of who would be running the company was vital in determining the direction Associated Newspapers would take in the future. The competition had, according to some, been a hot one, with Mick Shields producing statistics that showed his viewpoints were correct and Marmaduke Hussey producing similar charts and graphs that showed his own chosen course of action was wiser.

In a surprise move, Esmond himself took over the title of managing director of Associated Newspapers, but he made Hussey managing director of Harmsworth Publications. Thus was Hussey kept front-stage centre. What was the determining factor that caused Esmond to make Marmaduke Hussey his right-hand man? It was impossible to say, but certainly Hussey was at the time the more impressive. He was a war hero who had overcome grave injuries to rise in business. He was a member of the Establishment, married to a lady-in-waiting to the Queen. He was confident and charming, with leadership qualities.

Be that as it may, Mick Shields would always believe that the decision Esmond made then was the wrong one. Banished to a small office with only his secretary and a bright assistant, Ray Howman, he was put in charge of diversifying the company, a trend that had gained popularity in the face of monopoly rulings barring newspapers from unlimited ownership of media holdings. There were few visitors. Politically, Shields was out in the cold and it must have seemed to other top-ranking executives that his day was done.

One top executive whose interest did not lag was Vere Harmsworth, who was put in charge of overseeing the unit. Among the companies developed by Shields and his team was a computer-software company, which reaped handsome profits when it was sold. There were also schemes for give-away newspapers, a taxicab company, two furniture companies and even a chain of pizza restaurants. A young man from the Harvard Business School had the goal of becoming a millionaire by the time he was thirty and presented a business plan for a chain that he wanted to call 'Pizzaland'. By the time Associated Newspapers sold it to Associated Biscuit Company, the founder had indeed become a millionaire and Esmond's company had reaped excellent profits.

Mick Shields also had a hand in running Southern TV, the regional television franchise which had been acquired by Associated Newspapers in the wake of withdrawing from Associated Rediffusion. The franchise had gone a long way towards taking the sting out of that business fiasco, almost all the credit going to Brian Henry, who was instrumental in gaining the franchise and represented Associated Newspapers in the governing of it. Southern TV was the company's foot in the door of the television industry and, because of cross-media holdings laws, Associated Newspapers could not have owned Southern had they stayed in Associated Rediffusion.

But by far the most valuable experience Shields gained in the diversification projects he worked on was Blackfriars Oil. In September of 1964, the first licence interest in what would become Blackfriars was held by a company called Northcliffe Developments Ltd.

There had been continuing talk about the possibility of oil exploration in the North Sea, because oil had been found on shore for many years in very small amounts. Two brothers from Houston, Frederick Crawford Hamilton and Ferris Hamilton, had been doing excavation work for the Ohrstrom brothers before they decided to try their hand in the United Kingdom. In the UK, a well-known entrepreneur with an excellent track record in the mining business and connections with Kleinwort Benson was putting together the consortium that would eventually go in to drill for oil in the North Sea. His name was Sir Mark Turner and he was a close friend of Esmond Rothermere, as well as being an executor of his estate. But Rick Ohrstrom had also been married to Mary Ohrstrom, whose sister was married to Fred Hamilton and who would one day marry Esmond.

One night the Hamilton brothers, Sir Mark and Esmond had dinner together, and the Americans asked the Englishmen who would be a good partner for the project. Esmond responded without hesitation, 'We would. We would be good partners.' It was in this way that Esmond and Associated Newspapers became involved in exploration for oil in the North Sea.

Thus it was that Northcliffe Developments Ltd and Hamilton Brothers Oil Co., along with the Rio Tinto Zinc Corporation, applied jointly for a Production Licence under the Continental Shelf Act of 1964. It would eventually fall to Mick Shields to direct the development of this interest. The fifteen per cent participation in the venture agreed by Northcliffe Developments was transferred to Blackfriars Oil Co. Ltd, which, so goes the story, got its name from the musings of a secretary present at a meeting of the principals. She was looking out of the window of Carmelite House at the very moment a name was being sought for the company and, seeing the bridge, she said, 'Why not call it Blackfriars?'

Shields was said to be the man responsible for keeping Blackfriars in the consortium. After the first managing director of the company left the position, there was the inevitable debate on whether or not to stay with the investment. The process was costly and, for a number of years, fruitless. Shields made a trip to Houston, where he found the other investors cheerfully carving up the percentage about to be dropped by Blackfriars. He said later, 'Well, if they were already carving it up, it must be worth something.' When he came home, he recommended the company stay in and his advice was followed.

The second contribution made by Mick Shields was in settling a dispute between Fred Hamilton and Esmond over a small percentage, said to be less than half of one per cent of the investment, and the potential profits that might accrue from it. Esmond, a gentleman to the end, instructed Shields, 'We won't argue over half a per cent.' Essentially, Mick said, 'Oh, yes, we will.' Over the long haul, Mick would prove to be right. For after the oil came in, the half per cent would turn out to be worth millions. But the Blackfriars Oil bonanza would be many years in coming through – nearly eight. And in the meantime, the company's survival remained at issue.

In 1970, it was thought that Harmsworth Publications would show an internal profit, but this turned out not to be the case. And it was at this stage that a debate overtook the company as to what would be its ultimate future.

Said Marmaduke Hussey later:

My analysis of the situation then was that the damage the unions were doing to the newspapers was so devastating that they couldn't survive unless they really built up a strong force to prevent them carrying on the activity that they wanted to do.

When I was at the *Daily Mail*, I came to the conclusion that London could support only one evening newspaper. I also came to the conclusion – by then Rupert Murdoch had bought the *Sun* – that there would be a very strong development of the tabloid down to the bottom of the market and there would be room for only one middle-of-the-road newspaper – either the *Express* or the *Mail*.

And if [we merged the two], we would create two newspapers that were so strong, that would have such a hold, that would make so much money, we would be strong enough really to resist anything.

We'd dominate the middle and evening market and that would be a colossally strong position. Leave the gutter press to Rupert.

Looking back on it, I was clearly right about the evening newspapers. I haven't been proved right about the middle of the market, although I think I will be proved right in the end.

I think that in the next ten years the newspaper circulations will decline – we see that whenever television is strong – and the increased number of radio and TV news channels will put pressure on middle-of-the-road newspapers and on tabloids. I think that will lead to closures. I don't see how the *Star* and the *Mirror* and the *Sun* can go on. Certainly one will go.

It is more difficult to see what will happen to the *Daily Mail*.

It was this difficulty to envisage the *Daily Mail* as a market leader on the part of its management that would lead to the remarkable events of 1970 and 1971.

12

Chaos

During the month of October 1970, an American management consultant group, McKinsey & Co., carried out a comprehensive survey to
determine the state of health at Associated Newspapers. The study was
intended to aid executives of the company in determining the most cost-
effective methods of halting what looked increasingly like the imminent
failure of the company.

Some general fiscal truths were revealed in the report. First, if the
trends of the past five years continued into the next, the group's cumu-
lative losses on the *Daily Mail*, the *Daily Sketch* and the *Evening News*
would reach £14 million. More significant, if the losses continued at the
rate of the past *three* years, they would be *£32 million*.

The report underlined other ugly facts of life. The taking of economies
was all but useless since the only way to economize was by cutting staff.
But rises in costs, redundancy payments and higher wages would oblit-
erate any savings that could be made in this way. Therefore no stringent
measures, or sensible economies, or cut-backs in hours or people or supplies or promotions, could in any way help to remedy the situation.

In a market whose profitability was declining as a matter of course,
all three of the company's national newspaper titles showed terminal
weakness. *The Mail* was caught in the middle of the quality and downmarket press, and was losing readers to both; it was no longer able to
compete successfully against the *Daily Express*, long considered its main
rival. The *Sketch* had lost twenty-two per cent of its circulation since
1968 and enjoyed only 2.6 per cent of the market's advertising. The
Evening News was unable to attract the same advertising revenue as its
direct competitor, the *Evening Standard*, and television, too, had taken a
big bite out of its advertising profits.

No salvation could be found by closing the *Sketch* because such an
action might bring about industrial action that would affect the other
titles. Alternatively, any slimming down of the *Mail* staff might further
erode that newspaper's advertising base; the loss in personnel could
change the character of the surviving *Mail*, thus contributing to circulation decline.

The closure of all three newspapers, however, might possibly make a signal difference in the fortunes of Associated Newspapers in that the company would be freed from any future downturns in the newspaper business. By closing before their competitors, their losses would be smaller.

The suggestion that a tabloid *Mail* might turn the tide had merit, but McKinsey argued against it unless new research proved that circulation would not decline and that the majority of the readership would remain in the highly desirable ABC1 category.

The best course of action, and the one the management consultant firm now recommended, was the merger of Associated Newspaper with the Beaverbrook group.

The final report from the American consultant did not reach the desks of Associated Newspapers' executives until March 1971. By then the company had adopted a different set of imperatives from those recommended by McKinsey & Co. Perhaps, under the circumstances, it was fortunate that the new chairman, Vere Harmsworth, had never bothered to read the report.

Harmsworth didn't actually *believe* in management consultants. He suspected that all too often they did a lot of interviews and a lot of running around and at the end of the day they came to the conclusion favoured by whoever had engaged them.

The managing director of Associated Newspapers, Marmaduke Hussey, and his opposite number at the Beaverbrook group, John Coote, had known each other since the mid-Sixties, when each managed his company's evening newspaper. Both knew that the circulation of the *Daily Mail* had been in steady decline for the past twenty years, with only a couple of upward jags of short duration. At the *Daily Express*, the death of Beaverbrook in 1964 appeared to have affected the vitality of the newspaper and Beaverbrook's son, Sir Max Aitken, though an individual of great charm and an able combat pilot who had flown heroic missions in the Battle of Britain, was not a newspaper man. Everyone at the Beaverbrook group could see the handwriting on the wall. The *Daily Express* was beginning a downward slope symptomatic of what was happening in the newspaper industry as a whole – and there was no longer any Beaverbrook to save it.

With this as a continuing background, Hussey and Coote had for some time knocked around the idea of merging the *Express* and the *Mail* and creating one invincible newspaper that would dominate the middle market. Its circulation, by some estimates, might climb as high as 4.5 million. There was also the idea that the evening papers could be merged, creating a single market leader for London readers. The companies would be organized under a joint operating agreement, a device popular in the United States at the time – one that had been improvised to prevent newspapers about to fold from going under. Thus, two former competitors merged in order to split operating costs and preserve two editorial voices in a given community. Under the terms of the present joint operating agreement, the proprietors would alternate running the merged titles by five-year periods.

As early as autumn 1970, and perhaps before, Hussey and Coote had begun meeting for lunch to discuss the practical aspects of the merger. At Associated Newspapers, where the situation was somewhat more dire, the McKinsey team was drafted to start its consultancy work to see what alternatives still existed to restore the company to its former glory.

But word of the meetings between the two rival managing directors spread quickly throughout both companies, despite the secret code names attached to the project. Inside the companies the talks created a kind of momentum as high-level executives, worried about their future careers, began to jump on to the bandwagon. Eventually it seemed as if the entire management was involved in lining up jobs for themselves with the new company that would be created when the titles at Associated and Express merged.

This snowball effect was of some concern to Esmond's son, Vere Harmsworth, who had been vice-chairman of the Board since 1963. At forty-five, Harmsworth had gone through all the levels of management in the company and felt a great deal of affinity with the newspaper business. He said later that his birth into the newspaper industry had been an accident, 'but it was no accident that I remained there'. Unlike his father, who had had the newspaper business thrust upon him when his two elder brothers were killed in the First World War, Harmsworth lived and breathed newspapers. Whether through genetic disposition or simple inclination, he had known intuitively that he could run the newspaper business he was heir to and was eager to get on with it.

In January 1971, Vere and his family were in England, having spent their Christmas holiday at their country house, Stroods, as usual, when word reached him that an important meeting was to take place in London at Warwick House between his father and Sir Max Aitken. Vere had attended several meetings already, but this one was billed as the meeting that might change the course of the company for good. It was not unusual for Vere and his wife to have a holiday in January in their house in Jamaica, but this year Vere stayed home in order to attend what would go down in the lore of Fleet Street as one of the most significant evenings in modern newspaper history.

In one version of the story, a ghostly significance marked the event when a power cut took place and a servant fetched a candelabra. Thus, an appropriately mysterious atmosphere was achieved for a meeting at which the 'presence' of Beaverbrook was said to be felt. Several of those in attendance said afterwards they had no memory of the power cut, the candelabra or the ghost of Beaverbrook. Nevertheless, as events unfolded, there was an unsettling sense of intrigue and the struggle of one will against another. Present were Max Aitken; Arnold Goodman, who was the lawyer for the Beaverbrook group; Esmond Rothermere; Vere Harmsworth; Dennis Walsh, Associated's legal representation; and a number of lawyers, trustees and other minor functionaries for both companies.

At last, the moment arrived for Esmond Rothermere to concede in favour of the proposed merger of the *Daily Mail* and the *Daily Express*. And to this Esmond agreed, as had seemed inevitable. But Esmond now surprised everyone by making a moving plea that the *Evening News* should be allowed to continue under his proprietorship.

The significance of his request was not easily understood by those present. Esmond's son, Vere, however, immediately knew how to interpret his father's request. The *Evening News* had been the first title taken over by Northcliffe and the first Viscount Rothermere. Three years before the founding of the *Daily Mail* in 1896, the then Harmsworth brothers, Alfred and Harold, toiled to save the *Evening News*, a title that was all but defunct. Their success then had led to the founding of the newspaper dynasty that had lasted until the present time. Esmond wanted to preserve that last reminder of the Harmsworth achievement; his eloquent plea was rooted in a regard for the past and a sense of nostalgia. Vere later said,

> Max Aitken said he would be prepared to yield the point. But Arnold Goodman held up a hand and said, 'Stop. As your lawyer and friend I must prevent you from saying things which your natural generosity of heart would lead you to say but which are against your own true interests.' So Max then shut up and Goodman said it wouldn't do, they must have the whole thing, and Max said he was afraid Arnold was right and the conditions must be the total handing over of the whole empire, *News*, *Mail*, everything. Whereon my father said, 'In that case I can't do it. I shall have to think again.' The meeting broke up and the two sides never met again. That was the end of the merger talks. I must say I've always been grateful to Goodman for intervening as he did. As soon as he said it I realised my one opportunity would be arriving.

Harmsworth believed that the failure of the merger talks was what made his father decide to retire at last as chairman of the company. According to Vere, 'I think he wanted to see it through, to tidy things up before he went. When he saw it wasn't going to happen, I think he felt there was nothing more he could do. He sent for me and told me I was free to do anything I thought fit.'

On the next day, 18 January 1971, Rothermere resigned as chairman of the company and handed over to Vere. The following day he and his wife Mary set sail for an extended trip to South Africa. The trip had been planned for nearly a year and the timing carried no special significance. But for those who had just witnessed the significant events, Esmond Rothermere's absence cemented the finality of his decision.

The circumstances of Vere assuming the leadership of Associated Newspapers were as dramatic as an opera, and the company's situation so dire that his chances of saving it were minuscule. If he failed, no allowances would be made for the conditions he faced; he would simply be the heir who presided over the collapse of the Harmsworth empire.

Inside the company virtual chaos reigned. If Harmsworth were to succeed, he would have to cut right through it without making a single false step.

In January of 1971, David English was going through something of a personal crisis. He knew that the newspaper he was editing, the *Daily Sketch*, was about to fold and his own future was hazy. At precisely this moment, Max Aitken offered English the editorship of the *Daily Express*.

English had always wanted to edit the *Express* and until he had taken over the *Sketch* he had had this goal singly in mind. For David, the offer was the culmination of many years of dogged hard work, of honing skills and of learning how to cultivate the talent of others, at last establishing himself as the most promising young newspaperman of his generation. Now all he had to do was wait for the *Sketch* to close, pick up a generous pay-off and then waltz across to the *Express* building and take over the high command.

Ironically, English couldn't do it. It seemed to him that, after gaining the confidence of his colleagues and subordinates, this act would be viewed as such perfidy that he would never again be able to regain the trust of those who worked for him. When he talked the matter over with his wife, he found she shared his view.

By now, Irene English enjoyed a sort of cult status within the journalistic establishments where her husband had worked. Everyone knew that English, unlike so many newsmen, had a strong marriage. Women who might have been attracted to him were warded off by the instinctive knowledge that he was a happily married man who was not on the make.

Now, David and Irene English, talking over Sir Max's offer, agreed that if David were to accept, he would lose the respect of his subordinates and his success would be a joyless affair, bringing him little personal satisfaction. English made the decision to stay with Associated Newspapers, come what may, and he and his family went on a skiing holiday. Nevertheless, in his own mind, David prepared for the worst. When and if the *Sketch* did collapse, he would leave newspapers behind and go into the hotel business.

But when he returned from his holiday, English had a message to go directly to Vere Harmsworth's office. The new chairman, it seemed, had an offer for him.

At the time of the London merger talks, John Winnington-Ingram was managing director of the Manchester office. He had gleaned some inkling of the plan for the merger between the *Mail* and the *Express*, but he had nobody in particular to tell that he thought the idea was doomed from the start. He believed that such a merger would have carried very little dynamism and, like the merger in 1960 between the *Daily Mail* and the *News Chronicle*, the new paper would have dwindled away to nothing, taking both companies with it.

Winnington-Ingram was slated to take over from his boss, Bobby Childers, as general manager when he retired in March or April 1971. But he now received a message that Vere Harmsworth wanted him to come down to London for a meeting. Winnington-Ingram had just put together a joint printing consortium between the *Guardian* and the *Manchester Evening News*, something he was particularly proud of. His assumption was that having succeeded in putting this operation together, he was now wanted to play a part in bringing together the two merging companies in London. With no particular faith in the project, he agreed to go down to London and talk with Harmsworth.

Associated Newspapers was not the only newspaper company attempting to enter the oil industry. The Thomson Corporation was looking for a Number Two to Gordon Brunton, chief executive of Thomson North Sea Oil. The company had a sizeable interest in the Piper Field, which would eventually bring them a bonanza.

Word of Mick Shields's growing expertise in this side of the business had reached Thomson's North Sea Oil, and in late 1970, Shields was offered the number two position to Brunton, with the understanding that he would help to develop the oil interests of the newspaper company. After careful deliberation Shields decided to reject the offer.

At about the same time Shields was declining Thomson's offer, Marmaduke Hussey decided to accept an offer from Thomson's Corporation as their chief executive and managing director. When Hussey went to Esmond Rothermere to explain he was leaving, the proprietor at first refused to accept his resignation. But Hussey explained his resolve and Esmond at last acquiesced.

Shields also went to Esmond, but to him he explained that, although he had been offered the high-level position he had in fact rejected it. In Shields's mind ever after, his loyalty was the deciding factor in Esmond offering him the position of managing director, not only of the newspaper business, but of the entire group.

But Shields was wrong. The offer Esmond extended was on Vere's behalf and at Vere's request. At this critical juncture in the company's fortunes, Vere Harmsworth believed that if he were to succeed in saving the company he would need Shields's business acumen. Shields, Harmsworth would later say, had valuable skills in market research and an excellent background in advertising. He was good with the unions and had a great deal of personal charm. Most conclusively, he was an excellent leader and good at commanding and inspiring people – important at a time when company morale was sagging.

It was Shields's *enthusiasm* that Harmsworth most needed now. In explaining his choices many years later, he would say, 'I wanted David English to edit the *Daily Mail*. I wanted Mick Shields to become managing director. And I got them.'

He also wanted John Winnington-Ingram to take Marmaduke Hussey's place with the new title of general director, in order to free Shields for his more widely defined powers as managing director of the entire firm.

Vere had assembled his team in a very short time and indeed there was none to lose. He now considered exactly what kind of newspaper the *Daily Mail* would have to become if it were to leave behind its old-fashioned image and carry the company into a new era of publishing.

The executive personnel who led Associated Newspapers' management team leaned heavily towards the literary and their memoranda were not written in the predictable jargon-ridden, self-protective prose style that usually characterized men at the top.

Promotions manager Norman Heath set the tone of the discussion when, in a note sent to Mick Shields before the collapse of the merger between the *Express* and the *Mail*, he invoked the prayer composed by the American preacher Reinhold Niebuhr:

> God, give us the serenity to accept what cannot be changed;
> Give us the courage to change what should be changed;
> Give us the wisdom to distinguish one from the other.

Heath wrote to say he was very much against any joint operating agreement that would include a merger of the *Evening Standard* and the *Evening News*. He thought such a combination would simply provide Rupert Murdoch with 'an ideal opportunity to introduce a bouncing tabloid into the evening market'. A better idea might be to turn the *Sketch* into an evening tabloid.

What Heath was actually referring to was the growing recognition that the *Daily Sketch*, under David English's editorship, had developed into an energetic, breezy and pugnacious read, and it would be a shame to shut it down – although the fortunes of the company at the moment might seem to warrant that course of action. Heath simply wanted to keep the newspaper alive, as did several others among the managerial staff.

An alternative to shutting down the *Sketch* might well be to close the *Daily Mail* itself and, in the chaotic events leading into the New Year of 1971, this far-fetched scenario was seriously considered in management discussions.

A third possibility lay in transforming the *Mail* into a tabloid – although this was a frightening prospect. Rupert Murdoch's new *Sun*, launched in November 1969, had shown Fleet Street that the newspaper market was capable of being revived if a product were put before the public that they really enjoyed and therefore wanted to buy. But the *Sun* was downmarket, as was its successful tabloid rival the *Mirror*, also enjoying a high level of prosperity despite the new competition provided by the *Sun*'s editor, Larry Lamb, and his brash young Australian proprietor. What worried Associated Newspapers' executives was that they might be tarred with the tabloid brush of the *Sun* and the *Mirror*, and their middle-class readership would flee to the safe havens of their rivals, the *Express* or the *Telegraph*.

Could there not be a fourth possibility, then? It was postulated by the circulation manager of the *Daily Mail*, Bert Irvine:

> During the coming year the battle between the *Mail* and the *Express* may well reach a point where a dramatic policy change is the only way to avert a disaster. If it should have to be a fight to the finish, the suggestion that the *Mail* should be relaunched as the first serious, really upmarket tabloid must again be considered. The risk is indeed great, but as a last-ditch stand it could well come off. We should be introducing a new kind of tabloid journalism.

It was an idea. But a slightly different scenario was being advanced by the advertising manager, Brian Henry. In a report addressing the choices facing the company, Henry suggested it might be possible to close the *Sketch* and pour the money saved into updating the *Mail*'s ethos.

At the moment, wrote Henry,

The Mail's tone is too often sad and nostalgic, it seems to yearn for a return to the standard of a society which has all but vanished.

[What was wanted] was a more youthful, positive and optimistic tone ... a more buoyant and optimistic spirit...

The moral platform for its brash and materialistic optimism [should be] a sort of Victorian evangelism, which seems to combine the virtues of hard work with a belief in personal salvation and rewards in this life as well as the hereafter.

David English himself wrote a paper in which he outlined what he envisaged a new *Daily Mail* should provide in order to attract a new readership.

There should be more and better coverage of sport and television. News coverage should be upgraded, and photographs should be better and cleaner. An opinionated columnist, as well as a clear and outspoken political stance that wasn't afraid to examine particular political *policies* would be highly desirable. The *Mail* should appeal to people who were

traditional without being reactionary; who are believers in the individual being independent; who are ambitious (not yet rich, they hope to be some day) and who very much believe in this country. This does not mean they are all fuddy-duddy colonels; there is still a 'British is best' attitude among the young and the working class as well as the middle class.

Finally, John Winnington-Ingram wrote that whatever the outcome, the 'flagship mentality' that had made the *Mail* resistant to change needed 'an explosion'.

With so many different courses being plotted, so many strategies pursued, deciding a clear course of action had become a difficult matter indeed. As Vere Harmsworth considered his alternatives, only one thing was clear: if he followed the wrong one, the *Mail* and Associated Newspapers were finished.

Help came from an unexpected source – the *Financial Times*. On New Year's Day 1971, a letter appeared in its pages that summarized recent research completed by Bill Gregory, the head of *Codata*, that was about to be published in more detail in *Advertiser's Weekly*. Gregory was the former director of the Gallup Poll, where he had been responsible for advertising and media research.

In 1966, he had initiated a project comparing the behaviour of readers of tabloids and broadsheets. Gregory's conclusion was that the smaller newspaper was superior to the oversized broadsheet because the tabloid was more user-friendly.

It was easier to handle, more nearly the size of pages of paper used in other areas of readers' lives, more familiar, the advantages went on. Moreover, since it was easier to manage, the reader enjoyed a longer attention span and was generally more receptive to the content found in its pages than in that of a broadsheet.

The tabloid, in addition, held 'the answers to the escalating costs of newsprint, wages and transport. If the broadsheets went tabloid, they could cut their newsprint bills and related costs by at least twenty per cent, yet hold present advertising revenues, maintain unimpaired service to readers, and maintain, if not increase, circulation.'

But the most convincing part of Gregory's research was that advertising that took up a half-page in a broadsheet would represent a full page in a tabloid and, most significantly, *could be charged as such*. At the moment, Gregory concluded, the rate card for a tabloid was being undervalued by at least fifty per cent.

Gregory's research was highly interesting insofar as the *Sun* and the *Mirror* were concerned – but not crucial. Their income was based roughly eighty per cent on circulation and twenty per cent on advertising. But for a middle-market newspaper like the *Daily Mail*, whose split between circulation and advertising was closer to fifty–fifty, Gregory's findings were highly significant.

Gregory offered a single catch-phrase that embodied all his research into the advantages offered by the tabloid over the broadsheet: 'A page is a page'. Within Associated Newspapers it was destined to become one of the most oft-repeated aphorisms of the next twenty-five years. But Gregory was not the first to notice the obvious advantages of the tabloid.

On the first day of the twentieth century, 1 January 1901, Alfred Harmsworth was invited by Joseph Pulitzer to edit his New York *World*. Alfred's response was to cut in half the usual size of the *World*, taking as his format the 'small, portable and neatly indexed publication' he frequently cited as the most convenient size for a newspaper. Alfred gave this new miniature the name 'tabloid', meaning compressed, which he appropriated from a British manufacturing chemist's term for a large effervescent pill or tablet. The tabloid, Alfred said, was 'the newspaper of the future'.

It was Northcliffe, then, the actual founder of the *Daily Mail*, who had given the tabloid its name. If Harmsworth was looking for a rationale for the relaunching of the *Daily Mail* as a tabloid, he had found it. There were now compelling practical and historical reasons for following that course of action.

But Northcliffe had also advocated another innovation and in the early days of the *Daily Mail* it was one that helped ensure the newspaper's success by building the high circulation that would make the *Mail* the flagship of his press empire. He incorporated women's pages in his newspaper and the very first issue of the *Daily Mail* had contained feature material of great interest to female readers.

The lesson had not been lost on Vere Harmsworth, who had given the name 'FeMail' to the *Daily Mail*'s women's pages run by Shirley Conran during the 1960s. 'FeMail' and 'Money Mail' had been found to be two of the most popular features of the newspaper and instrumental in attracting a new, young, affluent readership. Now, in looking for an ethos for the *Daily Mail*, Harmsworth turned to what he called 'the last unexploited market in newspapers, the vast group of almost totally emancipated women that has risen since the war'. Said Vere then,

> Northcliffe's *Daily Mail* was aimed at the new lower-middle class. Beaverbrook imported American-style optimism and *Time Magazine*'s brittle and vivacious English. The *Mirror* discovered the working class. I believe ... that women are going to save this paper. We have to direct ourselves to women right through – not to producing a women's paper but a paper for women.
>
> The difference is subtle; you don't publish a lot of women's pages, you give a news coverage that women want to read; that way you hold your men readers too.

The way seemed clear. The new *Daily Mail* should be a tabloid newspaper aimed at attracting the interest of the new, independent woman reader. The only decision left was whether or not to use the actual term 'tabloid'.

The downmarket slant of the *Mirror*, and now of Rupert Murdoch's sensational *Sun*, seemed to the small group considering the question to taint the term and, fearing that middle-market readers would be turned off by the name, a new, more neutral word was selected – 'the compact'. It was an attempt by the *Mail* to adopt all the advantages of the tabloid size without the downmarket connotations.

At about this time, Howard French went to visit Vere Harmsworth in his office and, as the pair chatted, French became aware of a small sheet of paper on Harmsworth's desk. Vere lifted it up, saying,

> I've just had a telegram from my father in South Africa. Whatever I decide to do about the *Daily Mail*, he will support me.
>
> Of course, if I turn it into a tabloid and I fail, I shall have to leave the country. Everything will be in ruins. The family will blame me for doing it and failing.
>
> Well, I'm going to do it.

The first meeting of the tiny group of men responsible for the planning of the new compact *Daily Mail* met in the old and lonely boardroom that had been Room One, Northcliffe's imposing office, during the heyday of the newspaper's early existence. Vere Harmsworth later described the scene: 'The room was worn and in need of redecorating, the windows and the heating broken. I had the flu and wore long-johns from neck to ankle ... It was here that David came up with his great battle plan called "Fox and Fury".'

English selected the word 'Fox' as his code name for deceiving the enemy. It was a label to convince the unknowing that the *Daily Mail* was to be a broadsheet, improved, yes, but no radical departure from the earlier prototype of the past fifty years. The word 'Fury' was chosen because it conveyed a sense of power, aggression and urgency. It became his code name for the secret plan – making the *Mail* into a compact newspaper appealing broadly to a new female audience.

The extent to which David English succeeded in his deception was shown in a memo written by one of the executives, Circulation Manager Bert Irvine, who believed implicitly in the 'Fox' propaganda circulated by English and who deplored his and Harmsworth's intention of carrying on producing a broadsheet: 'In view of the risks attendant upon our present plan, I feel I must set my thoughts down for your consideration ... the task we have set ourselves is a much less logical and considerably more difficult operation [than the production of a compact *Daily Mail* would have been].'

The deception was further advanced when Arthur Brittenden was invited by Vere Harmsworth to lunch at Claridge's. Brittenden said,

> Over lunch, he was incredibly courteous and anxious not to be upsetting. And during this lunch he told me that I would be going. They had decided to go tabloid, so wanted an editor who had done a tabloid. 'Well,' I answered, 'I understand perfectly, I've had a marvellous time. I will go back this afternoon if you like and quietly clear my desk and disappear over the hills.'
>
> 'Oh no no no, that's not what we want. We want you to stay on for several months. What we want you to do is to keep the paper running and to leave David with the time to make his plans.'
>
> I felt uncertain about this, because it seemed somehow wrong. But Vere was very persuasive, saying, 'You would be helping us and everybody else.'
>
> So I agreed: 'Yes, of course I will do it.'
>
> Then he said, 'My father has asked me to tell you that he would like to be generous to you for all the work you have done in the last seven years. What he wants you to have is ...' and he took out of his pocket a piece of paper, and Esmond must have written these things down and handed the bit of paper to Vere.
>
> Vere started to read it and couldn't read his father's writing. Then he said, 'I

can't read it. You know my father's handwriting, perhaps you can.' And he handed me this bit of paper.

I said to Vere, 'He wants me to have X here and Y here and Z here, and I think it is very generous.'

So that is typical with a civilized Vere and Esmond. You get fired over lunch at Claridge's and you read your own scrap of paper as to what the terms are.

The new head of Associated Newspapers was a quixotic character. He could be as remote as his father and yet, even in business dealings, he was unfailingly courteous, even warm. Like his grandfather, Harold Rothermere, he was trusting and ingenuous. He gave the impression of being a man who needed to be protected and projected a sense of vulnerability. But, like Northcliffe, he was also dangerous. Woe to the disloyal employee, the pompous executive, the duplicitous courtier, the overconfident competitor.

The paradox, the contradictory impulse, the Harmsworthian ability to pursue two opposing goals simultaneously – these qualities were embedded in his personality. He was an original thinker and in this sense he was unpredictable. But for all his dreamy quiescence, he had a kind of charisma that was difficult to resist.

Each of those men who worked for Vere Harmsworth now set about imposing upon his personality the differing characteristics he sought in a figurehead. Harmsworth had a personality that lent itself well to such an exercise. Ambiguity was his wellspring. And for his own part Harmsworth could foster and support a high diversity of skills and talent.

But of all the characteristics routinely attributed to him there was one upon which everyone could agree. Vere Harmsworth was unusually stable. He could be relied upon to remain calm during periods of panic; he was immune to pandemonium.

As word spread of Esmond's resignation and Vere's take-over of the company, a wave of fear and anger overtook many of the workers. Predictions of mass sackings circulated throughout the building and Vere Harmsworth became the focal point for a hate campaign. Critics blamed him for the decline of Associated Newspapers. Competitors predicted that his attempt to save the *Daily Mail* would fail. Characterizations of him as a fool and a dupe proliferated in the popular literature of his rivals, and it became a commonplace to portray him as a buffoon.

Overnight, he changed from an invisible man to a figure of public scorn. And yet he was the same person.

For over twenty years he had watched the slow disintegration of Associated Newspapers, virtually powerless. He believed he had learned from the mistakes he had watched others making – and from his own.

Despite the hostility he engendered, he would try to stay the course. He wanted to restore the company's fortunes if he could; he wanted to save the Harmsworth publishing empire from extinction.

Now he had his chance.

EPILOGUE

It fell to the *Daily Mail*'s South African correspondent, Peter Younghusband, to meet the ship that carried Esmond Rothermere, Mary and his young son to South Africa after Esmond had handed over to Vere.

To Younghusband, the press lord seemed weary and distracted. He had the impression that he was glad to leave behind all the difficulties presently transpiring in London. Younghusband later said,

> I had been warned beforehand that really all he wanted was peace and quiet and a good rest, so we had made all sorts of arrangements for him to stay at pleasant places and to be quiet.
>
> I remember the first indication that I got that he was actually very nervy was when he arrived. He lost his hat, his hat was left on the ship, and he got in a terrible state. I leapt into a car and drove down to the docks and rummaged through this Union Castle liner from stem to stern to find his Homburg hat which eventually was found in the purser's office.
>
> He seemed very tired then and Mary told me that he was exhausted.

Younghusband took Esmond on the usual social rounds with all the prominent local people. They also had dinner with the British Ambassador, and Younghusband arranged a meeting with the Prime Minister, John Vorster. But it eventually became clear that all Rothermere wanted was to rest and to be quiet. Then the reporter took him to the beaches and for drives in the country, and Rothermere enjoyed that more.

The family were about three months in South Africa, and Younghusband was careful not to tell him that in the merging of the *Sketch* into the *Mail*, a brutal process that required the sacking of hundreds of journalists and printers, Younghusband himself was among those who had been made redundant. Eventually, however, when the pair were having tea in the garden of the Mount Nelson Hotel, because of the direction of the conversation, Younghusband felt obliged to make the fact known.

> At this, Rothermere became very embarrassed and indignant and he said, 'This is impossible, they can't let you go. I'm going to talk to the editor and you are going to be reinstated immediately.'

I asked him not to and I said I was quite happy with the arrangement because the *Daily Mail* had given me quite a generous redundancy pay-off and I had already committed the money to the purchase of a farm. In any event, after my retrenchment, I rejoined the *Daily Mail* on a contract basis.

Younghusband already owned a farm and the redundancy money allowed him to purchase a neighbouring one. 'So Rothermere came out on a couple of occasions, and he planted two Yellow Wood trees, he and his wife. They planted them near the house and they are still there. We actually christened them "Esmond" and "Mary" – although they've never grown very well.'

It gradually became clear that Esmond's role in the *Daily Mail* really was finished. He continued to chair the Daily Mail & General Trust, but effectively, when he handed over to Vere, it was the end of his involvement.

Esmond died in July 1978, when his second son was only eleven. One of the memories the boy had of his father was his delight in nature, how he would carry him about when he was little, telling him the names of plants. He seemed to remember being held up to look at a clump of fuchsia and pulling off some of the blooms.

For all his great wealth and power, Esmond's life had been less than satisfactory. He had lived in the shadow of his dead brothers, who died fighting in the Great War. He had taken over the business, although his own interests lay elsewhere.

Unlike his Uncle Northcliffe and his father, Rothermere, Esmond had been born inside the great British Establishment, but this brought him little happiness or peace of mind. He had dreamed of gaining his freedom from the beginning – when he was learning the demanding skills of becoming a gentleman, as his father and uncle had decreed. Instead, he took over the reins of the business as they expected.

Every generation of the Harmsworth family was obliged to re-establish control of the publishing firm. His father Harold had had to secure the company after Northcliffe's death and it was necessary for Esmond to do the same. Now it was Vere's time.

The routing by which Esmond became the head of the company had been a circuitous one. Had Northcliffe's wife Mary been able to have children, they would have been the ones to grasp the power. Had Harold's elder sons, Vere and Vyvyan, lived, it would have fallen to them.

Esmond carried out his responsibility from a sense of duty and, whatever his strengths or failings, without his commitment the newspaper dynasty would have been lost.

CHAPTER SOURCES

Prologue: Armageddon ... Again

Books include *Flight from Poland* by Cedric Salter (London: Faber & Faber, 1940); Unpublished Manuscript by G. Ward Price, 1949.

Articles include 'London Speeds Up Evacuation; 2500 a day'; 'Oxford Street Reopens' by Edward Tetlow and 'Night out in the West End' by Paul Bewsher, *Daily Mail*, 23 September 1940; 'Salute the Children' (anonymous poem), *Daily Mail Annual for Boys and Girls*, edited by Enid Blyton, *Daily Mail*, Northcliffe House, 1944; 'St Paul's Through the Smoke' by Herbert Mason, *Daily Mail*, 3 May 1951.

Interviews include the late Ralph Izzard, 1 September 1992; Rhona Churchill, 14 August 1992; Bill Benbow, 7 April 1992; Harry Brown, 6 April 1992.

1: The War Lovers

Books include *The Lords of Fleet Street* by Richard Bourne (London: Unwin Hyman, 1990); *The Letters of Ann Fleming* by Ann Fleming, ed. Mark Amory (London: Collins Harvill, 1985); *Laughter from a Cloud* by Laura, Duchess of Marlborough (London: Weidenfeld & Nicolson, 1980); *Ian Fleming* by Andrew Lycett (London: Weidenfeld & Nicolson, 1995); *A Late Education* by Alan Moorehead (London: Hamish Hamilton, 1970); *Alan Moorehead* by Tom Pocock (London: Bodley Head, 1990).

Correspondence includes Harold Harmsworth to Esmond (letter), Tuesday, n.m., 1923; Harold Harmsworth to Esmond (letter), 8 October 1924; Harold to Esmond (telegram), 23 January 1924; Lilian Rothermere to Esmond (two letters), n.d., 1937.

An interview with the late Aidan Crawley, 22 June 1922, is included.

As to Ann's appeal for Esmond:

Her aristocratic status may very well have been a confirmation of Esmond's social entrée – although none of Esmond's relatives or friends suggest this was the only basis for his attachment to her. It is not unusual, in fact, for Ann to be described as 'the love of Esmond's life'.

2: Bruisings

Books include *The Letters of Ann Fleming*; Unpublished MS by G. Ward Price; 'The Quiet Man of Fleet Street', unpublished MS by Arthur Wareham, n.d.; *Crusader* by Alexander Clifford (London: George G. Harrap, 1942); *A Late Education*; *Alan Moorehead*; *Ian Fleming*; *The Wanton Chase: An Autobiography from 1939* by Peter Quennell (London: Collins, 1980); *Laughter from a Cloud*; *The Diaries of Evelyn Waugh*, ed. Michael Davie (London, Weidenfeld & Nicolson, 1976); *The Noël Coward Diaries*, ed. Graham Payne and Sheridan Morley (London: Weidenfeld & Nicolson, 1982).

Interviews include Bill Benbow; Rhona Churchill; David Attlee, 10 June 1992; Tom Pocock, 4 June and 14 August 1992.

Correspondence includes Rhona Churchill to S. J. Taylor (letter), 4 September 1995.

3: 'The Monster'

Books include *Headlines All My Life* by Arthur Christiansen (London: Heinemann, 1961); *Publish and Be Damned* by Hugh Cudlipp (London: Andrew Dakers, 1953); 'The Quiet Man of Fleet Street'; *The Letters of Ann Fleming*; *The Wanton Chase*; *From This Day Forward* by Esme Cromer (Stoke Abbott: Thomas Harmsworth Publishing Co., 1991).

Articles include leaders, *The Times*, 1, 5 August 1944; *Daily Mail*, 4, 10 December 1936, 27 March, 5 April 1945.

Correspondence includes Esmond to Harold Rothermere, 'Memorandum on the Position of the *Daily Mail*, July 1931 (Private Papers of Vere Rothermere); Esmond to Lorna Harmsworth (letter), 7 October 1926 (Private Papers of Lady Lorna Cooper-Key); Esmond to Frank Humphrey (letter), 2 August 1944 (Harmsworth Archive); Esmond to Max Beaverbrook (letter), 25 August 1944 (Beaverbrook Papers, House of Lords Record Office); Rhona Churchill to S. J. Taylor (letter), 20 August 1992; Cecil Wilson to S. J. Taylor (letter), 30 April 1992.

Records include Twenty-First Ordinary Annual General Meeting of the Daily Mail & General Trust, formerly the Daily Mail Trust Ltd, December 1943.

Interviews include Vere Rothermere, 20 November 1990, 10 November 1992, 21 January 1993, 1 February 1993, 20 January 1994, 7 July 1996, 26 February 1997; Godfrey Howell, 15 July 1992; Sir Edward Pickering, 10 June 1992; David Attlee; Tom Pocock.

4: 'Ah, They're on the Woods'

Books include *Hitler's Rockets* by Norman Longmate (London: Hutchinson, 1985); *The Natives Were Friendly ... So We Stayed the Night* by Noel Barber (London:

Macmillan, 1977); 'The Quiet Man of Fleet Street'; *Beaverbrook, a Biography* by A. J. P. Taylor (London: Hamish Hamilton, 1972); *A Late Education; Alan Moorehead*. Correspondence includes Rhona Churchill to S. J. Taylor, 4 September 1995.

Interviews include Lady Cooper-Key, 1 June 1992, 2 February 1997; Titina Barber, 9 September 1992; Sir Edward Pickering; Tom Pocock; Donald Todhunter, 21 May 1992; Neil Swindells, 24 March 1992; George Johnson, 24 February 1992; Alan Watkins, 14 August 1992; Humphrey Lyttelton, 5 September 1992; Louis Kirby, 25 March 1992; Wally Fawkes, 17 June 1992; George Melly, 15 June 1992; Alwyn Robinson, 29 April 1992; Donald Edgar, 30 June 1992.

5: The Snowmen Were Abominable

Books include *A Private Life* by Molly Izzard (London: Faber & Faber, 1963); 'The Quiet Man of Fleet Street'.

Articles include 'To Everest Along a Primula Path', 21 April 1953, 'Yeti Track like a Human Foot Discovered', 6 January 1954, 'It Swam Its Way out of Snowdrift' and 'Now We Know the Yeti CAN Live Up Here', 15 April 1954, 'Sacred Yeti Skin Coming to Britain' and 'Why the "Snowman" Is Called "Abominable"', 9 December 1954, 'We Walk Right Through the Himalayas', 3 May 1954, by Ralph Izzard; 'A Murderous Attack on Noel Barber' by Noel Barber, 15 July 1954; 'Noel Barber, Shot in the Head, Insisted – "See that the *Mail* Gets the Story"' by Sefton Delmer, 30 October 1956; 'I AM AT THE POLE', 16 December 1957 and 'Jets Sent into Assam', 6 April 1959, by Noel Barber; 'A Peer's Niece', Anonymous, *Daily Mail*, 30 January 1932; cuttings 9 December 1932 from the *Daily Express*, 9 December 1930 from the *Evening News*; 16 January 1936 from the *Daily Star*; 'Four Days at the Races', 15 June 1953, 'Spring Diet', 17 April 1952 and 'The Queen's Gown Today', 2 June 1953, by Iris Ashley, *Daily Mail*.

Interviews include Ralph Izzard; Jeffrey Blyth, 28 September 1991; Gordon Mac-Kenzie, 1 April 1992; Alwyn Robinson; Penny Wigram, 9 September 1992; Vivian Hislop, 15 September 1992.

As to Spyros Skouras's offer to arrange an evening with Marilyn Monroe for Esmond:

Esmond hardly needed a procurer for women and the public courtship of starlets was exactly not his style. Not long before his death, at a chance meeting with Lord Hartwell in a dentist's office, he eventuated a guess that he had been involved with more than a thousand women. It was enough, he declared, vowing there would be no more. Nevertheless, he later admitted that had he realized the starlet 'Marilyn Monroe' would turn out to be *the* Marilyn Monroe, he might well have gone.

6: The Sons of Great Men

Books include *What I Said about the Press* by Randolph S. Churchill (London: Weidenfeld & Nicolson, 1957); Bert Irvine, Unpublished MS; *My Darling Clementine:*

The Story of Lady Churchill by Jack Fishman (London: W. H. Allen, 1966); *The Fall of the House of Beaverbrook* by Lewis Chester and Jonathan Fenby (London: André Deutsch, 1979); *Dangerous Estate: The Anatomy of Newspapers* by Francis Williams (London: Longmans, 1957); *The Lords of Fleet Street* by Richard Bourne (London: Unwin Hyman, 1990); *The Prerogative of the Harlot: Press Barons and Power* by Hugh Cudlipp (London: Bodley Head, 1980); *Strictly Personal* by Cecil King (London: Weidenfeld & Nicolson, 1969); 'The Quiet Man of Fleet Street'.

Correspondence includes Randolph Churchill to Esmond (telegram), 12 June 1961 (Harmsworth Archive); Geoffrey Wakeford to S. J. Taylor (letter), 14 September 1992; Esmond to Sir S. Hardman Lever (letter), 17 February 1947 (Harmsworth Archive).

Records include Daily Mail & General Trust AGM Minutes, July 1956.

Interviews include Vere Rothermere; Marmaduke Hussey, 11 May 1992; Gordon MacKenzie; Anne Scott-James, 2 April 1992; Donald Todhunter; Louis Kirby; Walter Hayes, 12 May, 21 July 1992.

As to Randolph Churchill's employment:

The *World Press News*, 16 October 1953, states that Randolph had just begun writing a television column for the *Evening Standard*.

7: 'The Invisible Man'

Books include *The House of Northcliffe: The Harmsworths of Fleet Street* by Paul Ferris (London: Weidenfeld & Nicolson, 1971); Bert Irvine, Unpublished MS.

Articles include 'She Got a Kick from Champagne' by Francis Wheen, *Vanity Fair*, November 1972.

Interviews include Esme, Countess of Cromer, 14 March 1992; Vere Rothermere; Lord Hartwell, 10 March 1994; John Edwards, 7, 15 May 1992; Sir David English, 29 November 1991, 14 May 1992, 9 December 1993; Gordon MacKenzie.

8: 'Popcorn and Pasta'

Books include *Canadian Wing Commanders* by George Brown and Michael Lavigne (Langley, Canada: 1984); *The Rise and Fall of Fleet Street* by Charles Wintour (London: Hutchinson, 1989); *The Lords of Fleet Street*.

Articles include 'The Friendless Ones' by Penelope Gilliatt, *Queen*, 13 April 1960; 'This Jungle Business' by Anne Scott-James, *Daily Mail*, 29 July 1960.

Correspondence includes Robert Morrow to Esmond (letter), 2 September 1960; Esmond to Robert Morrow (telegram), 13 March 1960 (Personal Archive of Robert Morrow QC); Robert Morrow to S. J. Taylor (letters), 29 August, 30 September, 10 October 1992.

Interviews include Robert Morrow QC, 14, 22 May 1992; Ted Jeffery, 12 March 1991; Sally Hardcastle, 26 August 1992; Monty Court, 5 May, 16 September 1992;

Donald Todhunter; Louis Kirby; Mike Randall, 13 April 1992; Alan Brien, 19 November 1992; Arthur Brittenden, 8 April 1992; Anne Scott-James; Christopher Fildes, 25 June 1992; Brian Henry, 22 July 1992; Neil Swindells; Peter Younghusband, 30 November 1992.

9: 'A Wind of Change'

Books include *Well, I Forget the Rest: The Autobiography of an Optimist* by Quentin Crewe (London: Hutchinson, 1991); *Simply Churchill* by Roy Howells (London: Robert Hale, 1965); *Listening for a Midnight Tram* by John Junor (London: Chapmans, 1990); *Strictly Personal* by Cecil King (London: Weidenfeld & Nicolson, 1969); *Shock! Horror! The Tabloids in Action* by S. J. Taylor (London: Bantam, Corgi Books, 1991); *Walking on the Water* by Hugh Cudlipp (London: The Bodley Head, 1976); *Out of the Wilderness, Diaries, 1963–67* by Tony Benn (London: Hutchinson, 1987); *Why, Why, Why* by Mike Randall (London: published by the *Daily Mail*, n.d. [c. 1966]); *Jeffrey Archer: Stranger than Fiction* by Michael Crick (London: Hamish Hamilton, 1995); *The Dawn Patrol and Other Poems of an Aviator* by Paul Bewsher (London: Erskine Macdonald, 1917).

Articles include 'The Mirror Tops 5,000,000', *Daily Mirror*, 9 June 1964; 'Benn: Harold Said that King Was Mad', *Guardian*, 29 April 1987; Fact Sheet circulated by Freddy Prince-White, Paul Bewsher's brother-in-law; 'Obituary for Paul Bewsher' by Vincent Mulchrone, 19 January 1966; 'How Many More, Mr Brooke?', 29 January 1964; 'A Life for 5d', 3 January 1964; 'The Red Meat Racket' (leader), 13 December 1963; 'Killer Tyres', 10 July 1964, *Daily Mail*.

Correspondence includes Esmond to Madame Floris (letter), 17 May 1962 (Harmsworth Archive); Max Beaverbrook to Esmond (letter), 29 May 1962 (Beaverbrook Papers, House of Lords Record Office); Godfrey Winn to Iris Ashley (letter), n.d. (Personal Archive of Penny Wigram).

Interviews include Arthur Brittenden; Gordon MacKenzie; Peter Younghusband; Robert Morrow; Ted Jeffery; Marmaduke Hussey; Mike Randall; Alan Brien; Jeffrey Archer, 11 June 1992; Sir Nick Lloyd, 22 May 1992; Dickie Herd, 8 May 1992; Shirley Conran, 25 May 1992; Monty Court; Joan Gabbedey, 25 March 1992; Ian Brown, 4 September 1992; Peter Lewis, 25 November 1992.

10: 'Walk Tall'

Books include *The Best of Vincent Mulchrone* by Vincent Mulchrone (London: Associated Newspapers Group Ltd, a publication of the *Daily Mail*, 1978).

Interviews include Jack Crossley, 30 April 1992; Gilbert Lewthwaite, 9 December 1992; Brian MacArthur, 13 July 1992; Patrick Mulchrone, 8 September 1992; Alwyn Robinson; Gordon MacKenzie; Alan Watkins; Sir David English; Jim Davies, 4 February 1993; Howard French, 21 May 1992; Louis Kirby; Vere Rothermere;

Marmaduke Hussey; Anthea Disney, 28 September 1991; Stan McMurtry (MAC), 23 November 1992; John Edwards.

11:   *The End of the Lunch Club*

Books include *The Lords of Fleet Street; The Letters of Ann Fleming; Laughter from a Cloud; The Fall of the House of Beaverbrook*; Bert Irvine, Unpublished MS.

Articles include 'Don't-know No More', 15 October 1964 and 'At the Election', 18 June 1970 by Bernard Levin, *Daily Mail*.

Records include Associated Newspapers Group Ltd, Minute Book, 16 September 1964.

Pamphlets include 'The Celebration of Major Aviation Anniversaries', published by the *Daily Mail*, n.d.

Interviews include Vere Rothermere; Lady Cooper-Key; Esme Cromer; Jane Gunther, 1 July 1994; Sarah Holcroft, 4 April 1992; Marmaduke Hussey; Arthur Brittenden; Norman Heath, 31 March 1992; Barry Norman, 21 April 1992; Julian Holland, 19 May 1992; Bernard Levin, 14 April 1992; Brian MacArthur; Lois Berman, 1 October 1992; Tom Shields, 3 September 1992; Ray Howman, 26 November 1992; Jack Lambert, 11 September 1992; Jim Johnston, 11 September 1992.

12:   *Chaos*

Books include *The Fall of the House of Beaverbrook; The Great Outsiders* by S. J. Taylor (London: Weidenfeld & Nicolson, 1996).

Records include McKinsey Report Findings, summarized in Peter Black's Unpublished MS, *The Saving of the Mail*, 1976; Minutes, 24 October 1963, Associated Newspapers Group Ltd Minute Book; Brian Henry, Unpublished Internal Report, December 1970; Vere Rothermere, Remarks Made at 21st Anniversary of the *Daily Mail*, 2 May 1992.

Correspondence includes Norman Heath to Mick Shields (memorandum), 11 January 1971; Bert Irvine to Esmond (memorandum), 22 November 1970.

Interviews include Vere Rothermere; John Winnington-Ingram, 22 April 1992; Marmaduke Hussey; Sir David English; Howard French; Arthur Brittenden.

Epilogue

Correspondence includes Harry Morison to Arthur (letter), 6 December 1940; Max Beaverbrook to Esmond (letter), 3 December 1942 (Harmsworth Archive).

An interview with Lady Cooper-Key is included.

SELECT BIBLIOGRAPHY

Annan, Noel, *Our Age*, London: Fontana, 1991.

Associated Newspapers Group Ltd, Annual Meeting Minutes Books, 1960–74.

Barber, Noel, *The Natives Were Friendly . . . So We Stayed the Night*, London: Macmillan London Ltd, 1977.

Barber, Noel, *Strangers in the Sun*, London: Geoffrey Bless, 1955.

Benn, Tony, *Out of the Wilderness, Diaries 1963–67*, London: Hutchinson, 1987.

Bewsher, Paul, *Captain Paul, The Bombing of Bruges*, London: Hodder & Stoughton, 1918.

Bewsher, Paul, *The Dawn Patrol and Other Poems of an Aviator*, London: Erskine Macdonald Ltd, 1917.

Bewsher, Paul, *Green Balls: The Adventures of a Night-Bomber*, London: William Blackwood and Sons, 1919.

Bielenberg, Christabel, *The Past Is Myself*, Chatto & Windus, 1968.

Bishop, Arthur, *Courage in the Air: Canada's Military Heritage*, Vol. I, Toronto: McGraw-Hill Ryerson, 1992.

Black, Peter, *The Biggest Aspidistra in the World*, London: British Broadcasting Corporation, 1972.

Black, Peter, *The Mirror in the Corner: People's Television*, London: Hutchinson, 1972.

Black, Peter, Unpublished MS, 1976.

Blyton, Enid, *Daily Mail Annual, Daily Mail*, London: Northcliffe House, 1944.

Bonham Carter, Violet, *Lantern Slides: The Diaries and Letters of Violet Bonham Carter, 1904–1914*, London: Weidenfeld & Nicolson, 1996.

Bonham Carter, Violet, *Winston Churchill as I Knew Him*, London: Eyre & Spottiswoode and Collins, 1965.

Bostock, Peter, *The Great Atlantic Air Race*, London: J. M. Dent & Sons Ltd, 1970.

Bourne, Richard, *The Lords of Fleet Street: The Harmsworth Dynasty*, London: Unwin Hyman, 1990.

Boyle, Andrew, *Poor, Dear Brendan: The Quest for Brendan Bracken*, London: Hutchinson, 1974.

Brendon, Piers, *The Life and Death of the Press Barons*, London: Secker & Warburg, 1982.

Brown, George and Michael Lavigne, *Canadian Wing Commanders*, Langley, Canada: 1984.

Buckley, Christopher, *The Road to Rome*, London: Hodder & Stoughton, 1945.

Bundock, Clement J., *The National Union of Journalists, A Jubilee History 1907–1957*, Oxford: Oxford University Press, 1957.

Calder, Angus, *The Myth of the Blitz*, London: Jonathan Cape, 1991.

Chester, Lewis and Jonathan Fenby, *The Fall of the House of Beaverbrook*, London: André Deutsch, 1979.

Chisholm, Anne and Michael Davie, *Beaverbrook: A Life*, London: Hutchinson, 1992.

Christiansen, Arthur, *Headlines All My Life*, London: William Heinemann, 1961.

Churchill, Randolph and Helmut Gernsheim (eds), *Churchill: His Life in Photographs*, London: Weidenfeld & Nicolson, 1955.

Churchill, Randolph S., *What I Said about the Press*, London: Weidenfeld & Nicolson, 1957.

Clifford, Alexander, *Crusader*, London: George G. Harrap & Co. Ltd, 1942.

Connor, Robert, *Cassandra: Reflections in a Mirror*, London: Cassell, 1969.

Coward, Noël, *The Noël Coward Diaries*, Graham Payne and Sheridan Morley (eds), London: Weidenfeld & Nicolson, 1982.

Crawley, Aidan, *Leap Before You Look: A Memoir*, London: Collins, 1988.

Crewe, Quentin, *Well, I Forget The Rest: The Autobiography of an Optimist*, London: Hutchinson, 1991.

Crick, Michael, *Jeffrey Archer: Stranger than Fiction*, London: Hamish Hamilton, 1995.

Cromer, Esme, *From This Day Forward*, Stoke Abbott: Thomas Harmsworth Publishing Company, 1991.

Cudlipp, Hugh, *At Your Peril*, London: Weidenfeld & Nicolson, 1962.

Cudlipp, Hugh, *The Prerogative of the Harlot: Press Barons and Power*, London: Bodley Head, 1980.

Cudlipp, Hugh, *Publish and Be Damned*, London: Andrew Dakers, 1953.

Cudlipp, Hugh, *Walking on the Water*, London: Bodley Head, 1976.

The Daily Mail All Channels TV Book, London: Daily Mail Publications, 1958.

Daily Mail & General Trust Ltd, Meeting Minutes, yearly from 1934 to 1990.

Driberg, Tom, *Beaverbrook: A Study in Power and Frustration*, London: Weidenfeld & Nicolson, 1956.

Driberg, Tom, *Ruling Passions*, London: Jonathan Cape, 1977.

Edelman, Maurice, *The Mirror: A Political History*, London: Hamish Hamilton, 1966.

English, David and the Staff of the *Daily Express*, *Divided They Stand*, London: Michael Joseph, 1969.

Farson, Daniel, *Wanderlust: The World of Negley Farson*, London: White Lion Publishers, 1972.

Farson, Negley, *A Mirror for Narcissus*, London: Howard Baker, 1956.

Ferris, Paul, *The House of Northcliffe: The Harmsworths of Fleet Street*, London: Weidenfeld & Nicolson, 1971.

Fishman, Jack, *My Darling Clementine: The Story of Lady Churchill*, London: W. H. Allen, 1966.

Fleming, Ann, *The Letters of Ann Fleming*, Mark Amory (ed.), London: Collins Harvill, 1985.

Four Hundred Famous Cartoons by Five Famous Cartoonists: Neb, Lee, Moon, Gittins and Illingworth, London: Associated Newspapers, 1944.

Fyfe, Hamilton, *Sixty Years of Fleet Street*, London: W. H. Allen, 1949.

Gannon, Franklin Reid, *The British Press and Germany, 1936–1939*, Oxford: Clarendon Press, 1971.

Gardner, Brian, *Churchill in His Time: A Study in a Reputation, 1939–1945*, London: Methuen, 1968.

Gibbs, Sir Philip, *The Journalist's London*, London: Allan Wingate, 1952.

Gilbert, Martin, *Second World War*, London: Weidenfeld & Nicolson, 1989.

The Great Adventure, 1896–1936, London: Associated Newspapers Ltd, Northcliffe House, 1936.

Hirsch, Fred, and David Gordon, *Newspaper Money: Fleet Street and the Search for the Affluent Reader*, London: Hutchinson, 1975.

Howells, Roy, *Simply Churchill*, London: Robert Hale, 1965.

Irvine, Bert, Unpublished MS, 1972.

Izzard, Molly, *A Private Life*, London: Faber & Faber, 1963.

Izzard, Ralph, *The Abominable Snowman Adventure*, London: Hodder & Stoughton, 1955.

Izzard, Ralph, *The Hunt for the Buru*, London: Hodder & Stoughton, 1951.

Izzard, Ralph and Molly, *Smelling the Breezes: A Journey through the High Lebanon*, London: Hodder & Stoughton, 1959.

Junor, John, *Listening for a Midnight Tram*, London: Chapmans, 1990.

King, Cecil, *The Cecil King Diary, 1970–1974*, London: Jonathan Cape, 1975.

King, Cecil, *The Future of the Press*, London: MacGibbon & Kee, 1967.

King, Cecil, *Strictly Personal*, London: Weidenfeld & Nicolson, 1969.

King, Cecil, *With Malice Towards None: A War Diary*, William Armstrong (ed.), London: Sidgwick & Jackson, 1970.

Koss, Stephen, *Fleet Street Radical: A. G. Gardiner and the Daily News*, London: Allen Lane, 1973.

Koss, Stephen, *The Rise and Fall of the Political Press in Britain*, Vols. I and II: Hamish Hamilton, 1981.

Laura, Duchess of Marlborough, *Laughter from a Cloud*, London: Weidenfeld & Nicolson, 1980.

Lest We Forget: The Horrors of Nazi Concentration Camps Revealed for All Time in the Most Terrible Photographs Ever Published, compiled by the *Daily Mail*, London: Associated Newspapers, 1945.

Levy, H. Phillip, *The Press Council: History, Procedure and Cases*, London: Macmillan, 1967.

Lewis, Peter, *The Fifties*, New York: J. B. Lippincott Co., 1978.

Longmate, Norman, *Hitler's Rockets*, London: Hutchinson, 1985.

Lycett, Andrew, *Ian Fleming*, London: Weidenfeld & Nicolson, 1995.

Lyttelton, Humphrey, *I Play as I Please: The Memoirs of an Old Etonian Trumpeter*, London: MacGibbon & Kee, 1954.

Mathias, Philip, *Takeover*, Canada: Maclean-Hunter, 1976.

Mendelssohn, Peter, *The Age of Churchill*, London: Thames & Hudson, 1961.

Monks, Noel, *Eyewitness*, London: Frederick Muller, 1955.

Monks, Noel, *Squadrons Up!*, London: Victor Gollancz, 1940.

Montgomery, John, *1900: The End of an Era*, London: George Allen & Unwin, 1968.

Moorehead, Alan, *The Desert War: The North African Campaign 1940–1943*, London: Sphere Books, 1965.

Moorehead, Alan, *A Late Education: Episodes in a Life*, Middlesex, England: Penguin Books, 1970.

Moorehead, Alan, *Mediterranean Front*, Bath: Cedric Chivers Ltd, 1973 (first published in 1941 by Hamish Hamilton).

Mulchrone, Vincent, *The Best of Vincent Mulchrone*, London: Associated Newspapers Group Ltd, 1978.

New York Times, Gaspesia, Unpublished MS, New York: Corporate Records Library, n.d.

News in Our Time: The Golden Jubilee Book of the Daily Mail, 1896–1946, London: Associated Newspapers, 1946.

Nicolson, Harold, *Diaries and Letters, 1939–1945*, Nigel Nicolson (ed.), London: Collins, 1967.

Norman, Barry, *Tales of the Redundance Kid or the Bedside Barry Norman*, Berkshire, England: Van Nostrand Reinhold, 1975.

Owen, Frank, *Tempestuous Journey: Lloyd George, His Life and Times*, New York: McGraw-Hill Book Company, Inc., 1955.

Pelling, Henry, *Winston Churchill*, London: Macmillan, 1974.

Pocock, Tom, *Alan Moorehead*, London: Bodley Head, 1990.

Price, G. Ward, Unpublished MS, 1949.

Private Lives: Correspondence between Mr Randolph S. Churchill, MBE and Mr Hugh Cudlipp, OBE, privately published, 1962.

Quennell, Peter, *The Wanton Chase: An Autobiography from 1939*, London: Collins, 1980.

Randall, Mike, *The Funny Side of the Street*, London: Bloomsbury, 1988.

Randall, Mike, *Why, Why, Why*, published by the *Daily Mail*, n.d. (*c.* 1966).

Reynolds, Rothay, *When Freedom Shrieked*, London: Victor Gollancz, 1939.

Roberts, Brian, *Randolph: A Study of Churchill's Son*, London: Hamish Hamilton, 1984.

Royle, Trevor, *War Report*, Worcester: Mainstream Publishing, 1987.

Salter, Cedric, *Flight from Poland*, London: Faber & Faber, 1940.

Taylor, A. J. P., *Beaverbrook: A Biography*, New York: Hamish Hamilton, 1972.

Taylor, A. J. P., *English History: 1914–1945*, Oxford: Oxford University Press, 1965.

Taylor, S. J., *The Great Outsiders*, London: Weidenfeld & Nicolson, 1996.

Taylor, S. J., *Shock! Horror! The Tabloids in Action*, London: Bantam, Corgi Books, 1991.

Vickers, Hugo, *Cecil Beaton*, London: Weidenfeld & Nicolson, 1985.

Vine, Colin M., *A Little Nut-brown Man: My Three Years with Lord Beaverbrook*, London: Reader Union, 1968.

The War Despatches, from the Pages of the Daily Mail, London: Marshall Cavendish, 1977.

Wareham, Arthur, 'Quiet Man of Fleet Street', Unpublished Manuscript, n.d.

Waugh, Evelyn, *The Diaries of Evelyn Waugh*, Michael Davie (ed.), London: Weidenfeld & Nicolson, 1976.

Waugh, Evelyn, *The Letters of Evelyn Waugh*, Mark Amory (ed.), London: Weidenfeld & Nicolson, 1978.

Williams, Francis, *Dangerous Estate: The Anatomy of Newspapers*, London: Longmans, 1957.

Williams, Francis, *Magnificent Journey: The Rise of the Trade Unions*, London: Odhams Press, 1954.

Wintour, Charles, *The Rise and Fall of Fleet Street*, London: Hutchinson, 1989.

Wood, Alan, *The True History of Lord Beaverbrook*, London: Heinemann, 1965.

Young, Kenneth, *Churchill and Beaverbrook: A Study in Friendship and Politics*, London: Eyre & Spottiswoode, 1966.

Periodicals

Boyle, Andrew, 'Bill Hardcastle: Portrait of a Friend', *The Listener*, 20 November 1975.

Braddock, John, 'One Bold Venture', *The Atlantic Advocate*, April 1968.

Churchill, Randolph S. 'The Press' *Spectator*, 27 December 1963.

Donnelly, Desmond, 'Mail in the Van', *Spectator*, 25 February 1966.

Gilliatt, Penelope, 'The Friendless Ones', *Queen*, 13 April 1960.

Hutchinson, Keith, 'British Press Trusts', *Nation*, Vol. 163, No. 6, 10 August 1946.

Ingrams, Richard, 'Sefton Delmer', *Spectator*, 15 September 1979.

McLachlan, Donald, 'How Lord Rothermere Lost his Nerve', *Spectator*, 30 December 1966.

Turnstile, Magnus, 'The Mail Affair', *New Statesman*, 23 December 1966.

Vallance, Aylmer, 'Inquest on the British Press', *Nation*, Vol. 164, No. 16, 19 April 1947.

Wheen, Francis, 'She Got a Kick from Champagne', *Vanity Fair*, November 1992.

INDEX